Democracy and Development in Latin America

For Ilona

Democracy and Development in Latin America

ECONOMICS, POLITICS AND RELIGION IN THE POST-WAR PERIOD

David Lehmann

Temple University Press
Philadelphia

Temple University Press, Philadelphia 19122
Copyright © 1990 by David Lehmann. All rights reserved
Published 1990
Printed in the United Kingdom

ISBN 0-87722-723-3
CIP data available from the Library of Congress

Contents

Gracias a la vida
Que me ha dado tanto,
Me ha dado la risa
Y me ha dado el llanto,
Así yo distingo
Dicha de quebranto
Los dos materiales que forman mi canto
Y el canto de Ustedes que es el mismo canto.
Y el canto de todos que mi propio canto.

Gracias a la vida que me ha dado tanto.

Violeta Parra (Reverte, 1983, p. 42)

Acknowledgements

I have incurred too many debts in writing this book – debts to those who have given help and support, and to those to whom I would, but for the priority of this task, have myself given help and support. The first person to thank therefore is my wife Ilona Roth, for her strength and encouragement.

The project started out thanks to the Twentieth Century Fund. Without their stimulus this would have seemed to me an absurdly ambitious project: it may still be absurd and ambitious, but at least it turned out to be feasible. They financed the research, and they supported me for half the writing of the manuscript.

Some friends and colleagues have been inordinately supportive in formulating the project and improving the text. I owe a special debt to Geoffrey Hawthorn, who read many drafts and commented in detail well beyond the call of friendship, and above all kept up my morale. Guillermo O'Donnell likewise has been extremely supportive, as in their various ways, have John Dunn, Zoë Mars, Stephany Griffith-Jones, Ernesto Laclau, Graham Howes, Lance Taylor, Joan Nelson, Cynthia Hewitt de Alcántara, Gustavo Gutierrez and my father Alfred Lehmann.

The book is the fruit of many friendships. For generous hospitality, advice and inspiration I am indebted to Roberto Batista, Maria Lia Pandolfi, Salvador Avilar, Graciela Shamis and Eugenio Díaz-Bonilla; Susan Joekes; Conceição Tavares, Mora Cordeu, Floreal Forni, José Nun, Ruth and Fernando Henrique Cardoso, José Bengoa, Al Stepan, Bill Rogers, Clarissa Hardy, Father Sebastião Eder, José de Souza Martins; Aníbal Pinto; Vainilda Paiva; Tom and Charlotte Carroll; Cristina Holmes; Emilio and Suzy Klein; Lucía Carrión; Francisco Carrión; Carlos Rodriguez Brandão; Gary Mceoin. Many of them gave me tips, leads and hints even when they were unaware they were doing so. Others gave their time in interviews which often also proved invaluable in unexpected ways: Padre Reginaldo of Casa Amarela, Recife; Padre J.C. Scannone of the San Miguel seminary, Buenos Aires; Wanderley

Guilherme dos Santos; Raimundo Faoro; Antonio Pierucci; Helio Jaguaribe; Delfim Neto; Persio Arida; Fernando Fajnsczylber; Pedro Morandé; Padre Lucio Gera; Edmar Bacha; Roberto Mangabeira Unger; Ann Drabek; Kevin Healey; Phyllis Pomeranz; Padre Crespo; Maria de Sá Barreto; Carlos Mesters; Pedro Jacobi.

Several institutions also generously offered me the use of their facilities: the Fundação Joaquim Nabuco in Recife; CEDES in Buenos Aires; and Sur and CIEPLAN in Santiago; CEPLAES in Quito; Cambridge University allowed sabbatical leave.

Finally, there are those who have, over the past twenty years, had an abiding and formative influence on my thinking: Solon Barraclough, Guillermo O'Donnell, José de Souza Martins, three people of remarkable intellectual and political integrity who have contributed in fundamental ways to my understanding of economics, politics and social movements.

As this long list shows, it has been impossible for me to work in and on Latin America without having the sense of being in touch with a collective and multifarious endeavour. We outsiders have made a career out of the sufferings of colleagues, friends, and also of the innumerable anonymous inhabitants whom we have interviewed in the city and the countryside, who have welcomed us into their homes, when we appeared from nowhere, have invited us to their parties, given us food and drink, and sent us away with a full belly and a full notebook. To all of them my thanks and a plea for forgiveness.

Quito-Cambridge, January 1989

Certain passages in Chapters One and Two have appeared in 'Dependencia: an ideological history', *Discussion Paper DP 219*, Institute of Development Studies, University of Sussex, July 1986, and in 'A Latin American political scientist, Guillermo O'Donnell', *Latin American Research Review*, 24, 2, 1989, pp. 187–200.

Introduction

This is the autobiography of a generation. A generation of intellectuals educated in optimistic, combative Latin nationalism, heirs to a vast array of revolutionary traditions, who for a time found themselves the depositories of the hopes of all the world's revolutionaries. They produced the most moving music of dissent melding the rhythms of the Spanish Civil War with the haunting tones of Andean flutes, or the rhythms of samba and jazz and bossa nova. From *Antonio das Mortes* or even *Black Orpheus* to *The Kiss of the Spider Woman*, *La Deuda Interna*, they produced a cinema which portrayed the culture of their compatriots through the universal themes of love, oppression and freedom. Born in the shadow of massively contrasting geniuses like Borges and Neruda, educated in a heroic self-mockery incarnated by García Marquez, they are marked by a permanent quest for yet another mode, yet another angle with which to capture the uniqueness of their history and their culture.

The list of other areas in which this generation, and that immediately preceding them, have enriched the culture of the Western world, is endless. In high culture it is only architecture, too heavily dependent on the commerical and monumental needs of the rich and powerful, which has been a disappointment. The popular culture of the United States, especially now, finds itself permeated by the headlong rhythms of salsa, not to speak of language, where Yinglish is replaced by Spanglish, 'garment' by 'garmento'. One common thread among many which cultural historians of the future will research for, is surely the intertwining of autochthonous Latin styles, traditions and themes with others drawn from Western European and North American modernism: Niemeyer's Brasilia, for all Le Corbusier's influence, is still Brazil. Borges' devotional tricks with Stevenson cannot hide the Latin violence. Neruda's luscious Gongorine imagery, his commemoration of the suffering slaves of Macchu Picchu share the same surrealist inspiration as his friend Lorca's *Poet in New York*. Now in the era of post-modernity, Latin America has thankfully continued to sustain her modernism, producing the literature and the films which feed the careers of literary critics in 'the North'. This capacity to assimilate and transform themes and styles from without shows a marked contrast with Asia, where music, art and literature remain proudly resistant, where cultural production resists individual innovation.

The permeability of Latin culture is nothing new. The colonial invaders may have decapitated an Inca empire at war with itself, and may have destroyed its idols, but they were also sucked into a pre-existing structure of domination, and the Christianity which subsequently developed drew on sources as varied as Spanish popular religion (imported by the friars), Indian devotional practice, and a popular imagination peopled by spirits of high and low, light and dark and white and black. Brazilian popular religion has been as open to Yoruba cults as to Sebastianist traditions. Latin American culture, in short, is not a syncretistic product, but a continuing interaction first with Western Europe and now also with North America, as well as between its own erudite and popular components.

The following chapters are a study of a small and very recent segment of this permeable and permeating cultural complex. They concern a generation of social scientists who have lived a particularly precarious life between *lo propio* – their own heritage, itself of mixed origin – and a variety of Western intellectual traditions. It has been precarious in the most immediate sense: they have lived through a heroic period of god-like youth, followed by political persecution, exile, and now economic indigence. They have resisted, and later welcomed the technical innovations of North American methodology, but they have produced a string of ideological and theoretical innovations which, through successive waves of enthusiasm and disillusion, have left an abiding mark on social thought far beyond their own frontiers. Of these the most significant are structuralist economics, 'dependency' and 'world system' theory, Liberation Theology, and most recently the 'grassroots' ideology of development, which I have termed *basismo*, from the word *base*, meaning base or, better, grassroots. Although there are many other, more specialized areas of influence too – post-marxism, discourse theory, psychoanalysis, come most readily to mind – these are my main themes. In describing their development I have sought to place them in their political context. The underlying question throughout is 'who is talking to whom, and why are they saying *that* to *them?*'

After a century or more in which the region's cultural life was marked by very little innovation, much self-indulgent romanticism, and a good measure of pretentious subservience to European ideas, the period following World War One was one of rebirth, under the influence of modernism and in response to the Depression and World War Two.

Nationalist political thought and *dirigiste* economics marked a new departure, and after the war structuralist economics – a systematization of dirigisme – became the acknowledged, though not undisputed, ideology of industrialization, in opposition to the doctrine of free trade. There followed a period of growth during which a new variety of populist nationalism intermittently dominated the political stage. But during the 1960s a concatenation of circumstances and socio-political awareness gave rise both to modernizing reformism embodied in the short-lived enthusiasm of the Alliance for Progress, and to an ideology of revolutionary socialism which in the wake of the Cuban revolution and subsequent military coups, proclaimed that no 'real' development was possible under a capitalist system, and that reformism was either insincere or doomed to failure. It seemed to the new generation of social scientists – the first generation with a modern professional training in economics, sociology and political science – that the capitalism under which they lived was not fulfilling its promise, and that even timid attempts to reform it would run into uncompromising opposition from the United States and the military acting as the instruments of dominant domestic and international economic interests. This intuition – which was a challenge both to reformists and to official marxism – became a doctrine in dependency theory. The high points of its influence were in the Popular Unity Government in Chile (1970–73) and in the period 1969–73 in Argentina, when the radical wing of Peronism contributed to the demise of the military regime which had seized power in 1967. Both these experiences ended in terrible suffering, and both gave way to an 'agonizing reappraisal'.

At the same time the Catholic Church went through a period of turmoil, initiated by the Second Vatican Council (1961–3) and deepened by the frustrations of lay movements such as Christian Democracy and Catholic Action. This led to a commitment to structural transformation expressed by the Latin American Episcopal Conference at Medellíin in 1968, and the fundamental ideological departure known as the Theology of Liberation.

Although the Theology of Liberation espoused marxist class analysis, dependency theory and in a general sense the cause of revolutionary transformation, its influence has eventually probably served to weaken both these schools: its underlying commitment to the inversion of the process of religious enlightenment, its call to 'listen to the poor' and to reshape the concept of theological truth in the light of the experience and the words of the poor, provided a crucial element in the reappraisal of *dependentista* Marxism. Its obsession with state power and its dismissal of individual rights as a bourgeois illusion, embodied an attitude which suffered severe blows as a result of the Brazilian, Argentine and Chilean crises, and was further questioned by developments in this unexpectedly friendly quarter. Although Liberation Theology did not meet with its unqualified approval, and occasionally met with open hostility, the official Church came to the fore in the defence of human rights (except in Argentina) while under hierarchical protection a vast informal Church of Base Communities, Human Rights Organizations and *Pastorales* (Pastoral Missions) regrouped, in new ways and on a larger scale, the social base which repression had tried to demobilize. The intelligentsia were being persecuted, exiled, expelled from the comforts of university life and sometimes they were killed; the parties in which they fought were dissolved, the politicians whom they advised and in whose shadow they lived were banned. But a new type of mobilization grew up from 'below', especially in Brazil, whose progenitors were armed with the Theology of Liberation and financed by a growing international community of non-governmental organizations. To these were joined another network of centres and institutes of social research, and later of social action, in which the intelligentsia in their turn regrouped, aided by those same clerical and international supports, but expounding a variety of ideological positions. It is the combination of these institutional forms and levels which I describe as *basismo*, even if, among the intellectuals involved, many would regard themselves as anything but *basista*. In the strong version of *basismo* the 'people' are viewed as the only legitimate source of political understanding, the formal institutions of liberal democracy are regarded (though not precisely despised) as a type of alienation, and collective-consumption trade unionism and communal self-management, as opposed to party militancy, constitute the prime elements of political mobilization. It has been a form of opposition politics well suited to authoritarian regimes, because it did not require easily repressed operational or command centres.

The authoritarian regimes have turned out to be less durable than was once thought, and if they turned some intellectuals away from formal politics, they stimulated others to revise more profoundly and systematically their previously held assumptions. The coincidence of their rise with apparently uncontrollable social pressures, and of their fall with the region's worst economic depression this century, also led to a reappraisal of the risks of quasi-utopian ideological invocations. In this climate Marxists turned to post-Marxism, resuscitated Gramsci as the saint of social democracy (in the place of Bernstein), and even looked again at the merits of liberal democracy. The critique of liberal democracy as a façade for oppression – so much more persuasive in the clientelistic and corporatist politics of the Third World than in advanced societies – became unacceptable in these circles, although *basismo* sustained it in a new form.

Basismo, in one form or another, like the Theology of Liberation, has spread throughout the world, especially in underdeveloped countries. Grassroots development is the favoured ideology of the burgeoning international non-governmental development community. But among the intellectual élite in Latin America the dominant movement has, if anything, been in the opposite direction. Neo-conservative and libertarian doctrines have had a strong influence among establishment ideologues and on economic policy itself, in parallel with the influence of European post-Marxism – almost indistinguishable from liberal democracy – on the now much-sobered left. The very 'Latin' division of the right between authoritarian inward-looking nationalists and outward-looking economic liberals is largely a thing of the past, as is the division of the left between metropolitan 'official' Marxism and the dissident 'national' Marxism of dependency theory.

The ultimate aim of this book is to bridge the gap between post-Marxist democratic theory and *basismo*, developing a version of *basismo* 'as if reality really mattered'. If rights and political stability are to be taken seriously, so too must the formal apparatuses of justice and bureaucracy, in such a way that the pursuit of social justice does not destabilize, and also in a manner which translates into sustainable practice the relationship between the two.

Largely in order to correct an enduring bias, I have paid some attention to the importance of formal (as distinct from social) justice in the daily lives and consciousness of the poor. Even if it does appear more relevant to many of them than wholesale economic transformation, that still requires a painful modernization of the state apparatus and a reduction of the political clientelism which has survived so long. The state has shown itself to be capable of modernization in the productive and infrastructural spheres, but the signal failure to modernize its own apparatus has lent substance to the identification of modernization with oppression. It is now time to develop the modernization from below, from civil society, which the much-criticized North American theorists of modernization were envisaging in the 1950s. This means transparency in the judiciary and in administration, and requires a mechanism whereby the state can relate to the proliferating social movements, and a strenuous effort to improve the quality of public administration.

There is a role here for the intellectuals, whose centres and institutes are rebaptized as either the 'informal university' or Grassroots Support Organizations (GSOs), as intermediaries between the state and social movements, leaving political parties to get on with the real business of ideological struggle. And finally there is a place for the international NGO community, though they must cease to evade or belittle the state and the intelligentsia, and learn that institutional development does not stop at the grassroots, but requires strong intermediary and bureaucratic organization as well.

Given the variety of these themes, at an early stage I had to take a decision to restrict the geographical scope of a project which otherwise threatened to go completely out of control. As a result the book is concerned principally with the countries I am most familiar with, namely Brazil, Argentina and Chile, although one or two of the most important writers it refers to are Peruvian. Nevertheless, I believe its contents are relevant to the continent as a whole.

I have not tried to provide a potted modern history, nor a potted comparative political analysis, for this is fundamentally a contribution to arguments – rather than stories – about development and democracy. In pursuing that ultimately evaluative course, it is extremely important to understand the political context in which ideas have been born and developed. In the first three chapters readers will find out more here about what underlay, for example, the theory of unequal exchange, or its offspring dependency theory, than about the evidence for and against its claims. I leave that to the economists, just as I leave to the theologians the debates about the God of the Poor. Chapter One traces the political economy of development and relates it to Latin American nationalism, from the 1930s, through the contribution of Raúl Prebisch and the structuralist school of economics, to depending theory. This requires references to Argentine economic history of the 1930s, but not necessarily to other economies at that period or to the Argentine economy since. It also requires reference to international politics at various points.

Chapter Two is a bridge chapter in which the stage is set for the ideological innovations which are the book's central concern. It explains, briefly, the crises of the pattern of industrialization prevalent in the region from the 1930s to the late 1970s, and then offers an account of how social thought reacted to those crises and the bureaucratic authoritarian regimes to which they gave birth. That reaction began by concentrating on the theme of the state and then shifted into post-marxism in various guises; elsewhere, there was a sudden spate of renewal in conservative thought, drawing heavily on North American neo-liberalism. Again, this chapter does not provide a documentation of human rights violations nor does it describe the debt crisis – in part because others have already done this, and as far as the latter is concerned, because I think that rarely has more high-quality brainpower been used to smaller effect than in the interminable discussions of the region's debt. My question is not how to solve the debt crisis, but rather how to make democracy in a bankrupt state.

At this point the book narrows its focus. It does not pursue political economy through to the neo-structuralist anti-inflation programmes of the mid-1980s; it does not pursue the various political forces, such as Peronism or Christian Democracy, which it abandoned on the eve of military coups. Instead it embarks in Chapter Three on a more detailed account of the modern history of the Church, as background to the Theology of Liberation and to the variegated political involvements of the hierarchy, of Catholic intellectuals, and of lay activists. This degree of detail is necessary because, in contrast to others I have touched upon, this is not a subject which would normally enter the consciousness of the sociologists, political scientists and economists for whom the book is primarily written. Yet Catholic politics have been particularly, and increasingly important in the region in the last twenty years and were also highly influential prior to that. I want to show that the study of religion, and of ideas about religion, should be integrated with the study of the politics of these countries. Like democracy, it has for too long been taken for granted. It is also important to convey to readers interested in contemporary religious thought – particularly Liberation Theology – some understanding of the context in which that thought is being produced.

At this point the book shifts from a concentration on ideas to the analysis not of contemporary political trends, but of contemporary social movements, since it is among them that we find the most important influence of Liberation Theology and it is also here that we can assess the potential of *basismo*. Chapter Four therefore provides an account of different types of movement in the countryside and the city, in Brazil and Chile, as a prelude to the explicitly programmatic concluding chapter which, as its title indicates, sets out some elements of a realistic *basismo*.

The book suffers from a lack of intensive field work. In particular the discussion of religion is too closely tied to the institutional life of the Catholic Church, pays too little attention to other religions, Christian and Afro-Brazilian, and too little to the meaning of religious belief, practice and institutionality in popular culture. It is a lack for which I do not apologize – the book is about ideology, after all, and the Catholics are among the most self-conscious producers of ideology in these countries – but I draw the readers' attention to it so as to warn them not to think that the coverage of religion is anything but partial.

One: In Search of a Development Project 'of Our Own': Social and Economic Thought in Latin America From 1948 to the Apogee of Dependency Theory

Introduction

Before World War Two Latin American political thought was concerned with two questions which did not necessarily admit of compatible answers: how could the region preserve its distinctive culture in the face of the growing economic supremacy of the United States, and how could the various countries create states capable of wrenching their people into the modern age? One response to the first question was that of José Enrique Rodó whose essay *Ariel* (1900) created a literary sensation from Buenos Aires to Santo Domingo. *Ariel* was a pretentious catalogue of vapid phrases which invoked innumerable great literary and philosophical names from Ancient Greece to the Enlightenment, none of them Latin American; the author thought that Latin America represented the higher reaches of the human spirit as compared with the 'Caliban' of the USA – the materialist and vulgar colossus of the North. Different from that aristocratic reaction was the response of the Mexican Revolution's most prominent educationalist, Vasconcelos, who, melding the racial and cultural in a uniquely ambitious and fantastical schema, predicted that the power of the United States would be surpassed in a 'third age' of the world ushered in by the 'mestizo' civilization, represented in Mexican Revolution (Brading, 1984).

The second question was of central concern to positivist thought, which appeared with greatest force in Mexico and Brazil, as an ideology of progress for intellectual elites who had difficulty in detecting an inner dynamic of progress in their own societies – such as the Enlightenment had detected in Europe. Positivism (of the nineteenth-century French variety) is not fashionable nowadays: it appears irredeemably optimistic, places naïve faith in science and – worse – scientists and, in its Latin American variant, was racist and authoritarian. But in the early part of this century it provided a framework which lent itself to a very diverse range of political projects, hardly any of which drew in any detail on the phantasmagoric utopia of the original positivist Auguste Comte, but all of which had in common the aspiration to a 'highly centralized state, in contrast to the more liberal aspirations of the previous period' (Terán, 1986, p. 20).

The post-Independence period was seen by many late-nineteenth- and early-twentieth-century positivists as one plagued by centrifugal tendencies, against which they called for centralizing and even authoritarian or caesarist projects, postponing the 'hour of politics' (i.e. of democracy) until the economic and social order had been constructed. In Brazil the military engineer and folk hero Benjamin Constant who transformed the military rebellion which brought the Empire to an end in 1889 into a 'republican revolution', publicly identified himself as a positivist even though he did not participate very actively in the small but tightly knit Brazilian positivist 'school' or 'Church'.[1] The Brazilian positivists took the unpopular step of opposing the abolition of slavery[2] on the ground that it would produce proletarian strata inadequately educated to deal with the insecurity of life. They were reluctant supporters of the republic, because they foresaw that it would be run by inefficient and corrupt politicians engaged in pointless squabbling. In a memorable phrase, they decried parliamentarism as the replacement of 'o absurdo teologico pelo absurdo metafisico' – 'of theological absurdity by metaphysical absurdity' (Cruz Costa, 1956, p. 239). They were paternalistic, calling for employers to pay a living wage, reminding them that the capital they invested belonged to society as a whole, and that they should therefore use it to the benefit of that society. However they opposed the redistribution of wealth on the grounds that the division between a minority of the rich and powerful and the impoverished majority was an inherent feature of any society, even a meritocratic one such as Comte envisaged; instead, although they advocated a remedy to extreme deprivation, they elevated

1 The positivist slogan 'Order and Progress' still adorns the Brazilian flag, and, more remarkably, continues to express very faithfully the message of Brazilian official nationalism.
2 Which came very late to Brazil, in a long drawn out process lasting from 1871, when the children of slaves were declared free, until 1888, when the institution was finally suppressed.

poverty to a dignified status (Cruz Costa, 1956, p. 255). In short, they shared the faith in progress of their Enlightenment forebears, but they did not share their faith in humanity.[3]

These two themes of cultural distinctiveness and state centralism were merged in the inter-war period in authoritarian doctrines, (to which some Catholic integrists also made a contribution) and also in the beginnings of the project of anti-imperialist liberation, ideas which had in common a hostility to capitalism, but diverged in their attitude to the popular sectors: the former despising them, the latter idealizing them. Although neither exercised pure or direct influence on holders of political power, their ideas were the most coherent available, and shaped the framework in which two different processes unfolded: first, the construction of state apparatuses which began to take a leading role in industrialization during the Depression and World War Two, and second the corporatist structure of the state designed to co-opt the social forces being born in the industrialization process. This last is more usually linked to the social doctrine of the Church, but it is possible that positivism was more important in shaping it, though the convergence of the two is most worthy of note.

After World War Two the two themes reappear, but the discourse of economics replaced one couched in biological, cultural or political terms. For the work of the most influential development theory in post-war Latin America – that of Raúl Prebisch, and his colleagues of the United Nations Economic Commission for Latin America (henceforth CEPAL: Comisión Económica para América Latina) – is once again concerned with the same themes: the distinctiveness of development paths in the periphery and the leading role of the state in an industrialization process.

A new era dawns after World War Two

CEPAL gave to the new generation of development planners a theory of their own. Its ideas were responsible for the creation of an entire UN institution – the Conference on Trade and Development (UNCTAD) in 1964 – and for the propagation of the term 'centre–periphery relations', and laid the bases for what became known as 'structuralism' and 'dependency'.

These ideas are indissolubly associated with the name of Raúl Prebisch

---

3 It is often difficult to distinguish between liberals and positivists, as can be seen from Mexico; but in Brazil the positivists were more of a sect than perhaps anywhere else in the world, so their positions are more clear cut. For Mexico see Brading, 1986.

(1901–1986).[4] Prebisch was a man of the 1930s but he shaped the outlook of a new generation who had not lived through the Depression as adults. He straddled two periods separated by a radical change in style, ideas and idols. He practised and encouraged technical professionalism in a field where dilettantism and inflated rhetoric had been the rule. Economists today might regard his efforts and those of his colleagues in the 1950s as hopelessly unsophisticated, but for Latin America they constituted a great step forward in rigorous analytical thinking. It is ironic that this man, who except in his very late years – with which we shall not be concerned – was not even remotely an ideologue or a technocrat of populism, or of nationalism, became the personification of Latin American economic nationalism. The man whom the Peronists detested, and whom Perón stripped of his academic posts because he would not serve him in a subservient capacity, was the progenitor of the economic policies which Perón stood for.

Prebisch came to CEPAL's Santiago headquarters in 1949, first as Director of Research and then, from 1951 as Executive Secretary, after notable successes as economic adviser to the Argentine military government in the early 1930s and then as founding Director of the country's Central Bank. In those positions he had contributed to guiding the country through the Depression with less suffering than many other countries, and in the process – whether as a result of governmental

4 Gurrieri (ed.), 1982; Rodriguez, 1986. Prebisch has for so long been an idol-like figure that we still lack the basic information which would enable us to understand the formative influences which later propelled him to the undoubted innovations of his work in the late 1940s and early 1950s. Writings about him, even before his death, tended towards the hagiographic, and were constrained by the bureaucratic character of the environment which Prebisch chose as his preferred working milieu throughout his professional life. Prebisch worked only briefly as an academic, and between 1949 and his departure from UNCTAD in 1969, his writings were mostly published as bureaucratic documents and thus lacked the usual scholarly apparatus which gives clues about influences. Likewise, his biographers chronicle his work as if it had fallen from the heavens and rarely place it in the context either of the man's biography or of the politics of his time, or finally of the politics of the UN Secretariat – a subject usually considered too hot to handle. Quite early on, Prebisch's persona gave way to Prebisch the institution, so that his personal history seems to have become a taboo subject. It is significant that Prebisch distances himself from both these works even though he is the author of the first (but appears disembodied in its title 'The work of Prebisch in CEPAL' while the author/editor is his long-time amanuensis Gurrieri) and the central figure in the second (for which he wrote a patronizing Preface explicitly disavowing many of the author's central points!) A less hagiographic account is that of Joseph Love, 1980. Díaz-Alejandro (1970) provides useful background material on Prebisch in the 1930s, which is largely reiterated in Love. Celso Furtado's recent autobiographical fragment, (A fantasia organizada, 1985), devoted to the early years of CEPAL offers a few insights; for example there is a tantalizing reference to travels in the Orient which may well have influenced Prebisch early in life (pp. 123–4).

sagacity or good luck and entrepreneurship – had overseen an impressive process of import substitution, using various unorthodox policy instruments which were to become the new orthodoxy after the war.[5] The theories of CEPAL can be regarded as a generalization of that experience but by the same token the weakness of CEPAL can be seen to derive from their continued obsession with the danger of another Depression during a period when, after World War Two, the world economy was in fact undergoing an unprecedented expansion.[6] In many ways the structuralists who followed Prebisch resembled the Keynesians in the industrial world, and indeed Prebisch was among the first to introduce Keynes's work to Latin America (Prebisch, 1947).

CEPAL's diagnosis of the prospects for underdeveloped countries first compared the role of the USA in the world economy with that of the previously dominant power – Great Britain – and then explored the implications of differing social structures for the distribution of the 'fruits of technical progress' between centre and periphery.

The USA, it was said, had a much lower propensity to import than Great Britain had had, and as a result the primary exporting countries no longer benefited as they had before from the upturn in economic cycles. They therefore had to follow a more 'inner-directed' development strategy. The argument was reinforced by the famous doctrine that primary exporting countries were at a constant disadvantage in world trade, reaping fewer benefits from gains in productivity as a whole than those accruing to industrialized countries. Economic orthodoxy held that 'commodity trade reduces (if it does not eliminate) international differences in wages, rents and other returns to factors of production' (Love, 1980). But, as Love goes on to explain, reality was seen to diverge from the orthodox predictions: 'according to the 1949 CEPAL Manifesto, as it came to be known[7] the purchasing power, in terms of industrial products,

5 Although import quantum fell by 28 per cent between 1925–9 and 1935–9, GDP grew during the same period by 20 per cent; after an initial dramatic fall, it rose by 33 per cent between 1932–9 (Díaz Alejandro, 1970, p. 95). One contribution to this was a managed and variable set of exchange rates, at that time an innovative policy and a highly successful one; also public expenditure was not reduced even though the aim was to balance the budget. In the midst of a world recession devaluation, as a response to balance of payments crises, would merely have reduced the prices of exports with no gains; intead the Argentine exchange rate went up in real terms between 1926–39.
6 Hans Singer's words, describing himself, Prebisch and their colleagues, in conversation, Summer 1987. Singer, who had studied under Keynes in the 1930s, was the first development economist hired by the UN and one of the foremost structuralist economists of his generation.
7 United Nations Economic Commission for Latin America: *The economic development of Latin American and some of its principal problems*, 1949. (Gurrieri, 1982, I, p. 108)

of primary exports, had declined from the 1870s to 1947, except for a boom period during World War Two'.[8]

The explanation of these trends was to be found in the different social – and not purely economic – structures of centre and periphery formations. In the centre, CEPAL claimed, working-class organizations were better equipped to defend what had been gained during the upturn and in response producers would shift the burden of recession to the periphery in the form of higher prices. Such an opportunity was not available to the workers on the periphery, on account of 'the characteristic disorganization of the working masses in primary production, especially agriculture' (Gurrieri, 1982, vol. I, p. 113; Cardoso, 1977). Thus the terms of trade would deteriorate, owing to the different class structures in different types of economy.

All this created something of a scandal: at the Mexico City Conference of CEPAL in 1951 the US delegation tried to have the Commission closed down, on the grounds that the OAS (Organization of American States) was a perfectly adequate institution to do the job (Furtado, 1985; Pollock, 1979).[9] Evidently Prebisch and his friends were viewed in some circles as dangerous radicals at the time. Elsewhere within the UN the period saw a series of rather distressing episodes, linked to the McCarthy period, such as the easing out of the distinguished Keynesian–Marxist economist Michael Kalecki from his position as chief of the World Economic Survey, and no doubt the attacks on CEPAL were related to these.

The small group of economists who worked in the organization felt that they were participating in a dangerous enterprise. In his memoir of the period, Celso Furtado, who was among Prebisch's earliest recruits, and became Brazil's first and foremost structuralist economist, describes his feelings after a trip to the USA in 1951 during which he met various eminent economists:

> I was convinced that we in CEPAL had advanced into unknown territory, and were occupying vanguard positions. I now began to realize that we would be attacked by overwhelmingly powerful forces and that we would probably get a shock when the research potential which was being built up in the United States was unleashed... But we had gained a slight advantage

8 Love, 1980. There is a vast literature concerning the empirical validity of this famous thesis, much of it dealing with statistical detail, base years, the period chosen etc. For further references see Love's paper.
9 Some of the attacks on CEPAL are to be found in Viner, 1952; Haberler, 1959. The atmosphere of polemic is well captured by Hirschman, 1961. For a defence of CEPAL see Nurkse, 1953. Nurkse's volume contains lectures given in Rio de Janeiro, as does that of Viner, in a series organized to discuss CEPAL's ideas.

and nothing could convince me that Goddess Fortune was not on our side.
(Furtado, 1985, p. 95)

The defeat did eventually come in the 1980s, but it was more of their own making, for the CEPAL economists were insufficiently critical of prevalent economic policy in the main Latin American countries, and had too naïve a faith in the reformability and potential administrative effectiveness of the state apparatus. Like the previous generation, though now with different, more modern instruments, they were searching for a destiny of their own, isolated from the wayward cycles of the world economy, in a development strategy known as Import Substitution Industrialization (ISI); and like the previous generation they had much faith in the state as an instrument of modernization.

Import substitution means the replacement of imported industrial goods by goods produced domestically; the policy instruments used to achieve this include, principally, government manipulation of the exchange rate, import tariffs or quotas, subsidized credit for substitutive investments and direct or indirect subsidies to hold down the cost of inputs required for substitutive production. It was at first an anti-cyclical response to the Depression, but eventually came to dominate the apparatus and content of economic policy to such an extent irrespective of the cyclical circumstances, that ISI became shorthand for a particular strategy of development.

The initial Prebisch argument was linked to foreign exchange shortage; but when the shortage had passed, interests and pressures were in place which enabled the protected activities to preserve their preferential access to still rationed dollars – while the state agencies which had gained power by their control of the dollars were reluctant to give it up. Furthermore, industrialists who enjoyed tariff or non-tariff protection were anxious to maintain their access to subsidized imported capital and intermediate goods through the burgeoning corporate state. Firms which enjoyed such a high level of protection from foreign competition were unlikely to develop international competitiveness, yet at the same time they were consuming a lot of foreign exchange by using imported capital and intermediate goods. It proved to be a recipe for continuing balance-of-payments crises.

It was not only the business class which joined the struggles to colonize portions of the state; the working class too, which grew fast during the early phases of ISI after 1930, was invited to join in as governments established corporatist systems of labour relations, especially in Brazil and Argentina. The outcome combined repressiveness and co-optation in varying degrees but, like the pattern of relations between state and business, it formed an integral part of the political economy of ISI.

CEPAL was not equipped to build the dynamics of these relationships into its model.

Prebisch had recognized, albeit in elliptic language, the difficulties import substitution would face from the viewpoint of allocative efficiency, while retaining a primary concern to devise counter-cyclical measures both domestically and internationally. He defended the higher cost of goods produced behind tariff barriers – and consequent loss of real income – by referring to the even greater loss of real income deriving from cyclical variations in the level of unemployment, describing the resultant stabilization of employment as a 'collective gain'. Nevertheless, already in CEPAL's 1949 'Manifesto' (CEPAL, 1949) he also recognized that 'the lack of raw materials and the inefficiency of labour' might lead to excessively high costs and thus no longer justify the protection of domestic production. He also recognized that domestic production would require capital imports and expressed the hope that these would be financed by 'international lending agencies' which would thus demonstrate that their 'counter-cyclical operations, in addition to helping countries of the periphery, can also maintain the level of demand for the capital goods industry of the countries of the centre' (Gurrieri, 1982, I, p. 149). The passage reflects either a naïve faith in foreign aid, or else a hidden awareness of the model's contradictions.

Prebisch deployed his theses from Olympian heights, disdaining the hurly-burly of routine political or ideological conflict and deftly evading commitment on certain crucial issues such as the limits to desirable constraints on free trade and the appropriate method to deal with inflation. Maybe such ambiguity is necessary if an innovative thinker is to have influence, for he needs both to undermine the assumptions of various established schools of thought and to bring together threads from a variety of schools if he is to avoid becoming imprisoned in an inherited framework.

The transformation of such initial subversive insights into a new school of thought requires systematizers, more polemical and more detailed in their approach, who 'stand on the shoulders of giants'. In Prebisch's case, these were the 'cepalino' economists Celso Furtado, Aníbal Pinto, Osvaldo Sunkel and Dudley Seers who, throughout the 1960s, wrote papers which took an integrated approach to the problems of trade policy, inflation and income distribution. Due partly to their contribution, the idea of the secular decline in terms of trade was to become the core of a whole new theory of imperialism, which revised marxist orthodoxy, and came to be known as dependency theory. Dependency theory was later marshalled to support a distrust of foreign capital investment, which became a feature of Latin American economic policy in the 1960s, though this was not Prebisch's idea at all. Indeed, on several occasions Prebisch made foreign investment part of his proposals for development in general and for Argentina in particular. And the structuralist account of inflation, though it fitted CEPAL heterodoxy, was not really an idea which he was concerned to propagate – rather the reverse. The very title of his essay 'The false dilemma between economic development and monetary stability' (Prebisch, 1971) shows that in dealing with inflation he was concerned to apply moderate structural changes, for example in land tenure and in the distribution of income generally, *together with* monetary discipline.

Enjoying a less exposed political position, his disciples took a more consistent line. Thus Furtado, in a highly influential book, (Furtado, 1959) argued that the rigidities of a dependent economy and the shallowness of its industrial base, prevented it from adapting rapidly to changes in the trade position which, whether favourable or unfavourable, tended to fuel inflationary pressures. This danger could be reduced by ISI. In boom times, when the trade position was favourable, the state could prevent excessive consumption, because protectionist policies discriminated against consumer goods imports and in favour of capital and intermediate goods. In times of recession, when foreign exchange was scarcer, the state could likewise sustain the manufacturing sector's capacity to import capital and intermediate goods by administrative means. From this point of view, protectionism could contribute to the control of inflation. As a classic example, he described how the intervention of the government to purchase vast coffee surpluses during the Depression had enabled Brazil to continue to industrialize and to experience fewer losses in income than even the USA.

But Furtado also recognized that the apparatus of controls gave rise to other rigidities, acting as a focus of pressure from a variety of interest groups whose 'catching up' pressures spurred on inflation; to decree stiff resistance to these pressures at any one time would inevitably favour some groups over others. Thus inflation was a question of income distribution both because the rich – especially the rural rich – had a low propensity to save, and because the process itself was stimulated by group and class conflict. This is the classic structuralist view of inflation arising from group or class struggle, which goes back a long way before Prebisch. The solution was not at all clear in Furtado's account, but it was a short step from this insight to the claim that income redistribution would reduce inflation by reducing class struggle once and for all. In addition, it would shift demand to the poorer sectors whose consumption goods contained fewer imported components, thus reducing capacity underutilization which would bring supply and demand back into balance. Finally, the redistribution of land completed the package of 'basic' or 'structural' reforms, on the grounds that large farmers had a low propensity to save while small farmers would respond more readily to changes in demand, thus reducing both pressure on prices and also the need for food imports.[10] As we shall see in the next chapter, these ideas became the core of the reformist programmes variously applied by Goulart in Brazil in the early 1960s, by Frei and Allende in Chile, and by the Peruvian military from 1968.

Prebisch would later also argue that the pure monetarist response to inflation failed because the standard package of devaluation, cutting public expenditure and controlling the money supply, presupposed for its success a market equilibrium which did not exist – and which could only be created once structural bottlenecks were overcome. Structural bottlenecks could be observed in the sluggish response of supply to the demand pressures which invariably built up during periods of growth: the agricultural sector, dominated by great estates whose owners were satisfied by incomes from a disorganized and underemployed labour force, responded to increasing demand in monopolistic fashion by raising prices rather than productivity, and landlords diverted increased profits to consumption rather than investment, while small farmers who might have responded more efficiently existed in insufficient numbers or had access to too little credit, inputs and technical assistance. The industrial sector for its part was heavily monopolized and cushioned by subsidies of various kinds, and thus likewise sluggish in its responses. Contrary to the oft-expressed view that income concentration acts as a stimulus to savings, he held that such concentration exercised a depressive effect on the savings rate and thus on the available resources for investment to respond to demand pressures. These were all structural – as opposed to monetary – factors which accentuated inflationary processes and made them resistant to orthodox treatment. Prebisch, though, was cautious: he usually avoids even mentioning the words land reform, and although he says that in the long run a redistribution of income would lead to a higher savings rate, in the shorter run 'the margin for savings by the mass of the people is extremely narrow'; to fill the gap, he once again appeals for the contribution of external resources – i.e. foreign aid.[11] The failure to

10 The theoretical basis for the argument on land reform was laid by Nicholas Kaldor when working with CEPAL in the 1950s (Kaldor, 1959). The basic arguments concerning inflation are set out in essays by Roberto Campos, Joseph Grunwald and David Felix in Hirschman, 1961.

11 Prebisch's cautiousness is reflected in the 1955 'Prebisch Plan', drawn up for the Junta which ousted Perón in that year. The plan advocated sound money and denounced the productivity losses arising from restrictive shop-floor work rules, imposed by the unions which enjoyed so much official support during the Peronist government. The plan was written – it must be emphasized – to deal with a classic inflation and balance-of-payments crisis, when some compression of real wages was inevitable (Díaz Alejandro, 1970, p. 116; Prebisch, 1955, 1956). As Díaz Alejandro reminds us, these reports show an aspect of

understand that structural remedies could only achieve the desired effects over the long run underlay several ill-fated attempts to bring inflation down 'at a stroke'.[12]

The process of radicalization continued. Imperceptibly, where Prebisch and his colleagues had criticized the system of international and to some extent internal economic relations in order to ameliorate them, the next generation and others from a more 'marxisant' background, took the view that the inadequacies of ISI or of the world trading system, were systemic and not remediable, and attributable to the weight of interests, to relations of power rather than to errors of reason or application. Thus the meaning of the word development itself came into question.

It all started with a dim awareness not only that ISI was not reducing the need for imported capital and intermediate goods in the process of industrialization, (that is, it was not 'self-sustaining') but also that it impeded further industrialization and perpetuated certain sorts of interests and privileges – an insight first expounded by Conceiçao Tavares, at that time working in CEPAL. Although during a first phase, the process had brought about a broadening of the incomes of all social classes, in a second phase the benefits were concentrated among the upper and middle classes, and this 'dual' pattern of income distribution constituted a 'structural barrier' to the expansion of the internal market for industrial production (Tavares, 1964). This was because the concentration of investment in labour-intensive branches producing consumer goods at relatively low levels of technology, which had prevailed in the first phase of ISI, could not be sustained due to the lack of a mass market for such goods, which was in turn a consequence of the unequal distribution of income. According to this account, if Latin American economies were to

---

Prebisch's thinking usually neglected or overlooked by Anglo-Saxon economists (Díaz Alejandro, 1965). It was not an ultra-orthodox IMF-style plan, but it was certainly not hostile to exports, as critics often say of unorthodox plans; indeed it proposed to redistribute from import-prone industry back to exporting agriculture by squeezing not wages but industrial profits, and to attract foreign capital into joint ventures so as not to penalize wages through the collapse of capital and intermediate goods imports. It was hardly 'structuralism' as the vulgar version might have had it in the 1960s and 1970s. Prebisch warned, correctly as it turned out, that if his recommendations were not implemented, the government would later have to take more drastic steps than those which then still sufficed. Further evidence of Prebisch's cautious attitude to the structural response to inflation comes from his treatment of the studies on the subject carried out within CEPAL itself: the results of the studies were never published as official documents by CEPAL, and instead their authors, Dudley Seers and Osvaldo Sunkel, published them under their own names in learned journals, where they became loci classici, but exiled nonetheless (Seers, 1962; Sunkel, 1958).

12 From Goulart, President of Brazil in the early 1960s, to Allende, Perón (in his second administration) and more recently the heterodox shocks of Sarney and Alfonsin in Brazil and Argentina.

make full use of their human and natural resources, the rate of investment would have to rise, but also thoroughgoing changes would have to take place in the 'mode of production' in various sectors, both modern and traditional. In short, industrialization was failing signally to provide employment for a rapidly growing labour force, and Furtado's optimistic assessment of 1954 was proved wrong, as he himself was gradually to recognize.

The conception which resulted, developed by Aníbal Pinto, Osvaldo Sunkel and Celso Furtado[13] – is summed up in the term 'structural heterogeneity' (Pinto, 1970). This refers to the enormous disparity of levels of productivity prevailing within and between sectors, which Pinto attributed to the model of development itself, and to the distortions and inequalities which arise when an attempt is made to reproduce the productive structures of wealthy countries in countries with incomparably lower income levels. Initiating what was in effect a denunciation of the entire system of ISI at least as applied in practice, Pinto attacked the heavy protection afforded to industries producing for upper-income groups enjoying 'opulent' consumption levels, pointing out that they were a subsidy to consumption. Structural heterogeneity arose because these capital-intensive industries did not create backward linkages, but rather coexisted in unstable equilibrium with a mass of low-technology units of production. The structuralists had turned against ISI, or at least against actually existing ISI.

Like Sunkel and Furtado, Pinto was particularly impressed by the rapid growth of the Brazilian economy in the late 1960s and early 1970s, which seemed to show, against their earlier belief, that structural reforms were not a precondition for growth, and therefore had to be defended on grounds of equity alone. The state was under the control of new élites, and the entire ISI process had produced an irremediably divided society: the problem was not how to achieve development, but whether development which came more easily than predicted would inevitably produce this type of society.

According to this new structuralism – now known as dependency theory but which I prefer to call neo-dualist – the modern sector was dominated by multinational corporations and characterized by an extreme concentration of the control of production and the integration of a global network of social groups all sharing a common lifestyle, projected globally through the mass media. The concentration of resources and the marginalization or co-optation of 'national' managerial and entrepreneurial classes excluded any possibility of autonomous development in

---

13 Furtado had left in the late 1950s; Sunkel was out of CEPAL for most of the 1960s, but returned in the late 1970s.

underdeveloped countries. Even the middle class and working classes were divided into 'modern' and 'traditional' sectors and could no longer be considered 'national'. The capital-intensive character of multinational investments meant that there was no prospect of integration of the masses of unemployed, and consequently even the 'cheap labour' arguments for integration into the world economy were excluded. At best there would be a 'selective and discriminatory' upward mobility of workers in the working and middle classes required by the transnational corporations and their associates (Sunkel, 1971).

The new pattern of development, dynamic though it was, actually required growing social inequality and political repression, because of the peculiar characteristics of late development on the periphery of the world economy. The principal of these, for Furtado, was the exogenous provenance of technical progress in dependent economies as compared with industrialized ones: development in the advanced countries was powered by technological progress whereas in dependent ones it was powered by demand. Income had to be concentrated among the upper and middle classes, if growth was to be sustained, for that was where the demand existed for the durable consumer goods and, indirectly, for intermediate goods, which multinational enterprises wanted to sell (Furtado, 1973).

The neo-dualist analysis was as critical of the state as of free marketeering. But it was so ultra-overdetermined – it offered a scenario so utterly hopeless for the mass of the poor and even many of the middle classes – that it contained very little ideological appeal and became a denunciation and little more. It fell to the more marxist version of dependency theory – with which these writers had little sympathy – to convert their account into a political banner by stating that socialist revolution did offer a way out of the black hole of underdevelopment.

Origins of dependency theory: 'national' marxism in the inter-war period

It was hardly surprising that the encounter between economic nationalism and marxism should lead to a revised, or 'neo'-marxism; for marxism in colonial and post-colonial countries, in China as in Latin America, has for long existed in tension with what is broadly thought of as nationalism. The tension finds an ideological expression in the opposition between a marxism which looks to universal historical trends and universalistic values and a nationalism which looks back to the roots and particularly the cultural roots of a civilization, in search of an inspiration for a future destiny. It has occasionally cost official marxism dear. In Latin America, the support of the Allied cause during World War Two, under guidance from Moscow, led several Communist Parties to align themselves with conservatives, who gravitated naturally towards the USA and Great Britain, and probably lost them a great deal of legitimacy among potential followers who would have preferred to pursue the class struggle irrespective of the international conjuncture.[14]

The first marxist thinker in Latin America who gave serious thought to the analysis of the 'national question' was the Peruvian José Carlos Mariátegui (1895–1930) whose combination of marxism with an understanding of culture and ethnicity has led some to describe him as a Latin American Gramsci. Writing in the 1920s, Mariátegui distinguished himself from Peruvian liberalism and positivism, and from the international socialist movement. As against the 'indigenists' of Peru, who idealized pre-Colombian society and sought to find a destiny for the country's *indio* masses in a return to a communal utopia, he took the view that although a transcendence of capitalist forms of production could build on the cooperative traditions of the indios, such a transcendence could not be a recreation of the past. He thus rejected the 'arcadian' variant of the indigenist tradition, as well as the generosity and sacrifice of *mestizo* ('mixed-blood', but also middle-class) groups; their activities merely served to highlight the 'moral insensitivity of a generation and an epoch' (Mariátegui, 1965, pp. 31–2). He also distanced himself from the evolutionist, or 'stage-by-stage' variant of marxism and indeed of all ideologies of modernization, by rejecting the idea that the problems of Peruvian development – and thus of the construction of a Peruvian nation – could be solved by overcoming feudal forms of domination and creating more modern capitalist forms to replace them. The overall message was that just as it was impossible to be a socialist without taking into account the people's cultural traditions; so equally it was impossible to be a true nationalist without being a socialist, because the division between the *indios* and the rest of Peruvian society was so closely bound up with that society's capitalist character. Although he was not a participant in Comintern politics, Mariátegui was taking up a theme which has been a source of conflict in the international Communist movement ever since the October Revolution. Although the Russian Revolution's very occurrence could be taken by some to raise questions concerning the validity of evolutionist ideas of history, the stage-by-stage view fitted nicely with the

14 This was known as 'Browderism': Browder was the secretary-general of the US Communist Party who dragooned his Latin American colleagues into these positions. It was not surprising that, after the war, the banner of anti-imperialism was available to corporatist movements such as Peronism, the Cuban labour confederation (CTC) and the Movimiento Nacional Revolucionario in Bolivia. Only in Chile did the CP retain a respectable share of the vote.

foreign-policy interests of a new Soviet state encircled by hostile im-perialist states. For Moscow, and for Lenin, the formation of as broad alliances as possible in colonial and semi-colonial countries, so as to weaken imperialism and support the October Revolution took priority, whereas from the periphery – in that case from Asia – came the call for immediate proletarian revolution, from delegates and political leaders who were not at all attracted by the prospect of collaborating with their 'national' capitalists in bourgeois democratic revolutions (Carr, 1953, III, ch. 26).

Although he saw capitalism at the root of the plight of the Peruvian people, Mariátegui did not claim that they would respond to a political ideology borrowed from advanced capitalist societies. On the contrary, the revolution would be based on a renewal of the mythical and religious components of Andean culture – a culture which he idealized perhaps more than he knew, since in his short life he spent very little time outside Lima, and when he did travel it was to Europe and not to the highland Andes.[15] He disagreed with official marxism which confounded progress with 'westernization': 'Faith in indigenous renewal comes not from a process of material "westernization" in quechua [i.e. Indian] lands. It is not civilization, or the Alphabet, which raises the soul of the indio. It is the myth, the idea of socialist revolution' (Mariátegui, 1928, p. 32). Or again:

> The propagation of socialist ideas in Peru has brought about an upsurge of indigenist demands. The young generation feels and knows that there will be no real development in Peru, or at least no Peruvian development, unless it is the work of and leads to an improvement in the welfare of the Peruvian masses, of whom four-fifths are indios and peasants. This same movement is manifested among artists and writers who increasingly value autochtho-nous forms and subject matter, hitherto despised by a Spanish colonial spirit and mentality. Indigenist literature seems destined to play the same role as that of the Russian populists in the pre-revolutionary period. The *indios* themselves are beginning to give signs of a new awareness . . . for the first time the indigenous problem, hitherto evaded by the rhetoric of the ruling classes, is being posed in social and economic terms, and identified as fundamentally a problem of land. With every day that passes, it becomes more evident that this problem cannot be solved either by a humanitarian formula, or by a philanthropic programme. (ibid., pp. 31–2)

Mariátegui is the founding figure of Peru's marxist left, just as Haya de la Torre – who was his ally, rival and eventually his ideological enemy but lived on until 1980 – is the founding figure of the country's foremost

---

15 Mariátegui was 'exiled' to Europe with a scholarship more or less forced upon him by the dictator Leguía in 1919. He returned to Peru in 1923 and died in 1930.

national–popular, and intermittently reformist, political party, APRA.[16] Like later marxist and radical theorists, including the theologians of liberation, Mariátegui values the indigenous cultural tradition yet needs to distance himself from its invocation and manipulation by conservatives of both paternalistic and authoritarian hue. Disputes over whether a workers' party (rather than a more broad-based and multi-class organiza-tion) with a socialist ideology (rather than a national–popular one) should play a vanguard role, led to the split between Mariátegui and Haya de la Torre in 1928, and to splits in other left wing movements – for example the breakaway of the socialists in Chile from the Communists, and in Argentina the development of a national–popular alternative within the Radical Party and later in the form of Peronism.

In the event, it was not in Peru but in Argentina that the 'national' call had most success, though many Argentine nationalist writers invoked Mariátegui's heritage. For some forty-five years, a deep division cut right through the Argentine intelligentsia, and right across the European conventions of 'right' and 'left': from the 1930s on, there would be 'national' and 'cosmopolitan' marxists, and, in fact if not precisely in name, national and cosmopolitan conservatives. The national left was anti-liberal and anti-British, to be sure, but was also ferociously hostile to (cosmopolitan) official marxism and to the moderate, modernizing socialism of the Socialist Party, known contemptuously to some as *socialismo cipayo*, in an allusion to the Indian 'sepoys' hired by the British Army to repress their own countrymen. On the right, an authoritarian, anti-liberal tendency, strong in Catholic and military circles, coexisted uneasily with the traditional liberalism of the beef and wheat exporters and the finance houses.

To clarify this Argentine picture we must return to the late 1920s when a group of historians known as *revisionistas* resurrected the figure of the nineteenth-century 'Federalist' dictator Rosas.[17] Previously thought of as the 'Caligula of the River Plate', Rosas was now reanointed as a founding father of Argentine nationhood, in a radical departure from earlier generations' veneration of his liberal, 'Europeanizing' junior contempor-ary Sarmiento.[18] This was part of a broader project, heavily influenced by

16 The Alianza Popular Revolucionaria Latinoamericana, founded by Haya de la Torre in Mexico in 1924, but always a Peruvian party (Bourricaud, 1967).

17 Governor of Buenos Aires Province from 1829–32 and 1835–52.

18 Sarmiento, apart from being one of the great liberal nineteenth-century statesmen, remains famous or notorious for the phrase 'civilization or barbarism' as a stark statement of the alternatives facing a society caught between the primitive customs of the hinterland banditry and the western culture of the towns. His classic account of banditry is *Facundo* (1848), 'Contemporary opponents reviled Rosas as a bloody tyrant and a symbol of barbarism, while a later generation canonized him as a nationalist hero, but he is more

European fascism and Maurras-style integrism denouncing the decadence of liberalism, the corruption of the Argentine state, and the need for an authoritarian system closely allied with the Catholic Church to save the state from further erosion by democracy and consequent overthrow by communism. The project failed; its protagonists had thought mistakenly that the military who overthrew President Irigoyen in 1930 would carry it out.[19] But the anti-imperialist tradition they had inaugurated was to live long in Argentine political discourse: before long populist historians had taken up the revisionists' enthusiasm for Rosas and also their definition of the nation in opposition to imperialism and its local liberal puppets. 'Imperialism' meant British imperialism, which had made Argentina into its 'sixth dominion' and in 1933 had imposed upon her the humiliating Roca–Runciman treaty. That document remained a byword for *entreguismo*, the attitude of submission – supine at best, treacherous at worst – of the local oligarchy in the face of pressure from great powers.[20] The puzzlement experienced by outsiders in the face of Peronism is explained to some extent by the movement's amalgamation of these themes into an apparently unified discourse, and in support of causes – such as trade unionism – which made the establishment shudder.

The 'national left' had a difficult relationship with Peronism, for if

---

accurately described as the embodiment of the Federalist *caudillo*, a conservative autocrat dedicated to the aggrandizement of his own province and to its ranchers' (Rock, 1986, p. 104). The publication *Criterio*, which first appeared in 1928, was the organ of this tendency.
19 A similar pattern was repeated in 1967. A useful survey of the literary expressions of this tendency is given in Rock, 1987. See also Navarro, 1965 and 1968. Note also the disdain with which Vargas treated the Brazilian integrists even after the establishment of his highly corporatist *Estado Novo*, modelled in essential features on Mussolini's *Carta del Lavoro*.
20 In the year 1929–30 Argentine export earnings fell 34 per cent, and aggregate output by 14 per cent (Rock, 1986, p. 220); a further shock came in 1933 as world wheat prices fell by 45 per cent in domestic currency terms and maize prices by half (ibid., p. 221). Britain was the country's principal trading partner, accounting in the late 1920s and early 1930s for a fifth of Argentina's imports and a third of her exports, also the major foreign investor both in Argentine bonds and in capital – especially railways and meat-freezing. But when the Depression hit primary product prices world-wide Britain agreed on an arrangement known as Imperial Preference, at the Ottawa Conference of 1932, which guaranteed a share of the British home market to her formal dominions, thus excluding Argentina, the (informal) 'sixth dominion'. The Argentine government was appalled and dispatched the Foreign Minister Roca to London, where the agreement was concluded in 1933. The pact may have preserved the amount of Argentine beef exported to Britain, and may have ensured that 15 per cent of those exports were frozen in Argentine-owned freezing plants, but otherwise it was extremely beneficial to both British exporters – who were in effect exempted from the emergency tariff imposed during the Depression – and British investors in Argentina, who were granted privileged status protecting them from devaluations. In the case of the railways they even obtained exemption from the legal obligation to fund pensions for their employees. On the left-right cross-fertilizations which ensued, see the excellent account by Halperin Donghi, 1984.

Peronism represented a social force that they all most fervently desired, they were far less enthusiastic about its political management and direction. The origin of the national left lay in a tendency within the Radical Party, which eventually became an independent intellectual force, known as FORJA (Fuerza de Orientacion Radical de la Juventud Argentina)[21] whose spokesmen were obsessed by the financial intrigues which had accompanied foreign investment, implying that the Argentine state was manipulated from abroad and that, because of the treachery of the country's rulers, the growth of the Argentine economy served foreign interests better than those of her own people.[22] We see here the early seeds of dependency theory, that is, of the idea that a ruling class can pursue its own interests by submitting to foreign economic forces in contradiction to the interests of the popular classes, and indeed that it cannot act in any other way without endangering its own existence as a class. The dependency theorists preferred to explain this by reference to the pattern of insertion into the world economy, and not to the venality and moral shortcomings which obsessed the nationalists of left and right.

The apologists of the national left placed themselves firmly apart both from the anti-democratic nationalism of the right and also from the socialist intelligentsia which in their caustic view applied an imported marxism but in practice propounded the same version of history as the oligarchy.[23] They claimed that the proletariat during the inter-war period was immature and its parties and unions had been 'imported'. The advocacy of class struggle – as opposed to national liberation – was for them merely a pretext adopted by the left-wing intelligentsia whereby they could avoid ever having to support 'the popular movements who gave expression to social and national advancement', a diversionary manoeuvre which facilitated the strategy of the oligarchy (Jauretche, 1974, p. 13). Where the liberal 'cosmopolitan' Sarmiento had pictured a struggle between civilization and barbarism, they saw Argentine history

---

21 Literally the 'Radical Orienting Force of Argentine Youth' – but more importantly an acronym which refers to the notion of a forge and thus, presumably, the forging of a nation.
22 Prebisch, of course, had been a member of the team which negotiated the Roca–Runciman pact. The classic work of historiographic muck-raking or demonology in this school was that of Scalabrini Ortiz which still was to gain renewed popularity in the late 1950s and in the 1960s. It is noteworthy that his most popular book, the *History of the Argentine railways*, which Halperin describes as characterized more by moralism and 'demonization' than by economic analysis was first published in 1940 and then not reissued until 1957, two years after the overthrow of Perón. The book concentrates on the financial manipulation which accompanied the construction of the railways by British capital and the complicity of Argentine governments in these murky deals.
23 Jauretche, 1974. This book too, first published in 1964, was republished in 1973 when Peronist nationalism was experiencing its headiest period as the Montoneros conducted their military assault on the state.

as a 'conflict between a reality which is seeking expression through its own modes and to advance in tune with its own being, and a falsified and shrunken country ["civilization"] which its opponents would create'. With the defeat of Rosas at the battle of Caseros, 'the real country and with it its people are buried (ibid., p. 40). Their dream was of a *capitalismo propio* – 'a capitalism of our own', no longer stunted by imperialist involvement. It is a vision later described by the same writer in an unforgettably morbid image: 'happy will be the day when an Argentine, on having his throat cut by another Argentine, will be able to look up and see that the knife which did the deed was made in Argentina' (Galasso, 1983, p. 95).

If writers such as these saw in Peronism the possibility that their dream of a 'national' capitalism would be realized, others, in the marxist tradition, reacted differently, signalling a division in the nationalist camp and illustrating the divisive potential of nationalist ideologies which seek to sustain all-embracing class alliances. The rise of Peronism after 1943, and perhaps especially the remarkable persistence of popular and especially proletarian support for Perón after his overthrow in 1955, constituted a fundamental intellectual challenge to marxism, especially when taken in conjunction with the growing awareness among the intelligentsia that the country's great economic expansion had given way to decline. The overwhelmingly Peronist working class seemed the very incarnation of the ideal of a solid collective actor mobilized in traditional causes of trade unionism and living standards, but ready for radical politicization. Yet they were also mobilized in the name of a leader rather than an ideology, and of a leader whose one and only consistent ideological stance was perhaps his anti-marxism. The other Argentine conundrum for marxists of any hue was the country's economic decline which, occurring without a cataclysmic revolutionary crisis heralding the socialist revolution, cast severe doubt over the historical stages which formed the core of the marxist canon. The development of underdevelopment really did occur in the most empiricist sense of the term in Argentina. Later on, that phrase would be used to describe a static structural condition in which capitalism develops at the expense of the wellbeing of the masses and of a polarization of social classes, but in Argentina it seemed to many that a process of increasing general prosperity had turned out to be constructed on foundations of sand because it was based on foreign investors who had no interest but to bleed the country dry. This idea, that foreign investment, far from contributing to accumulation, drains surplus away, was to become a central plank in dependency theory.

These challenges gave rise to a second dimension of the national left, whose constituency was strong among the vast student community of Buenos Aires, and who sought a way out of these theoretical difficulties by trying to shift Perón to the left through pressure from below, linking his vast class alliance to a socialist programme. This left Peronist tendency (often close to Trotskyism) flourished briefly in the period between Perón's overthrow in 1955 and the military coup of 1966, after which the attack on an academic community which was just beginning to acquire international renown, led many of its most prominent members to leave the country. Thus was born a diaspora of Argentine intellectuals which since then has not ceased to grow. The left Peronists and marxists among them probably contributed substantially to the tidal wave of dependency theory by applying their own Argentine experience to that of other countries. It is indeed possible to think of dependency theory as an adaptation of the Argentine 'national marxist' analysis to countries where the word underdevelopment referred to a set of self-perpetuating structures rather than a reversal of development[24] in the strict sense, and where the working class was far weaker and less solid than in Argentina.

Dependency theory

The confluence of marxism and nationalism known as dependency theory became extraordinarily popular among the Latin American intelligentsia during a brief period which ran from about 1965 to 1975. This popularity was the result of many factors, including the parallel failures of official marxism and of the reformism embodied in the Alliance for Progress, and the success of the Cuban revolution in defying both of them. The appeal and the originality of dependency theory lay in its claim to solve both the question of social injustice and that of national destiny in one single theoretical and ideological framework.

For the radical intelligentsia, concerned with doctrine rather than practical politics, Latin American nationalism appeared irredeemably provincial, just as Peruvian *indigenismo* had seemed to Mariátegui, and although the example of Peronism illustrated its mobilizing potential, Peronism also showed the limitations of national–popular ideologies, for it was anti-marxist, authoritarian and manipulative and when economic crisis loomed inevitably retreated to orthodox capitalist solutions.

Dependency theory found a way out of this impasse by offering an account of the world economy which explained the structural bases of underdevelopment in economic terms, and which thus showed how the world economy constrained the opportunities and choices open to states on the periphery and their leaders. The theory thus transcended a

24 This phrase is the title of a recent book by one of these émigrés (Waisman, 1987).

nationalist discourse based on culture or national destiny, and created a new discourse in which the 'anti-nation' was not a foreign or colonial power but a world system whose tentacles reached into the very fabric of peripheral formations. Dependency became an anti-imperialist doctrine of a new type because it saw the mechanisms of oppression analytically in the operation of a world economy and not in the subjection of some nations by others.

In the ensuing pages we see how dependency theory arose as a reaction against official marxism and reformism, and we also see the beginning of a concern with the state, which has to become so dominant in the intellectual debates of the 1980s.

Official marxism

The official doctrine of Latin America's Communist Parties was for long characterized by a primitive 'stage-by-stage' view of development and socialism, as originally formulated by the early Russian Social Democrats (Carr, 1953, I). The CPs of Latin America were imprisoned within the straitjacket of official dialectical materialism; a moderate political strategy; and a servile relationship with Moscow, which is difficult to understand because it brought so few rewards.[25]

The 'stages' theory is a combination of two elements: first, the evolutionist version of dialectical materialism as distilled from Marx by Engels and the early Russian social democrat Plekhanov (1857–1918), according to which socialism cannot develop until capitalism has fully exhausted its possibilities and succumbs to its internal contradictions. The second element is the model of a class alliance, in which 'progressive' and 'national' capitalists would ally with peasants and workers against the landlords and 'imperialism'. This image derived from a model of an enclave, or primary-export economy, in which foreign capital is invested in production for export and the domestic market is left to local entrepreneurs. The state does not use economic policy to expand the domestic market, preferring to stimulate exports and therefore support-ing both the landed oligarchy which produces them and the 'comprador bourgeoisie'[26] which lives parasitically off the import of foreign-made

---

25 The irony of the relationship is accentuated by the recollection that, when in recent years non-communist nationalist political forces have carried out revolutions, notably in Cuba and Nicaragua, the Soviet Union has been quick to support them and the official Communist Parties have climbed on the bandwagon rather late in the day. On Cuba, see Karol, 1972.

26 'Comprador' means purchaser; the term seems to have originated in South-East Asia where it refers to non-indigenous merchant groups with a distinctive ethnic (Chinese, Indian, European) identity.

goods for the wealthy minority. Domestic consumption levels are held down, and thereby the market for domestic producers of manufactures, or indeed of anything but primary products, who depend almost exclusively on that market, is restricted. From this it would seem to follow that the interests of all social classes except the landlords and the compradors would be served by a reorientation of the economy away from exports and a redistribution of land which would broaden the internal market and deprive the existing ruling class of its power base. The affinity with CEPAL's analysis and the 'basic reforms' strategy it inspired is clear. In China and Vietnam, this strategy was the rhetorical plank of revolution, but in Latin America and Africa the official marxist line, embodied occasionally in the term 'non-capitalist road',[27] was reformist, even though it claimed a monopoly of legitimate marxist revolutionary doctrine; and it was marxist even though it was allied with the conservatives in Argentina against Perón, with populism in Brazil against the status quo (1961–4), with the Socialists in Chile against dependent capitalism (1970–3) and with the military in Peru in favour of structural change (1968–75). Argentina was the only country where, before about 1967, the Communist Party did not hold hegemonic control of the field of marxism. In general, of course, CP moderation fitted well with Moscow's aversion to Third World revolutions which might escape Soviet control, and with the strategy of peaceful coexistence.

The Alliance for Progress and Latin American Reformism

CEPAL and official marxism offered two converging ideological projects, and they were further reinforced by the Alliance for Progress, in a brief moment of consensus during the early 1960s when reformism seemed to carry all before it.

The idea of a major cooperative international reformist development effort with strong financial backing from the United States was embodied in the Alliance for Progress, launched with much fanfare by President Kennedy in March 1961, and incorporated later that year into a Charter at a meeting of the OAS in Punta del Este, Uruguay, shortly after the Bay of Pigs invasion and six months before Cuba was definitively excluded from the Interamerican system. The Alliance was a response to the Cuban revolution, without doubt, but it started out as a liberal response, in the North American sense of the word, based on the view that, although counter-insurgency and other security measures were no doubt necessary to prevent a 'second Cuba', the root cause of the revolutionary threat was the poverty which created favourable conditions for revolutionary activ-

---

27 Also adopted by the Chilean Christian Democrats in their more enthusiastic moments.

ity. The themes of democracy and liberty were there, although the unmentioned theme of security was obviously implicit. But above all the call of the Charter was for economic development – with the accompaniment of massive injections of foreign aid – with an emphasis on drastic reform, especially agrarian reform, and its liberal inspiration was reflected in its emphasis on the role of the state and of planning in the development process, consistent with the New Deal heritage of its progenitors.

The Charter was preceded by a 'Declaration of the Peoples of America' which reminds us of the extent to which the tone and content of international official statements on development in the region have fundamentally altered in the last twenty-five years. In it the signatories agreed to:

> encourage, in accordance with the characteristics of each country, programs of comprehensive agrarian reform, leading to the effective transformation, where required, of unjust structures and systems of land tenure and use; with a view to replacing latifundia and dwarf holdings by an equitable system of property so that . . . the land will become for the man who works it the basis of his economic stability.

The appearance of the word 'latifundia', in an official – though admittedly not binding – international document of this kind was extraordinary, for it is an almost abusive term. The Latin American representatives must have thought that the USA was about to provide them with a very big pot of gold indeed if they were prepared to swallow it.

It was now possible to argue for reform invoking almost every available sacred cow, from official marxism to CEPAL and the Alliance for Progress. All these schools of thought believed that the landed oligarchies were vulnerable because, despite their undoubted political influence, their economic interests stood in contradiction with those of almost every other interest. They were said to be traditional, retrogade, backward, inefficient, paternalistic. They were the favourite butt of every reforming expert, local or foreign.

All these schools shared a stage-bound conception of what the dominant sociological theories of the time called modernization and others called capitalist development; they all believed that, in the inimitable phrase of Marx's Preface to the first edition of *Capital*, 'the country that is more developed industrially only shows, to the less developed, the image of its own future' (Marx, 1976, p. 91). For the Communist Parties, reforms plus an expansion of the state and controls on foreign capital were designed to hasten the process of home-grown capitalist development, and socialism remained an ultimate goal – but the crucial element was the underlying stage-by-stage conception. And although CEPAL had taken up to some extent a tradition of the search for a *pensamiento propio*, by affirming that the economic problems and strategies of these countries demanded a specific approach distinct from Anglo-Saxon and European orthodoxy, the goal they envisaged was clearly the conventional one of Western-style industrialization. The possibility that the distinctiveness of the means might imply the distinctiveness of ends received little attention.

Why did this wide theoretical consensus on reformism and evolutionary stages not translate into political consensus? The answer, as we shall see in the next chapter, is that the consensus, though real, did not reflect a confluence of political or economic interests, but merely a common terrain of argument: the political argument over how fast and how far reforms should go became a proxy for the argument over whether they should be implemented at all; and the complicated political management of reform offered fertile grounds for disagreement.

The reasons why, in the words of a graphic study, the Alliance for Progress 'lost its way' (Levinson and Onís, 1970) are many, and they have been the subject of much comment: they range from a lack of financial commitment in Washington to the shift in emphasis in US policy towards Latin America, from development and democracy to security and stability, to a lack of capacity or commitment among Latin American political leaders, and to a growing doubt among them whether reforms could be weathered without seriously destabilizing their institutions and social structure. The next chapter will give a more detailed account of how the politics of reform fell apart.

The reformist consensus, then, was short-lived. If we survey the 1960s, we see that at the very time when it seemed to come together in the 'Punta del Este chorus', where Che Guevara sang together with Dean Rusk, its ideological underpinnings were falling apart. The 'neo-dualism' of Pinto, Furtado and Sunkel was the first sign of disillusion from former members of the CEPAL camp. Other signs came from a new style of political science in the USA. Within marxism there was the earthquake represented by innumerable events ranging from the Chinese Cultural Revolution, which began in 1966, to the student uprisings of 1968, the Prague Spring of that same year, and nearer to Latin America, the Cuban revolution, the Bay of Pigs and the 1962 missile crisis. In the advanced countries generally the Vietnam War provoked a contestation of official doctrines – Western and Eastern – concerning the place of the developing countries in the international political and economic system which provided a favourable audience and a breeding-ground for radical Third Worldism.

In the USA dissent of one kind from the liberal optimism embodied in the Alliance for Progress was expressed by the political scientist Samuel Huntington, author of what might be described as the ideological handbook of the US military (Huntington, 1957), adviser to the Pentagon in Vietnam, and a friend of certain very prominent members of the Brazilian military.[28] In 1968 he published a highly influential – and highly readable – book which argued that democracy did not necessarily either favour development or emerge in consonance with it, that the primary aim of government was to govern and not to produce democracy or development, and that civil and human rights were a middle-class demand which governments in poor countries would do best to ignore unless they wished to create serious problems of instability. Not that the book was uniformly hostile to change: for example Huntington did support land reform, on the slightly cynical grounds that it would create a suitably conservative land-owning peasantry, though his analysis and data on the subject were seriously flawed.[29] These academic disputations are secondary, though, to the shift which Huntington reflected and perhaps produced in establishment perceptions in the USA, as one of the first conservative thinkers to challenge the optimistic nostrums of the liberal modernization theory which underlay the 'aid-optimism' of the time.

In Latin America, the conservative reaction was delayed, and the initial intellectual assault on the reformist consensus was predominantly from the left. The growing awareness, in the light of the Cuban experience, that reform was not going to be tolerated either by the USA or by local ruling elites, provided a backdrop to the merging of marxism and the CEPAL tradition in the potent formula of 'dependency theory'. Although Furtado and Sunkel did produce one version of this, they had too little political sensitivity to write it in a way which would be ideologically resonant: the key to such resonance was the ability to invoke both the marxist and the nationalist traditions. The universalistic references of the CEPAL tradition and its descendants, and of official marxism, needed to be tempered by an awareness of or even an expression of faith in a special destiny for Latin America and the Third World.

Thus was born the economic analysis of backwardness and poverty as inherent features of an entire class of states and populations oppressed by the world economic system. The nationalism of the patriot and of state defensiveness was overtaken in political discourse – though hardly in

28 Huntington is said to be highly admired by General Golbery do Couto e Silva, long-time participant in various plots, culminating in the coup of 1964, founder of the Brazilian National Intelligence Service, top official advisor to various subsequent military Heads of State etc. According to Skidmore (1988), Huntington was consulted extensively by Golbery on the management of the military's gradual withdrawal from power in the period 1974–84.

29 Huntington, 1968. For a critique of his account of land reform, see Lehmann, 1971. An account which shows how Huntington was also reacting to the turmoil on some US campuses at the time is to be found in Cruise O'Brien, 1972.

political practice – by a 'multi-nation' nationalism. In the place of a nationalism which calls on the particularities of a people's history as a sign of their destiny an alternative was produced which defines a people in terms of their common exploitation by great economic forces and describes their destiny as the struggle against those forces. Hence the role of marxism.

An available audience

Although, as we have seen, radical development theory had many precursors, its international success was heralded by André Gunder Frank, a Chicago-trained economist writing in the early 1960s in the American marxist journal *Monthly Review* (Frank, 1969, 1970).

Frank launched an attack on three different orthodoxies: that of economics, that of CEPAL, and that of official marxism. Where orthodox economics said that trade spread wealth, Frank said it spread poverty; where it said that gains from productivity increases are spread evenly throughout a free trading system, Frank said that free trade creates polarization and concentrates those gains among those best endowed initially; where that theory taught the virtues of comparative advantage Frank taught those of autarky, in a much stronger sense than CEPAL had ever done. Frank's ideas caught on like wildfire, and if we put ourselves for a moment in the minds of students (especially North American students) brought up on an unadulterated diet of orthodox economics we can see that to them this at least was comprehensible. The discourse of Marx and Lenin would have seemed like a foreign language to them. The early to mid 1960s were a time when Marxism was scarcely even mentioned in American university courses in the social sciences, let alone in economics; in Britain too it was given fairly cursory treatment. The formulation of a dissident theory in pure undiluted marxist terms would have found hardly any audience at all.[30] Similarly, student protest found expression in Europe and even North America in unorthodox marxism and in a radical libertarianism deeply hostile to the official versions put out by the Soviet Union and her friends.

In Latin America too, Frank set the cat among the pigeons, but the contestation was perceived as directed against official marxism as much as

30 Educated at the University of Chicago and taught by some of the best known economists associated with that institution, he took their paradigm and turned it upside down – in a manner reminiscent of Althusser's account of the young Marx 'standing Hegel back up on his feet'. That is, he turned orthodox trade theory on its head, but the trade theory remained the same trade theory, or rather its 'problematic', the questions it posed, remain the same: see Althusser (1966, p. 70).

against conservative politics. Although he attacked CEPAL grievously for its reformist illusions and what he regarded as its 'underdeveloping' development plans, Frank took out of CEPAL's book a vulgar version of the theory of the secular decline in the terms of trade. He christened this a 'metropolis–satellite' relationship – as distinct from Prebisch's 'centre–periphery' image – in which not only was the 'gap' widened, but 'surplus' was siphoned off from periphery to centre even as economic growth was proceeding, so that 'the richer the countries became, the poorer the people became'. In adopting this usage he was adding a marxist tinge to a non-marxist analysis, but he was also using the term 'surplus' in a very un-marxist way.[31]

Frank's thesis was also an attack on the orthodox views of Communist Parties. The message of orthodox economics, after all, was in some ways not different from that of Marx when it came to development. In his writings on India, Marx had also pointed to the positive effects of capitalist expansion on the hinterland, the colonies, the periphery: it would produce growth and transform social structures, modes of production, values and ways of life. Frank confronted deeply-rooted assumptions, namely that all countries go through essentially the same development path, pointing out that since the progress of the early industrializing countries had depended on the exploitation of today's developing countries the latter's chances of following them was seriously undermined. They had been part of the world capitalist system from the first years of their incorporation into the world trading system in the sixteenth century and therefore the current plight of their populations was indissolubly tied to that fact. Just as developed countries had never been *under*developed even if they had been *un*developed, so underdevelopment was a creation of capitalism, not a condition preceding it – let alone one which might be overcome by it. One of Frank's favourite paradoxes was the claim that the purportedly 'feudal' structures of Latin American agriculture were the creation of capitalist expansion, beginning in the colonial period, not a

31 The term surplus has a specific meaning in marxist economics, and Frank's usage is not in conformity with it. In marxist economics it refers to that part of production which is left over after paying variable costs and replacing capital at the best available technology. It is not therefore the same as profit, since if non-optimum technologies are needed some of the surplus will go towards paying labour or replacing capital, and not towards profit at all. The sense in which Frank uses it here is utterly different, since he refers in essence to a purely notional difference between what would accrue to the satellites if terms of trade moved in their favour – or did not move at all – and what actually occurs when terms of trade move against them, as he assumed them to do, after Prebisch. Whereas in Marx's schema the extraction of surplus by the wage labour relationship was part of a mechanism of accumulation and thus of development, in Frank's it is, in effect, an extortion with no built-in mechanism to channel the pseudo-surplus back into the accumulation process. This example of his usage shows well how right Frank is when he denies that he is a marxist.

stage prior to it. For him the 'marginalized masses' had not been left out: rather they had suffered precisely by being integrated into a pattern whereby capitalist development proceeded at the expense of their persistent poverty.[32]

It was illusory to believe that the capitalist classes in poor countries were in any sense progressive, as official marxism liked to think. On the contrary, Frank described them as an integral and supportive part of the metropolis–satellite system. Their way of life and their economic interests were dependent on the continual exploitation of the poor, they were mere links, agents or intermediaries in long macro-historical chains of exploitation linking successive metropolitan centres to successive satellites from the great financial and industrial centres of the world down to the last syllable of exploited peasantry, and sucking 'surplus' back in the opposite direction. They would therefore resist any change. This is what, in a phrase destined to seize the imagination of many, he termed the 'development of underdevelopment'.

Frank is an extraordinary, perhaps unique case in intellectual history, and the nit-picking polemics surrounding his work have obscured its real historical significance. He should be treated not as an interlocutor but as a phenomenon, a social fact. What is extraordinary is that a person writing in this paranoid and intemperate style, the antithesis of the dispassionate academic, should have had such a profound influence both within and outside the university. He burst onto the stage with a set of iconoclastic generalizations formulated more as slogans (albeit brilliant ones) than as scientific or historical statements, and with little identifiable immediate meaning if taken too literally, supported by only the flimsiest evidence and much argument from (and against) authority ('the well-known Centre for Research ... says ...'). Yet he redefined the whole area of development research and teaching, he recreated the questions to be asked, and since then he has been a constant – though now dwindling – point of reference for development theory.

32 This claim was to run a long way, for it provided an initial basis on which marxist theorists could take into account the proliferating informal sector and peasantry, who hardly fit the category of an industrial proletariat. If these could be shown to be exploited by mechanisms inherent to the process of capitalist development, then there was still a good reason for socialist revolution. The most systematic exposition of this view is in de Janvry, 1981. This view of marginality also gave rise to the idea of the articulation of modes of production, according to which 'surplus' is channelled not only between classes, but between different modes of production, through the mechanism of unequal or manipulated trade – viz. the control of food prices, or of foreign exchange, or of export receipts etc.

Conclusion

Frank's intervention was seminal, but he was not alone. The Latin American intelligentsia was becoming part of a broader Western intellectual community. On the Latin American left the view gained ground that Soviet anti-imperialism was a sham and that the Soviets and the Americans were intent upon carving out mutually accommodating spheres of influence under the guise of détente. A serious rift developed between the Cuban Communist Party and other Communist Parties, which only began to heal after Castro's speech in 1968 in apparently reluctant support of the Soviet invasion of Czechoslovakia.

In 1966 the Cuban government sponsored the formation of two ephemeral organizations called OLAS (Organización Latinoamericana de Solidaridad – the Latin American Solidarity Organization) and Tricontinental (strictly OSPAAL: Asia–Africa–Latin America Solidarity Organization) devoted to the promotion of immediate and violent revolution in Latin America and the Third World in general. At the same time Régis Debray – a Frenchman who had gone to Cuba and become a confidant of Fidel Castro – issued a call to arms in his *Revolution in the revolution* which provoked scandals on the left and right in Europe and Latin America, advocating the immediate formation of guerrilla *focos* in Latin America on the (seriously misinterpreted) model of the Cuban revolution;[33] relations between Havana and the Latin American Communist Parties were at their nadir, especially in the wake of Che Guevara's Bolivian debacle, for which the Communists were blamed and which they in their turn regarded as dangerous adventurism. In Chile, Colombia, Guatemala and Peru 'extreme left' or 'Castrist' groups had also formed and were challenging the legitimacy of orthodox Communist Parties.[34]

The attack from the left was reinforced when in 1964 the capitalist

33 Debray's misinterpretation consisted in an undervaluation of the contribution of urban guerrillas to the revolution and an overvaluation of the role of the tightly-knit band of men in the mountains. The latter, of course, had been led by Fidel, whereas the former were a network in which many different organizations participated as well as a large number of others providing logistical support. Debray's book offered a rationale for Guevara's ill-fated Bolivian campaign in 1967. It claimed that all urban political forces were corrupted by the tempting, 'bourgeois' environment of the cities, and that the masses were likewise co-opted by reformist or conservative ideologies. The only solution, then, was the *foco*.

34 The accusations of 'reformism' against the Communist Parties were in fact somewhat unfair. By 1970 the Chilean Communist Party had made it abundantly clear that it looked with no more favour upon the 'monopolistic' elements of the 'national bourgeoisie' than it did on their multinational partners. If it advised caution, that was for tactical reasons and also because of the party's continued distaste for violent political action.

classes – and indeed much of the middle classes – of Brazil lined up with the military in the first of a series of unprecedently repressive regimes, closely allied to the USA and to multinational capital. Although the high rate of economic growth achieved in Brazil after 1967 seemed to cast doubt on Frank's theses if one interpreted him to be saying that economic growth and integration in the world system were incompatible, if he was taken to mean that development, in the wider sense of the eradication of poverty and social injustices, was incompatible with such integration, then this Brazilian experience of 'savage capitalism' reinforced his point. This was underlined by various writers, especially the Brazilian Teotonio dos Santos and the Argentine sociologist José Nun (dos Santos, 1969; Nun, 1969).

Dos Santos and Nun went beyond Frank by taking into account the reality of Latin American industrialization: the region could no longer be described only as a 'primary producer', and foreign capital was now investing in manufacturing as well as in primary production. Yet despite industrialization, unemployment remained very high and was increasing. (In this they were too emphatic, at least for Brazil, the region's most dynamic case of industrialization.) It seemed that the conditions of peripheral industrialization in the twentieth century made structural unemployment inevitable: the labour available in poor countries was so cheap, relatively, that multinationals could even make a profit while paying high wages, in local terms, and using capital-intensive, labour-saving technologies. From a political point of view, structural employment on a large scale seemed to favour the perpetuation of an 'available' and pliant populist mass, unlike the more familiar marxist account of capitalism and its demise which relied heavily on the system generating that very working class which would overthrow it.

The voluntarism and vanguardism of the various Castrist organizations which grew up in Latin America in the 1960s can be related to this type of image in which classes and modes of production from all countries fit together in a global capitalist system seemingly without internal contradictions. The independent action of guerrilla *focos* and other tightly-knit conspiratorial bands came to appear as the only way of producing those contradictions – by an intervention from outside the system.

In addition, there grew up the idea, reminiscent of the late 1920s in Europe,[35] that, as in the title of dos Santos' book, the alternatives for the people were fascism or revolution. There was no middle way. Underlying

---

35 From 1925 Stalin decided that, as against previous doctrine, Social Democracy was to be regarded merely as the moderate wing of fascism, as 'social fascism'. This line was, as Claudín observes, to have 'baneful consequences', for it laid the way for Hitler's electoral victory. Similar problems were to recur in Spain before and during the Civil War (Claudín, 1975).

this there was a perception that the ruling economic classes were too weak to resist even moderate or peaceful popular mobilization or reformist working class or peasant demands (such as land reform). Instead of establishing their ideological hegemony in civil society they were beholden to the state apparatus and on their own they lacked the capitalist dynamism which would enable them to respond flexibly to those demands. Indeed, dependency theory itself, in one version, revealed its neo-classical velleities in an underlying, though undeveloped, thesis to the effect that, if markets were left to act perfectly, then the global development process would not be uneven; the ruling classes in the periphery and semi-periphery existed by virtue of their dependence on the interventionist apparatus of the state and thus ensured that markets were interfered with and resources misallocated.[36] The ruling class of the Third World were, in this respect, a pale imitation of the *bourgeoisie conquérante* which had led the industrialization process in Europe and North America, in both economic performance and political leadership, for they were not truly entrepreneurial and presided over a 'distorted' form of capitalism.

The result was perceived as a brittle political system, a zero-sum game, in which reformism found no space, and in which the structure of the state and its particular role in the mode of accumulation played a central part. In the face of the slightest tremor, the domestic ruling classes and the USA would turn immediately to the military to seize power – a military which was incomparably more powerful than the coercive apparatuses which had been available in earlier processes of industrialization.

A climate of doubt was setting in with respect to democracy. In addition to the traditional marxist reservations about 'bourgeois democracy' as the 'dictatorship of the bourgeoisie', and to equally traditional reservations on the right, serious doubts were being expressed in non-marxist circles about the efficacy of either political democracy or economic growth in providing a framework for overcoming poverty or social injustice – in other words, in achieving the objectives of the Alliance for Progress. Doubts about democracy not in principle, but as actually practised in Latin America, were expressed, for example, in the work of a moderate Christian Democrat and 'cepalino' Chilean economist like Jorge Ahumada (Ahumada, 1958), and in the declarations of the Latin American Episcopal Conference which met in Medellín, Colombia in 1968. Those declarations, in lending ecclesiastical authority to denunciations of 'institutionalized' and 'structural' violence, implied that the

---

36 This is the strong implication of the writings of both Samir Amin and Immanuel Wallerstein, see Amin, 1976; and Wallerstein, 1979, 1984. For an elaboration of this point, see Lehmann, 1986a.

prevalent democracy was a sham. These positions all had in common the idea that formal democracy was not a value to be placed above all others, nor an efficient but malleable system of government, but rather that it was one value among many and could, under certain circumstances, be accorded a lower priority than, for example, the correcting of social injustice or the saving of a country from Communism. In any case, the distinction between democracy as an attribute of political institutions and democracy as an attribute of social structures was cast aside: the assumption among reformists and revolutionaries of the left was that no democracy was worthy of the name if it exhibited high degrees of social injustice. These same groups also placed enormous faith in and accorded high priority to the capacity of the state apparatus to develop and apply effectively policies designed to bring about complex social changes. The risk that 'democratic' social changes might endanger political institutions, which has become a commonplace in the 1980s, was unthought of in the 1960s, or else was considered well worth running. There were few candidates for the title of 'democratic institution'; there were few countries which had had more than a few years of uninterrupted elected civilian government since the 1930s; and the experience of repression under military, or indeed civilian, regimes before about 1967 was not comparable in intensity, scale or degree of organization to that which was to be experienced under the new breed of bureaucratic authoritarian regimes after 1964. Revolutionaries could take their rights for granted because perhaps they did not think that their actions would have any serious consequences.[37]

37 A recent book by Cristóbal Kay, *Latin American theories of development and underdevelopment* (London and New York, Routledge, 1989) offers an excellent, detailed and scholarly survey of the schools of thought discussed here, and their offshoots.

Two: From Dependency to Democracy

The congruence of corporatism and import-substituting industrialization (ISI)

The period following World War Two saw fairly steady economic growth in the three countries we are mainly considering, accompanied by varying rates of industrialization and urbanization. However, the period was also marked by endemic inflation and balance-of-payments crises, by a high degree of inequality in income distribution, and, in Brazil and Argentina, by persistent political instability.

Although total industrial output was rising, its quality left many things to be desired. Its ownership was heavily concentrated and it tended to generate less employment than the real supply of labour might have led one to expect, on account of the generous subsidies offered to labour-saving capital investment and to the import of capital and intermediate goods. Industrial exports were very few and the countries continued to rely on primary commodity exports for their foreign exchange.

Agriculture in Chile and Brazil, as in many other countries, was hampered by two sets of problems. For structuralists, as we have seen, the slow growth of agriculture and the instability of the economies were attributable to a land tenure system which held down land productivity and rendered the sector as a whole slow to respond to changes in demand. From this it followed that an agrarian reform was needed which would redistribute land and satisfy not only the needs of the peasantry, but also those of industry and the urban middle and working classes. In this diagnosis the landed elite were seen as isolated and politically weak.

The orthodox diagnosis, in contrast, held that the effects mistakenly attributed to these structural problems were in fact due to misguided protectionism and state intervention: over-valued exchange rates and domestic price controls discriminated against agricultural producers. If these macro-economic policies were changed, the sector's production and exports would increase.

Although the supporters of these different approaches were locked in polemics, it is not difficult to see that they were not incompatible. The claim that the price regime for agricultural output was unfavourable did not take into account the subsidies obtained by the landed elite from other sources, namely very cheap credit, a very generous tax regime, and legal and administrative measures which, by repressing the organization of the rural labour force, held the rural wage rate down. Except in Argentina, where the agrarian structure was very different, these could be seen as concessions from the urban to the rural élite in exchange for their 'delivery' of the votes of the peasantry in support of conservative parties. They also meant that whereas the agricultural *sector* was placed at a disadvantage in price and exchange policy, the costs of this unfavourable treatment were born by wage-earners and by those who did not have access to subsidies from which the landlord class benefited. This pact of domination contradicted the standard model of development shared by marxists and modernization theorists alike, according to which there is an abiding conflict between landlords and urban capitalists and the development of capitalism requires that it be resolved in favour of the former. It also meant that the traditional argument that industrialists would have an interest in land reform were not valid: they were obtaining numerous advantages from cheap imported inputs and low urban food prices, obtained in exchange for the subsidies to the landlords, already mentioned; and in any case they feared reform for the inevitable accompanying political mobilization of the peasantry and the implicit threat it posed to the principle of private property.

In all three countries, despite variations, this pact rested on a corporatist state. The corporatist state underwent a process of consolidation during the inter-war period in Chile and Brazil and in the early post-war period in Peronist Argentina, when social welfare legislation, labour relations legislation and the apparatus of import substitution were institutionalized, but it should not be forgotten that it was based on long-standing foundations in the legal system itself – what Alfred Stepan and others have described as the Iberian tradition in which the state regulates private association through a 'charter' mechanism (Stepan, 1978; see also Wiarda, 1981).

Corporatist labour legislation in Brazil and Chile set out to enable unions to exist but also to restrict their autonomy, especially in Brazil, and their size, especially in Chile. Under the constitution of the Estado Novo (1937) an elaborate set of rules rendered Brazilian unions dependent on the Ministry of Labour which collected dues from employers and then redistributed them to the unions, retaining the power to inspect union books at any time, as well as to remove union officials at any level. All union officials had to present a certificate of 'ideological suitability' in order to have their appointment confirmed by the Ministry. This created a clientelistic relationship between union bureaucracies and the ministry, but it also enabled politicians of the left to reach positions of union power during their period of ascendency in the early 1960s. The labour legislation (CLT–Consolidaçao dos Leis do Trabalho) also placed severe restrictions on the right to strike, by linking it to security of tenure in employment. Workers who were properly registered rapidly gained quite strong rights to redundancy payments, but these might be forfeited if they went on strike without going through a series of procedures including compulsory cooling off periods and compulsory arbitration in the labour courts (Erickson, 1977; Humphrey, 1982). In Chile the mechanism was slightly different: the restrictions on the right to strike without forfeiting job security were also there, but the labour code allowed the unions more autonomy; on the other hand it contained various provisions which prevented the development of very large unions, and the clientelistic relationship with the Ministry of Labour was absent (Angell, 1972). In neither country was the unionization of agricultural workers a feasible proposition until the 1960s.

In Argentina a rather different system was created in the period beginning 1943, when Perón become Minister of Labour and set about undermining and co-opting the unions, detaching them from their prior Socialist or Anarcho-Sindicalist loyalties. After Perón's election in 1946 the union movement was institutionalized through the all-embracing Confederación General del Trabajo (CGT) which had powers to requisi- tion and otherwise intervene in the affairs of its affiliated unions, not dissimilar to those exercised by the Brazilian Ministry of Labour. Unions were able, but only with government approval, to become 'institutions of public law' and not mere civil associations, by acquiring a type of legal status known as *personería gremial*, *gremio* being a generic term to refer to a representative association (Ciria, 1983, p. 27). So long as Perón was in power, he and his political associates were able to impose the appoint- ment of their nominees as union officials, but they often had to give way to pressure over pay and conditions, especially in the early years. After the overthrow of the government in 1955 though, the CGT became an extremely powerful organization in its own right, despite various attempts to rein it in and requisition it, because of its powers of intervention in the affairs of its affiliates. In addition, the unions controlled vast financial resources, as well as hospitals and holiday homes for their members, and after a decree passed by the military government in 1970 (Abós, 1983, p. 92), they administered social benefits on behalf of the social security system, thus gaining access to further abundant financial resources. These were used to pay for habitual ballot-rigging, violence and corruption in the union apparatus (James, 1978).

The corporatist apparatus also provided a framework for a social security system. The system drew a clear boundary between monthly paid salaried workers and wage-workers paid on an hourly, daily or weekly basis. By more or less compulsory discounts from wage packets individuals gained the right to the hospitals or pension schemes of their particular category, and the lowest paid gained access only to more humble provision (Mesa-Lago, 1978). In Brazil for most workers, especially from the 1964 coup until the late 1970s, the most important role of the union was that of administering medical attention and pension payments, enabling it to develop a bureaucracy and the concomitant patronage.

Despite these structures of co-optation and control, in all three countries, when governments friendly towards the union leadership came to power, they were vulnerable to union leaders' economic demands because of the capacity of the unions to penetrate, directly or indirectly, the decision-making processes of the state. This occurred through the Peronist movement in Argentina after 1972, through the Ministry of Labour in Brazil after 1961, and through the political parties in Chile after 1970, and rendered the task of coping with economic volatility almost impossible.

The literature on corporatism has tended to emphasize its importance in relation to the unions, but the pattern of co-optation and imbrication of business associations and the state bureaucracy likewise fits the general features of corporatism. This may take the form of the establishment of official bodies with strong formal representation of organized business interests, for example in the regulation of an activity or in the allocation of scarce foreign exchange. Or it may take on a more informal appearance through the pressures of individual or collective interests. Thus although dirigisme appears to dominate, it is not a centralized dirigisme of a powerful technocratic apparatus such as that established, for example, in Korea under President Park after his coup of 1961. Rather, private interests were in a position to colonize agencies of the state, especially those concerned with the allocation of foreign exchange and subsidized credit, in such a way as to make it very difficult to impose overall policies. As in O'Donnell's conception of *corporativismo privatista*, interest groups could colonize the state, while relying – not always successfully – on the statist dimension of corporatism (*corporativismo estatizante*) to co-opt and control the popular sectors (O'Donnell, 1977). The state was 'central', but not 'centralized'. ISI's weakness lay not in the inefficiencies of protectionism, but in the way both its institutional and financial resources could be controlled by dominant economic groups.[1]

These institutional resources consist of the power to create monopoly. By imposing high tariffs and quantitative import controls, ISI created a monopoly for domestic industry, or for foreign investors in domestic production. The corporatist decision-making process in which interest groups sat on boards and committees and had to reach agreement constituted an incentive to an oligopolistic share-out of markets rather than competition. It left a great deal of discretion in the hands of government officials, by avoiding broad uniform protection in favour of narrow categories of protected activities.[2] The profitability of industrial activities, then, depended heavily on the capacity of owners and managers to gain access to more or less fixed market share through the allocation of protection, to rationed, but cheap foreign exchange, and to subsidized credit. This is what Anne Krueger and others have described as 'rent-seeking' (Krueger, 1974).

Why was the ISI system so prone to economic and political volatility? Is it not, on the face of it, a perfect balance of dominant interests designed to fend off popular pressure from below? The answer rests partly on the contradictions built into the ISI system, and partly on the impact upon it from without of growing popular mobilization, both urban and rural.

The political economy of ISI suffered from an unstable relationship between economic growth, the exchange rate, domestic inflation, fiscal deficits and the balance of payments. These countries may have industrialized, but in the period prior to the advent of bureaucratic–authoritarian regimes the industrialization continued to be heavily dependent for foreign exchange revenues on primary exports. As a result an increase in industrial production and investment brought about increased needs for imported capital and intermediate goods. Export receipts from agriculture could not keep up with these demands in the short run, resulting in inflationary pressures, which in times of expansion were compounded by rapid growth of public expenditure on subsidies and wages. The sluggishness of agriculture production, and the bargaining strength of labour in growth cycles further exacerbated inflationary

1 This point is particularly worthy of emphasis now, in the 1980s, when the examples of Korea and Taiwan are being adduced as paragons of free-market policies; the truth of the matter is that these are economies subject to tight but effective central planning which has succeeded in creating incentives to exports while keeping imports out of the domestic market. The lesson they hold out to Latin America concerns institutions, not policies.

2 Susan Kaufman Purcell, 1977. It bears saying that it is difficult to know how much weight to attach to the effects of these relationships on industrial performance; after all, Japan and Korea, with their superior industrial performance, are hardly noted for the transparency of decisions in industrial policy or for the distance between decision-makers and their sponsors within the state machine.

pressures. For a time the relative cheapness of imports repressed price inflation as the exchange rate held up or was made to hold up, but the longer it held up the harder it would fall when the crisis eventually became unavoidable. The expectation that periodic crises were inevitable generated what O'Donnell has called the plunder economy (O'Donnell, 1982), as businessmen concentrated on making money out of the market imperfections which accompanied the almost certain knowledge that the government would eventually be forced to devalue the currency and reduce price controls and subsidies.

Meanwhile, government expenditure would run out of control, propelled by the indexation of wages which was an institutionalized feature of all these economies. The government borrowed from the Central Bank to make up the difference between expensive hard-currency borrowing and cheap local-currency lending, to finance wage increases in the public sector, and to repress prices of food, utilities and other 'basic' goods and services through subsidies. Eventually, the IMF would be called in, standard stabilization-cum-recessionary recipes were adopted, and a period of stagnation ensued.

During the periods of stagnation installed capacity became underutilized, so that after a year or two governments seemed to be in a position to reflate their economies without running the risk of renewed inflationary pressure. Demand would be stimulated and for a time prices could be held down by controls as capacity utilization increased and profits rose as well, but eventually a ceiling would be reached where new investment was required to meet the increased demand. Meanwhile, the pressure of demand against limited and monopolistic productive capacity led to a renewal of the inflationary cycle.

The structuralist theory of inflation seemed to offer a way out of these cycles, via a policy combining economic reactivation and income redistribution, and it was applied in a variety of contexts: in Brazil in the early 1960s under the inspiration of Furtado, in Allende's Chile under the inspiration of former 'cepalino' Pedro Vuskovic, and in Argentina by Perón in 1973. In the Brazilian case the redistributive element was limited to a proposal for land reform which was never seriously applied; in Argentina it was absent; but in Chile the redistributive element – though not ultimately very successful – was strong, confronting both foreign and domestic capital under the influence of neo-dualist dependency theories, which emphasized the negative effects of technology transfer and foreign investment on employment and income distribution.

Three observations require emphasis at this stage. The first is that the technocratic instincts and assumptions of policy makers were ill-suited to vulnerable state apparatuses severely lacking in the capacity to respond and to manage. The second is the contradiction between their conception of structural change as a process managed – though not, in any strong sense imposed – from above, and the reality of social movements which proliferated in response to the structuralists' own reformist and occasionally revolutionary appeals. The third concerns the 'colonization' of the state by forces from civil society. In Chile and Argentina in particular, the periods of left-wing or Peronist government were marked by an intensification of the practice of awarding bureaucratic positions to political supporters. Political factions were allocated control over particular positions or even departments and this meant that several contradictory policies were being pursued at the same time.

As the experience of those years recedes into the distance, so it has become increasingly clear that the cataclysms which followed upon these reformist efforts were more than a reaction of the privileged to the threat of revolution from below – which in any case was only serious in the Chilean case, and even then was in no way an armed threat. This was the crisis of the ISI system as a whole, of the corporatist state, and in Brazil and Argentina of populism as its ideological superstructure, torn asunder by popular mobilization and its penetration of the state apparatus. The degree of mobilization varied, and its ideological thrust varied as well, but the essential characteristics of the crisis were present everywhere.

Structuralism and reformism: blueprints and popular mobilization

The rest of this book is concerned with intellectual responses to the crisis of ISI and the bureaucratic–authoritarian regimes which ensued. It will show how the responses consisted of both a reappraisal of the idea of the state and of democracy, and also a renewed attempt – mostly among Catholic intellectuals – to inspire popular movements.

The three cases under consideration are Brazil (1961–4), Chile (1965–73), and Argentina (1970–6). In each of these cases economic reactivation was attempted, combining a wage-led expansion of demand with administrative price controls, and in each case the outcome was a balance-of-payments-cum-inflationary crisis. But there were important variations deriving from the nature of the state, the class base of the ruling alliances, and the invocations underlying popular mobilization.

Brazil

The Brazilian episode begins with the inheritance left by President Juscelino Kubitschek (1956–60). Kubitschek's administration is noted for the initiation of the building of Brasilia, the new capital, and for his

attraction of large-scale multinational investment in manufacturing industry, especially in the automobile sector. This did not generate immediate
inflationary pressures, but by the time he handed over to his elected
successor Janio Quadros those pressures were beginning to be felt, and
within six months Quadros resigned, unable to put together the necessary
stabilization package. His successor was the Vice-President João ('Jango')
Goulart, but Goulart's succession to office was interrupted, briefly, by an
attempted coup. Although the coup was prevented at that time, it was in
effect only postponed to 1964 (Skidmore, 1967). Opposition to Goulart
came from anti-nationalist quarters in the army, who viewed with
considerable distrust the anti-imperialist or nationalist factions within the
institution (Sodré, 1968), and from the powerful but small liberal party,
the UDN (União Democrática Nacional), led by the redoubtable Rio-
based State Governor Carlos Lacerda. Lacerda and the UDN were able to
brand Goulart anti-democratic by identifying him as a protegé of Vargas
(whom he had served as Minister of Labour in 1950–4), and a representative of the authoritarian style of the Estado Novo, thus avoiding basing
their attacks simply on his closeness to organized labour. In Brazil, as in
Argentina, even while openly plotting a coup the anti-populist forces
could invoke democracy against organized labour without seeming
anti-democratic; in Brazil their task was made all the easier by the
Communist Party's enthusiastic support for Goulart's reforms.

   Goulart's three years in office were marked by a rhetoric of *reformas de
base* or structural reforms, combined with an almost total inability to
deliver any of those reforms. With his rhetoric he upset the coalition on
which post-war Brazilian politics had been based – a coalition between
the two parties which Vargas had created as the foundation of political
coexistence: the Social Democratic Party (PSD: Partido Social Democrático) which was dominated by the landed elites of the hinterland, and the
Brazilian Labour Party (PTB: Partido Trabalhista Brasileiro) which was
close to the trade-union apparatus. His announcement of a land reform
provoked a ferocious response from the Church, in alliance with the
UDN and the PSD, leading to mass demonstrations by the middle classes
in major cities, especially São Paulo. To compound his difficulties, he
definitively alienated the military high command by encouraging a
half-cocked NCOs' revolt.

   Goulart was not helped by the use to which the Communist Party put
their alliance with him. The party exploited its control of crucial positions
in the union movement to encourage parallel hierarchies and exacerbate
economicist demands which undermined attempts at stabilization. This
was further complicated by a sub-plot in the north east of the country. In
this, Brazil's most characteristically *latifundista* region, dissident leftists
operating on the margin of or even against the Communist Party, were

beginning to mobilize the peasantry, and in response progressive sectors within the Church began to do the same. Both were helped by Miguel Arraes, elected Governor of Pernambuco state in 1962, who simply instructed the police to keep to their proper role and not intervene in labour disputes, thus allowing legitimate union activity for the first time in the region, and producing paroxysms among the landed élite (Hewitt de Alcántara, 1969; Azevêdo, 1982). After the coup the repression of these activities and their leaders was particularly severe.

When the military seized power in 1964 they started out with an orthodox stabilization plan and also a commitment to an early return to democracy. But this commitment did not last: once the inflation rate had been brought down economic policy returned to a modified version of ISI, while a return to open politics with freedom to form parties and present candidates was postponed indefinitely in 1968, to be restored, at least partially, only in 1979. The regime had experienced too many difficulties in putting together a political alliance which would perpetuate its policies and alliances behind a democratic façade (Kinzo, 1985).

The Brazilian BA regime did not constitute such a radical break with the past as was to occur with its Chilean and Argentine successors in 1973 and 1976. The development strategy pursued by Delfim Neto from 1967 relied heavily on the apparatus of controls and subsidies developed by Vargas and Kubitschek, and except for a brief period after 1968, the regime never closed down political life entirely: although after 1965 direct elections for state governor were not held until 1982, Congressional elections were held at regular four-year intervals, though often under legal and physical constraints which made it impossible for even the official opposition to campaign effectively. But local-level elections continued to be held almost uninterruptedly. Instead of banning political activity altogether, the military and their technocratic associates co-opted much of the political elite and adopted many of the habits of the past which in the first flush of their 'revolution' they had intended to erase. Local politicians beholden to the regime were eased into office even while parties and individuals were banned from political life.

The corporatist system of trade unions remained untouched. Indeed, union membership rose fast during the period, consequent upon the very fast rate of industrialization, and in the countryside as a result of the institution of a pensions system for farmers which was administered by the agricultural union CONTAG (Confederação de Trabalhadores Agrícolas). But because of the repressive measures in force, especially the AI-5 (Institutional Act no. 5, 1968, revoked in 1979), labour could not make itself heard as an independent voice.[3] The period between the promulga-

3 The AI-5 granted the President the following powers: to decree a recess of legislative

tion of that Act and the accession to power of the following President, Geisel, in 1974, was characterized by a degree of repression previously unknown in South America: systematic torture, the centralization of control of the security apparatus, 'disappearances' – all practices which became even more pervasive in Chile and Argentina later, but first made their appearance during this period in Brazil. By the late 1970s, though, it was becoming increasingly difficult for government to control unions and a series of major strikes in the automobile industry of São Paulo heralded a new era of union independence (Tavares de Almeida, 1984). Furthermore, the military high command took fright at the independence of their own repressive agencies and this was one reason for the very gradual *abertura* (opening) initially by Geisel in 1974 (Skidmore, 1988).

Under the military, development strategy constituted a modification, but by no means a reversal, of ISI, though the combination of expanding credit for the middle classes and wage repression for wage-earners, to pump supply of and demand for modern manufactured consumer goods was perhaps an innovation. Massive state investments were made, especially in industry and capital goods (Evans, 1979; Castro, 1985). State intervention expanded through the use of policy instruments ranging from subsidized credit to production quotas to tariff policy and price policy. The intervention may have become more centralized in the sense that more decisions were now taken by the federal government at the highest levels, and more technocratic in the instruments used, but case studies show that basic decisions continued to be taken in the time-honoured fashion, that is through economic and political pressure from property-owning and producer groups: for example, efforts to rationalize the Institute of Sugar and Alcohol succeeded in installing technically qualified personnel, but not in changing 'adherence to personalistic, non-technical norms', while private monopolies (disguised as 'cooperatives'!) rose meteorically to a position in which they dominated both sugar and alcohol production and policy-making towards that sector.[4]

---

bodies at local, state and federal levels; to legislate during the recess; to intervene in state and municipal government, taking over their powers; to suspend any citizen's political rights, cancel political mandates, decree a state of siege, confiscate properties, and issue complementary instruments to implement the Institutional Act itself. It also suspended habeas corpus and the tenure of public employees, and excluded judicial review of decisions and actions taken under the authority of the Act.

4 Nunberg (1986). After the oil crisis of the 1970s, of course, alcohol became extremely big business and extremely profitable in Brazil. Government investment in its production by private corporations rose from $59 million in 1975 to $1.4 billion in 1981, and the methods of allocation described by Nunberg illustrate graphically the intertwining of public and private domains which is so characteristic of modern Brazilian capitalism and corporatism. Nunberg also gives abundant evidence of the polarizing effects of sugar and alcohol policy as small and medium-sized cane producers were squeezed out of the market and the position of wage-earners grew increasingly precarious.

Another study – of the steel industry – speaks of 'a new clientelism' based on 'organic association between state apparatuses and fractional or sectoral interest blocs, rather than on the political manipulation of favours and prestige' – which was the style of the oligarchic state before the 1930 Revolution. It describes periodic reorganizations as devices to minimize rather than improve bureaucratic constraints.[5]

The strategy eventually ran into a severe debt crisis, as is well known, but it did produce record rates of growth and of industrialization. Industry grew by 11 per cent between 1965 and 1973, and by 10.1 per cent between 1970 and 1980, and although this was followed by a severe recession in the early 1980s, growth resumed, led by exports, in the second half of the 1980s (World Bank, 1985). Durable consumer goods and capital goods together, which had accounted for only 6.8 per cent of industrial production in 1950, rose to 28.2 per cent of that – vastly increased – production by 1980 (Faria, 1984). This, to be sure, was at the cost of a notorious polarization in income distribution. The data are subject to debate, but all studies (for example, Bacha and Taylor, 1978) produce the same trend: according to Faria (1984) the top 10 per cent of income-earners raised their share from 39.6 per cent in 1960 to 46.7 per cent in 1970 and 50.9 per cent in 1980, while the bottom 20 per cent – mostly rural dwellers – found their share declining from 3.9 per cent to 3.4 per cent and 2.8 per cent in the same years. It was a period in which the structure of agrarian society underwent definitive and often violent changes, involving the colonization of Amazonia, the very rapid development of capitalist agriculture on the basis of coffee, sugar and soybean in São Paulo and states to the south, the rapid decline of resident permanent labour on north-eastern estates, and the rise, therefore, of vast contingents of seasonal rural wage-labourers in both the south and the north east (Lehmann, 1982; da Silva, 1981).

Why did dirigiste policies produce such a high rate of growth in Brazil

5 Abranches (1978, p. 398). This is a study of the management of the state-owned steel industry and emphasizes the central role of CACEX, the office of the Banco Do Brasil charged with determining levels of protection. Abranches describes the repeated failure of the state bureaucracy to impose a rationalized, centralized plan over the various 'fiefdoms' represented by the state steel-making enterprises and the private sector which relied on them and on the state for orders and subsidies. 'Comprehensive plans have almost no other function than that of providing ideological grounds for negotiations and for the legitimation of governmental actions. Therefore, most policies are effectively made by sectoral agencies, state banks and enterprises' (p. 440). CACEX – which controls the licensing of imports where they compete with domestic products – grew out of the Bank of Brazil's total control over foreign exchange transactions during the Depression, from 1929, and has preserved that power to some degree ever since. It also supervises negotiations over the balance between imported and domestically produced goods in big projects worth more than $7 million, which is a very important role.

when compared to Chile and Argentina? The answer must surely lie in the political weakness of the urban working class and the peasantry. During the military government the indexation mechanism was manipulated to keep wages down, and trade union activity was, until the late 1970s, severely constrained. When a gradual *abertura* began in the late 1970s, pressure from below did mount, and although the government imposed a draconian stabilization between 1981 and 1983, the inflation rate did not come down. Subsequently, through a series of more and less spectacular attempts to reduce inflation, the economy has experienced both an export boom and a stagnant or even declining trend in real disposable income. Thus while GDP grew by only 1.3 per cent p.a. in 1980–5, exports during those years grew by 6.6 per cent and imports declined annually by 9.1 per cent (Carneiro, 1987; World Bank, 1987). The position in the late 1980s is paradoxical: the persistent high inflation reflects the foreign debt, to be sure, and also the indexation system which the Sarney government has not dared to abolish, and thus also the power of the trade-union movement which has defended it; yet the unions have still not been able to halt the decline of real wages.

Chile

In Chile, reformism got off to a much more promising start. Unlike Goulart the Christian Democrat President Frei was elected with an absolute majority in 1964 and gained a supporting Congressional majority shortly after. He raised rural wages and instituted a land reform as well as allowing rural unions to form. He pulled the economy out of recession and managed to restrain it before inflation ran out of control. But in the process he undermined the centre-right coalition which had brought him to power, and although he slowed down the reform process in the face of growing conflict in the countryside in 1968, it was too late to rebuild confidence with the right-wing parties. These had been alienated by his unwillingness to repay their electoral support with positions in government, and were also undergoing their own independent shift away from patrician attitudes towards a more authoritarian conservatism.[6]

Thus the pact of domination on which the country's political stability had rested was broken. The absence of any desire – or indeed any social basis – to renew the centre-right electoral pact of 1964 opened the way for

6 The literature on Chile is vast. On the politics of the period see for example Stallings, 1978, Valenzuela, 1978. But the literature has not, to my knowledge, given sufficient weight to the shift in emphasis on the civilian right towards anti-democratic authoritarianism after 1964, though the origins of the 'high monetarist' economics for which Pinochet is so renowned are well documented.

a narrow victory of a coalition of left-wing parties in 1970, known as Unidad Popular (Popular Unity). The relatively centralized structure of the Chilean state – far less prone to venality than elsewhere – was still not enough to resist the colonizing ventures of political parties with strong ideological motivation. First the Christian Democrats and later the various parties of Unidad Popular invaded the state apparatus. This did not have serious decentralizing effects under Frei's one-party government, but under his successor Allende, each party was awarded agencies, or ministries, as its own to make appointments and, in effect, policy as well. Thus after Allende's election in 1970 the state was extremely vulnerable to external pressure from a civil society mobilized on all sides to a far higher degree than was, for example, the case in Goulart's Brazil.

This vulnerability was compounded by a high-risk economic policy: drawing on the structuralist theory of inflation, Unidad Popular stimulated demand and controlled prices and initially succeeded in bringing down inflation, but at the cost of a rapid deterioration in the balance of payments and also a rapid exhaustion of existing productive capacity. At the same time it embarked on a programme of nationalizations which gave workers a strong voice in the management of their companies and allowed them to make spiralling wage claims, often supported by political groups who were part of the governing coalition. Popular mobilization also grew in the countryside, incorporating hitherto unorganized sectors such as the dispossessed Mapuche peasants of the south, and exacerbating pressure for land reform. The reform proceeded apace, but in the process production and marketing of agricultural goods and inputs was inevitably disrupted, thus exerting further pressure on food prices. In addition, inhabitants of working-class districts (*poblaciones*) mobilized in support of price controls and collective goods.

In 1972 and 1973, as the class war grew in intensity, factory workers began to take over installations which they attempted to run themselves. This was countered – and indeed provoked – by growing mobilization on the right, as factory owners boycotted or undermined the government's attempts to control the economy, and as their activities broadened to encompass middle-class groups such as lorry owners, irritated by attempts to regulate their activities or merely frightened by the threat to their social position embodied in the rising tide of revolutionary fervour.

Rarely can a counter-revolution have been so openly invited and so little prepared for, yet there was little, in the end, which the reformist and revolutionary forces could do to prevent it: they lacked any central co-ordination, either to mount a seizure of power or to hold their forces back; and they lacked arms. They could not even pact with the Christian Democrats at party level, since the latter had embarked, by mid-1972, on a strategy of destroying the government at any price.

In Brazil the 1964 coup spelt the end of a style of electoral politics but not of the ISI strategy or of the corporatist state. In Chile, where the class confrontation was fiercer and the actual reforms carried out deeper, the coup of 1973 spelt the end of both ISI and the corporatist state.

Argentina

In Argentina the pact of domination prevalent under the ISI system was more complex, because the working class was, from 1943, more powerful and more autonomous of either political parties or the state and also because it was much more difficult to sustain a pact of domination between the property-owning classes in both industry and agriculture (O'Donnell, 1978a). Since the country had no peasantry to speak of except in the Andean north east bordering on Bolivia, the fertile heartland of the pampas being managed without recourse to servile relations of production, the industrial sector could not rely on a supply of cheap labour from an underemployed or marginalized peasantry. Therefore, one element of the pact of domination the repression of rural labour, was unavailable. The country's industries were reliant on a domestic mass market, and could only with difficulty weather the storms of periodic stabilizations. Whereas in Brazil and in Chile industry produced more for a middle-class market which tended to survive better in hard times, the power of Argentine labour to resist wage reductions forced domestic industrial interests into intermittent populist alliances with the unions.

The dominant agricultural and meat-producing interests in Argentina had a vested interest in a relatively cheap currency, which would open external markets to them and/or hold up the domestic value of their exports. But not only were the compensating mechanisms which elsewhere mediated the conflict of industry and agriculture absent; their interests as far as exchange-rate policy was concerned were diametrically opposed: the industrialists and the working class both needed an 'over-valued' or at least 'highly valued' currency, for in addition to the protection it offered their markets, it also held down the price of imported inputs and, by making export markets relatively unattractive to agriculture, kept the domestic food market cheaply supplied.

In other countries, these conflicts would have been overcome by holding down agricultural wages and prices and compensating the landlords for the cheap prices with cheap credit, and other subsidies. But Argentina's land tenure structure was, in comparison, relatively egalitarian, and this could not be achieved so cheaply. Farmers also successfully resisted a tax on differential rent, the ever-present demand of the intellectual spokesmen of the 'national' path to capitalist development, and an obvious incentive to improve productivity. For a brief period the military regime of 1966–73 succeeded in breaking this Gordian knot, by devaluing and at the same time impounding a portion of the extra profits which exporters gained therefrom. The result was a couple of years of rapid growth, which then ground to a halt for political reasons.

Thus Argentina lived through a series of crises, a spiralling vicious circle in which the 'national bourgeoisie' oscillated between a populist alliance with the Peronists and, when popular mobilization made them too uncomfortable, a tactical defensive alliance with agricultural interests; between alternating periods of expansion and stagnation-cum-stabilization (O'Donnell, 1978a). The only way out, it seemed, was a restructuring of industry such that its development could be led by a more modern, more multinationally dominated infrastructure producing not for a mass market but for the upper and upper-middle income groups, along the lines which, it was thought – wrongly[7] – characterized the Brazilian boom of the late 1960s and 1970s.

This pattern had begun to emerge during the 1960s: it was a period of relatively high economic growth, punctuated by political instability and uncertainty, during which the growth of wages lagged behind that of industrial productivity. But this became politically unsustainable under the pressure of internal dissension in the armed forces and the pressures from without of a revived worker militancy among middle-class groups and also among the workers in the most advanced industries. When the Peronists returned to power in 1973 they more or less forbade new foreign investment and increased the share of wages. Like the dependency theorists, they were convinced that the two were related. Although they managed to sustain a negotiated wage freeze for a brief period, the death of the vault-key of their entire project, Perón himself, and the usual contradictions of expanding wage-based demand and frozen prices heralded the collapse of the economic project. Like their neighbours in Chile, their assumptions were far too optimistic and they failed to compensate for increasing demand and faltering investment by controlling public expenditure. A belated attempt by Perón's widow and successor Isabelita to apply a more orthodox stabilization plan was politically unsustainable. The unions – under severe pressure from below on account of the successes of radical activists on the shop floor and in the streets – forced her to back down.

At root, the problem was not a lack of foresight or economic understanding, so much as an institutional failure which could not be blamed on a particular group: the porousness of the state enabled parties

---

7 A refutation of this, Furtado's (1973) and O'Donnell's interpretation of Brazil (O'Donnell and Linck, 1973), is to be found in Wells (1977). Wells shows that the Brazilian boom was accompanied by an expansion of demand in lower-income groups for consumer durables.

and factions – in Chile – and trade unions and business interests – in Argentina – to gain control of crucial portions of the policy process and neutralize any effort to negotiate a minimally consistent outcome (Canitrot, 1978; di Tella 1983). The resulting spiralling inflation was accompanied by the beginnings of the war between Montoneros and para-police forces which then merged with the 'dirty war' against the educated intelligentsia and working-class activists after the formal seizure of power by the military in 1976.

The ideological moment of the early 1970s

How might one characterize, if not explain, this ideological moment – reminiscent of the 1930s in the high drama of the events and in the apocalyptic quality of rival calls to political action?

The moment begins with the legitimacy conferred on reformism by a 'centre–left' consensus, and the rapidity with which reformist experiences were either suffocated (Brazil) or discredited (Chile). The United States' commitment to even moderate reform was quickly seen to be a fraud; the economies of the region seemed extremely brittle, in that even moderate social democratic policies, of the sort implemented in post-war Europe, led to inflation and balance-of-payments crises. Whereas the mature ruling classes of Europe had tolerated and survived such moderate reforms, their Latin counterparts reacted ferociously to the merest hint of change. Did they not attack Frei ferociously as the 'Chilean Kerensky'? Did they not react to Perón, a deeply conservative and anti-communist leader, with speechless outrage? Did they not resist even that quintessentially capitalist reform, the dismemberment of great landed estates? The 'system' did not seem to be able to tolerate change.

The notion of a 'system' was crucial because political discourse was dominated by the assumption that, taken together, all the problems of underdevelopment had mutually consistent solutions. If the existing system failed to ensure development or social justice, then it needed to be replaced *in toto* by its opposite. That 'system' was defined as both dependent and capitalist, and thus the domination of the USA had to be shaken off at the same time as the domination of the ruling class – though some concluded that nothing would change until the working classes of the rich countries had themselves overthrown capitalism, and others, rejecting the Eastern European model of socialism, awaited a parallel uprising in those countries too.

This accent on the systemic character of the diagnosis of the region's ills and their remedy is central to understanding the ideological moment: whatever the content of the solutions proposed they were systemic in scope, both at the level of slogans and at that of more elaborate theoretical and practical proposals. It reflected the region's own intellectual history, the heritage of Catholic social doctrine, with its strong organic component, and also European structuralist marxism, developed by Althusser and popularized in Latin America by Marta Harnecker, with its emphasis on the capacity of the capitalist system to 'over-determine' the structures of economy, polity and ideology (Althusser, 1966; Harnecker, 1971).

It would be too simplistic to attribute the systemic character of the proposals to their marxist character. The Peruvian military reformers, who from 1968 embarked on an all-embracing project involving a thorough land reform, the transfer of major industries to co-operative ownership or self-management, and the subjection of multinational corporations to state ownership or control, were extremely hostile to marxism. In Chile, the ideological vanguard of Popular Unity emerged from the generation of students who had been in the forefront of Frei's Presidential campaign in 1964, and brought with them a transfusion of Catholic social thought and activism. In Argentina the Peronist left which originated in the combination of popular invocations and national capitalist advocacy of the 1930s and 1940s, was radicalized by the overthrow of Perón in 1955 and the Cuban example of 1959. It then came under the hegemony of the Montoneros who proclaimed a 'national' variant no longer of capitalism but now of socialism (*socialismo nacional*). The Montonero proposals' component parts were extremely heterogeneous: from their integrist origins they brought a strong Catholic identity, while they drew from the earlier history of Peronism a banner which proclaimed the only way forward as a very broad nationalist alliance, including the capitalist classes, against any form of external dependence or imitation, capitalist or socialist (Gillespie, 1982).

The Montoneros are the most puzzling. Within some seven years they achieved a dominant position among the Peronist youth, able to mobilize hundreds of thousands of people at a mass meeting, and created a small but powerful armed apparatus supported by a large penumbra of sympathizers and collaborators. They embodied an entire generation of educated middle-class youth – as distinct from the working-class youth who were more active in grassroots trade unionism, where the Montoneros gained little acceptance. Their discourse was marked by an idolatry at once shrill and hollow for a leader who had used them in paving the way for his return but then turned his back upon them. Their invocation of the leader made him into a flag, or an emblem (Sigal and Verón 1986), in the absence of a project which might conciliate their evident appeal with their political impotence. After Perón's return in June 1972, and the accompanying massacre of Ezeiza airport, they were excluded from decision-making and had no means of expression other than the force of arms and mass demonstrations. The repression carried out first by the parallel police and later by the army after 1976 was pitiless (Gillespie, 1982).

Common to all the radical projects of the time was the vision of a final stasis, in which the contradictions of society and economy would be overcome and a state of harmony achieved – again reflecting the influence of Catholic thought. It is not surprising that, when the reaction finally arrived, these experiments, so concerned with the pursuit of the final goal and unmindful of the need for political strategy, were utterly defenceless.

Socialism was a handy slogan for the alternative, but the few diehards who truly believed that the Eastern European model offered a feasible or desirable alternative tended to preach political moderation. The new generation of activists and ideologues rejected repressive regimes of all kinds including those represented by official marxism. They derived from the *zeitgeist* a rejection of exploitation and of capitalist values, but as citizens of the Third World they derived from developmentalism a faith in the state which their European contemporaries of 1968 had so brazenly discarded. Anarchism was not an affordable option in the midst of poverty. Furthermore, finding themselves in power, in Chile in particular, in a period of transition and great confusion there was no option other than to nationalize idle industries and to entrust the state with a planning role.[8]

This theme of the state is the hinge of ideological change: in the wake of the coups in Chile and Argentina, it became the dominant issue among social scientists. On the surface, this was a reaction to the onslaught of a new Leviathan; but the underlying issue was more complex, namely why was the state unable to regulate and arbitrate social conflict without risking a fundamental change of regime?; what was the specific weakness which affected Latin American states? Or, alternatively, what was the specific strength of the ruling élites who had been able so successfully to retain their dominant position in society even after losing control of the state in democratic elections – as in Argentina and Chile?

Initially, as we shall see, the instinct of leading writers was to see the rise of authoritarian regimes as a natural outcome on the assumption that

8 Some Christian Democrats proposed a co-operative model as a basis for agreeing criteria for nationalization with the Popular Unity government in 1972, but the proposal failed for several reasons. Firstly, the distrust between the two sides; secondly the unwillingness among leading sectors of the Christian Democrats to lend any helping hand whatsoever to the government; and thirdly, the worry among the government parties that the co-operatives would be redoubts of Christian Democrat activism. Prominent figures on the left also foresaw that co-operatives would stimulate individualist, profit-minded attitudes which were at odds with the ideological thrust of a transition to socialism. Had it succeeded, the proposal might have changed the entire subsequent course of events, and it would have been a small price to pay on both sides.

the state is, 'in the last instance', a reflection of the relations of production prevailing in society. But this view progressively lost ground; the intellectual arguments for its abandonment or attenuation have been numerous, but the main reason was its political sterility. Eventually two broad currents of thought emerged in the radical tradition: the one, expressing a deep distrust of formal politics, emphasized the potential for liberation in social movements, in 'politics beyond the state', deriving much inspiration from the Theology of Liberation and its numerous ideological and practical offshoots; the other, which I shall call post-marxism, rediscovered the democratic strand in marxist theory and emerged in the late 1980s as a supporter of social democracy. To these we now turn. In addition, we shall give an account of neo-liberal (or neo-conservative) thought on account both of its practical applications and of its effect on ideological discourse generally in the region.

A new theory of the state?[9]

The crucial intervention in developing an understanding of the Latin American state was probably that of the Argentine political scientist Guillermo O'Donnell between 1974 and 1977. O'Donnell's first academic publication (*Modernization and Bureaucratic Authoritarianism*) came out in English in 1971. Written 'while doing graduate studies at Yale in 1968–71', it is both an attack on and a development of certain central tenets of comparative politics as practised in the United States at that time. Although the book did not place itself declaredly in the dependency tradition, some of the doubts it expressed concerning modernization theory bore a similarity to the much shriller attacks coming from the dependency school.[10]

The book is concerned to interpret 'the evidence that (to put it mildly) the manifold changes that South American countries have been under-

9 Much of the following account has appeared in Lehmann (1989).

10 Later, O'Donnell took that tradition on board enthusiastically, but in the early 1970s, fresh from an abandoned (and meteoric) political career, he was still wrestling with the transmitted wisdom of his North American mentors. The book is couched in the language of 'modernization theory' and 'comparative politics' even though it issues a challenge to both, and in particular to the latter. The vast numbers of references – resembling what I imagine to have been the sum of every 'pol.sci.' reading list at Yale in the early 1970s – and the effusive recognition of the inspiration of the prominent theorists of political moderniza-tion – David Apter in particular – should not deceive: the book challenges one of the principal substantive claims of modernization theory and one of the principal methodolo-gical features of comparative politics. It is a pervasive feature of O'Donnell's work that he dislikes polemics and often seems to quote in support of his claims people who argue the exact opposite, under the guise of a phrase such as 'on this point see . . .'

going in recent decades do not seem to have increased the probability of the emergence and consolidation of more open political systems, or of collective action that might effectively diminish the conspicuous inequalities and injustice in these societies' (O'Donnell, 1971, vii). It proceeds to give an inside account of how political institutions became vulnerable to military takeover. It was an 'inside' account in two senses: one, that it was inside a particular political system, namely the Argentine one, the other that O'Donnell himself had been an insider. Indeed, he had been something of a child prodigy in Argentine politics: leader of the University Students' Federation at the age of 18, a qualified lawyer at 20, and 'Sub-Secretario' (equivalent of Assistant Secretary in the USA) of the Ministry of the Interior at 27, during the military government which took over after the overthrow of Frondizi in 1962. This experience, unique in a social-science community whose members tended to be associated with governments of the centre and the left, provided him with a rare insight into the workings of the military 'mind', and of the military institution.

O'Donnell offers a detailed account of institutions and factions, of plotting and counter-plotting, of a political system in which the military act as a (frequently disunited) veto group imposing rules which make the game virtually unplayable. Even so, contortions of style betray the sense that he was still wrestling with a straitjacket, that he was reluctant to renounce the neat grid of modernization theory for the messiness of political history:

> different levels of modernization, in all the dimensions that this concept entails, generate different constellations of issues that define each country's problematic space. In turn, the set of political actors and their political responses ... are moulded by these different constellations and by the different structures in which these constellations have emerged. (O'Donnell, 1971, p. 68)

The circumlocution in this passage hardly conveys a sense of either clarity or comfort. If he thought modernization theory was ridiculous, why did he not say so? Out of politeness? Perhaps, but more likely because he was still searching for the security of an alternative paradigm.

O'Donnell pays especially close attention to the incumbents of what he calls technocratic roles:[11] frustrated by the 'irrational' politics of the short term, he sees these people coalescing into what eventually becomes a coup-coalition. Out of this interest in technocratic role-incumbents emerges the term 'bureaucratic–authoritarian': it adds to the 'genus' of authoritarianism a word which suggests 'the crucial features that are specific to authoritarian systems of high modernization': the growth of organizational strength of many social sectors, the governmental attempts

11 This is inspired by David Apter.

at control by 'encapsulation', the career patterns and power-bases of most incumbents of technocratic roles, and the pivotal role played by 'large (public and private) bureaucracies' (O'Donnell, 1971, p. 95). In a kind of genetic engineering, O'Donnell has taken two terms out of the vocabulary of day-to-day 'pol.sci.' and has begun to transform pigeon-holes, stages or labels into actually existing social processes in which real struggles for power take place. The bearers of modernity, far from being the enemies of military authoritarianism, turned out to be its best allies.

It was not long before O'Donnell entered a much more outspokenly *dependentista* phase, as evidenced in the book he wrote in 1973 (O'Donnell and Linck, 1973). It was, in the words of its Preface, a 'premature book' written as a contribution to the political life of the country during the dying days of the 1967–73 military regime.

The book fell into the 'neo-dualist' school of structuralist/ *dependentista* economics, which held, as we have seen in the work of Furtado and Sunkel, that integration into a newly dynamic world economy dominated by multinational corporations had brought about an accentuation of dualism at both national and international levels. In this account the Argentine state and most if not all Argentine classes were powerless in the face of the multinational juggernaut. O'Donnell's proposed solution was a form of self-managing socialism in the image of Yugoslavia.

As the Argentine drama unfolded, though, these issues seemed to pale into insignificance: if a returning *caudillo*, wily and instinctively conservative by now, in whom the dominant classes had placed their hopes for stability and the mobilized Peronists of all stripes their hopes for liberation, could not impose a modicum of political coexistence, then the country's political problems were surely not of the kind which could be resolved by an economic blueprint. The structural faults lay in institutions, and not only in economic structures. O'Donnell's subsequent contributions, which centred on the institutional mechanisms of the state and their interlocking with the mechanisms of economic power, came just at the right time.

The analysis appeared in three articles which went through overlapping periods of composition and revision: 'Corporatism and the question of the state' (1977), 'Reflections on the patterns of change in the bureaucratic–authoritarian state' (1978a) and 'State and alliances in Argentina' (1978b). They all came out as the full force of Argentina's by then openly declared 'dirty war' was being felt, after the final overthrow of Isabelita's surreal regime in April 1976. The sense of impending doom was reinforced by the 1973 debâcle in Chile and by the persistence of military rule in Brazil.

The influence of *dependencia* could most clearly be seen in the idea (elaborated in the 'Reflections ...' paper) that the bureaucratic–authoritarian state marked a particular stage in the process of development when a crisis of 'deepening' had been reached. The process of import substitution had been exhausted, and a renewal of capitalist development required a more regressive income distribution (as the neo-dualists were saying, following the Brazilian case) and also large-scale infrastructural works required to further the development process: this is what he meant by 'deepening'. This deepening, he said, could not be carried out in the existing institutional context, and required major investments of which only the state and multinational corporations were capable. The other argument in the paper concerned the political economy of import substitution which had encountered serious contradictions and created conditions in which powerful sections of society called for an authoritarian solution. He described the instabilities and populist mobilizations which had arisen – especially in Argentina and Chile in the early 1970s – as interrelated with the crisis of ISI. As for the concept of deepening, its author might well wish it to be quietly forgotten, and he did not take it up subsequently, though it has generated a good deal of academic disputation (Serra, 1979; Hirschman, 1979; Cammack, 1985; Remmer and Merkx, 1982); though it did fit the Brazilian BA regime and Argentine one of 1967–73, it clearly made no sense in the later Argentine and Chilean ones. Analytically, whether 'deepening' is necessarily or statistically related to these repressive governments is a secondary question: the primary one is to understand the processes whereby ISI unravelled and BA regimes first rose up and later declined or retreated in an orderly fashion.

O'Donnell was poised between two rival schemata: in the one the BA state, brought on by political processes, and by the crisis of the political economy of ISI, constitutes a radical break with the past. In the other, the BA state is a restoration, a shift of bias within a fundamentally unchanged institutional structure. The former favours a more economistic interpretation – and finds some support in the radical changes in economic policy which accompanied the establishment of BA regimes in Chile and Argentina; the latter favours a more politico-institutional approach, in which the military are brought in from the wings to centre stage, in which the balance between coercion and co-optation, between repression and participation, is shifted towards the former, but within a framework which, deep down, remains unchanged. The concept of corporatism proved helpful in resolving the dilemma.

The paper on 'Corporatism' takes up the definition of the term given by Schmitter – which is a radically different definition from the standard contemporary Western European concept in that bias, co-optation and class power are built into it.[12] O'Donnell, in practice, departs from – and develops – that definition, by pointing to two dimensions of corporatism – *corporativismo privatista* and *corporativismo estatizante* – which go to form an *estado bifronte*, a Janus-faced state.[13] Noting that despite their structured biases, the corporatist institutions and practices inherited from the ISI period at least had offered a platform for the intermittent activation of the popular sectors, he describes how the BA state uses that structure to suppress, through direct control as well as repression, the mobilization of the popular sectors, while allowing privileged access to dominant groups, in particular to big business. In short, he introduces in subterranean fashion, the concept of class, of a class-divided society, into the otherwise over-institutional view of corporatism. The BA state, from this viewpoint, does not constitute as fundamental an institutional rupture as one might think.

By linking institutional and class analysis, this conception also makes it very difficult to sustain the conceptual opposition of 'class' and 'state' which is at the heart of so much talk on the subject. For in the O'Donnell formulation real power is exercised by real class representatives not only through, but in and on the basis of the state. The fragmentation of the state apparatus combined with corporatism produces an image of an apparatus which has decentralization and parcellization built into it: it is thus a departure from familiar assumptions both of modernization theory and of marxism, even while drawing on both traditions.

For a graphic account of a society in which the forms assumed by corporatist politics are shown to be a dimension of state autonomy (or the lack thereof) we can turn to his article 'State and alliances in Argentina'. He writes twice of the state dancing 'to the tune' or 'to the pendular rhythm' of civil society; and describes the pattern of politics generated by the corporatist state in that country as 'intrabourgeois struggles' which 'usually occurred, in contrast with other Latin American cases, at the very heart of a national state which was continually fractured by them' (1978b, p. 14). Again, this time with reference to the popular sectors:

---

12 'a system of interest intermediation in which the constituent units are organized in a limited number of singular, compulsory, non-competitive, hierarchically ordered and functionally differentiated categories, recognized or licensed, if not created, by the state, and granted a deliberate representational monopoly within their respective categories in exchange for observing certain controls on their selection of leaders and articulation of demands and supports' Schmitter (January 1974). For a 'standard' Western European approach, in which corporatism is synonymous with a system of bargaining among the most powerful interests in society, see Panitch (1980) and Winckler (1976).
13 A contrast reminiscent of Stepan's 'exclusionary' and 'inclusionary' corporatism; see Stepan (1978).

the moments of political victory and reversal ... were those when the temporary victors took the state apparatus by storm, seeking to strengthen institutional positions from which they would fight future battles when the situation was once again reversed – as experience taught them it would be. Of course the unions were no exception to this: the history of the defensive alliance is also that of the extraction from the state of important institutional concessions. These, in turn, reinforced the possibility of renewing the mobilization of the popular sector. The conquest of institutional positions enabled the unions to cover the popular sector with a fine organizational net, from which they could direct it repeatedly toward a militant economism, towards the polyclass alliance and towards the mirage of the 'other' capitalist path which *peronismo* proclaimed. (1978b, p. 24)

And finally, in general:

The state was recurrently razed to the ground by civil society's changing coalitions. At the institutional level, the coalitions were like great tides which momentarily covered everything and which, when they ebbed, washed away entire segments of the state – segments which would later serve as bastions for the piecing together of a new offensive against the coalition which had just forced its opponents into retreat. The result was a state apparatus extensively colonized by civil society.... Civil society's struggles were internalized in the state's institutional system.... As a consequence this colonized state was extremely fragmented, reproducing in its institutions the complex and rapidly changing relationships of dominant and subordinated classes – classes which could use these institutions to fuel the spiralling movements of civil society. (1978b, p. 25)

In this schema class conflict in itself need not undermine the capitalist bases of society: it is the structure of the state which enables or even imposes sustainable outcomes to that conflict.

O'Donnell was transcending the state–society polarity which has hobbled marxism as much as the old chestnut of economic determinism. As against the marxist nightmare of a state assumed to be centralized and unified, even (or, in a sense, especially) if it is governed by a bloc, coalition or congeries of ruling class fractions or their representatives, in the defence of an equally centralized and unified monster called capitalism, he postulates an unstable state and an unstable capitalism. Maybe one had to be an Argentine to take that crucial step. Class struggle then finds not an arena in the state, which would imply a game with stable rules, but a resource in the various apparatuses of the state – and the plural 'apparatuses' is crucial here. Corporatism departs from Schmitter's hierarchical, hegemonic apparatus and becomes a word describing the use made of the state by the organizations representing and inventing class interests. The state creates the classes and is shaped and misshapen by their struggle, but it is not 'set apart' from civil society.

The articles in which O'Donnell has himself attempted general theory have been less successful, but their very failure has been perhaps a crucial element in bringing back political agency and subjectivity. In 'Tensions in the bureaucratic authoritarian state and the question of democracy' (1979), the first in which the possibility that the BA state too may generate its own contradictions, was raised, the eight principal character-istics of a BA state are enumerated (Collier 1979, pp. 292–3). The political exclusion of popular sectors is related to long-term strategies designed to produce a highly transnationalized and polarized pattern of growth. But the paper then goes on to show how the suppression of mediations – namely of citizenship and of *lo popular* – turns out to be far more difficult than might appear, and also that talking about such suppressions is not easy. The BA becomes a speaker, an utterer of discourse, as it 'claims to be a national state', as it 'statizes the meaning of the nation' (1979, p. 295). In short, the theory turns out to be disappointingly simplistic: 'domina-tion becomes naked . . . manifests itself in the form of overt physical and economic coercion'. Legitimating mediations disappear, and the state begins to look less secure than its repressive appearance might lead one to believe. 'Tacit consensus is a foundation too tenuous to sustain the state' (1979, p. 297). (Is this Weberian legitimacy in new clothes?) Such a state is 'permanently haunted by the spectre of an explosive negation' (1979, p. 309).

Subjectivity, then, turns out to be central to what started out as an apparently structural dynamic. What counts in the end is whether the people will have the opportunity and capacity to organize and join 'a struggle for the appropriation and redefinition of the meaning of demo-cracy' (1979, p. 317). The Achilles heel of the BA state is not foreign debt, or military wrangling; it is simply 'the issue of democracy' (1979, p. 316) raised by 'voices' which, though temporarily silenced, eventually and inevitably will come to be heard again (1979, p. 318). Once again, structuralism gives way to hermeneutics, the march of history to the consciousness of the people. But how this subjectivity develops and operates remains a mystery.

But in Latin America electoral government does not by any means necessarily bring more social justice, and although the BA state may be ephemeral, the social structures which underpin it and whose defence was its main raison d'être, survive its demise. O'Donnell has tried to deal with this in various places by writing a very general theory of the capitalist state (O'Donnell, 1978c; O'Donnell, 1982, ch. 1). Thus he describes the state, in general, as the 'guarantor and organizer of capitalist social relations' and these are 'relations of production which are unequal and, in the last instance, contradictory' and they are 'established in a basic cell of society, namely the labour process and the workplace', and the state is in its origin and constitution, part, or better, an aspect of those social relations. And finally: 'the state is a mediation imbricated in and imposed upon a relation among other social agents. This is why usually the state is something more than just an agency of coercion, rather a consensually articulating mediation among social actors'.[14]

This attempt at general theory was doomed because it set out on the assumption that it was possible to say something about the state in general which would encompass the marxist critique of liberalism, and the structuralist marxist critique of traditional marxism, and yet remain faithful to a certain sense of structural necessity. Thus the state had to 'guarantee' capitalist social relations – to be anti-liberal; it had to protect capitalism as a whole, but not any particular capitalist class or fraction thereof – to distance itself from traditional, vulgar marxism; but it was not allowed to 'do' anything, to be either agent or actor, for that was a belief characteristic of what the author contemptuously describes as *la conciencia ordinaria*.[15]

Like many others of his generation and background who, having attempted to scale the heights of the general theory of the state, found themselves ineluctably thrown back into the world of agency and subjectivity, O'Donnell had to recognize that if he wanted democracy he could not sustain a hyper-determinist theory of the state. When the book he was writing throughout the 1970s – of which the three articles on the BA state were by-products – finally emerged in 1982, it turned out to be remarkable not for its high theory, but for the intimate account of military and élite politics, of the judgements and misjudgements which individuals and factions formed about each other, and also for the integration of politics and economics not at a level of high theory, but at that of day-to-day decision-making: it was not what his readers of the mid-1970s might have expected. By the early 1980s O'Donnell was calling for a cultural renewal as a precondition of democratic consolidation,[16] and his audience were beginning to read Hobbes and

14 O'Donnell 1982, p. 15. I reproduce here the original Spanish of the last quotation: 'el estado es una mediación imbricada en, y emanada de, una relación entre otros sujetos sociales. Esta es la razón que el estado sea habitualmente, además de coacción, una mediación consensualmente articuladora de sujetos sociales.'
15 Best translated as 'conventional wisdom' and used in Spanish in opposition to 'la conciencia crítica'. 'Ordinario' is also used (in Chile, but not, perhaps, in Argentina) to refer to ill-behaved, cranky children: cf. American 'ornery'.
16 See his 'Democracia en la Argentina *micro y macro*' (1984b). While hotly denying that he wishes to denigrate the importance of political life and institutions writ large, he insists (in the first footnote) that the consolidation of democracy in Argentina requires a change in the deeply rooted authoritarian habits of a society which had survived despite – or maybe because of – its relatively egalitarian character. He denounces the racism of Argentine culture, the recurring manicheism and paranoia which he perceives as characterizing the

Locke,[17] to listen again to North American liberals like Robert Dahl, and even to listen to the voice of religion which they had so steadfastly ignored for many years. The simple fact that in the forefront of the struggle against dictatorship stood priests and nuns armed with the Theology of Liberation, was not lost on them, though few if any could assimilate that fact in their theoretical work. As we shall see, the subsequent reappraisal was still couched in the marxist tradition, but now reformulated almost unrecognizably, as 'post-marxism'.

Post-marxism

Latin American marxism – that is, the marxism associated with the dependency school, not the official marxism of the Communist Parties – has in the last few years lost the unifying assumption that political institutions, social structure, the mode of production, and the international system of domination all hold together indissolubly; attempts to reform the one without all the others no longer attract the pejorative label of 'reformism'. So long as this assumption held sway, more implicitly than explicitly, participation in political institutions was merely a tactical concession. Within this discourse, *real* democracy was distinguished from formal democracy; it referred to the degree to which an institution, a policy or even an individual, was substantively in tune with the interests, aspirations and even the sentiments of the 'people', that is to say the poor, the workers and the peasants. The institutions of elected government were largely regarded as devices for the perpetuation of the status quo. The interests of the workers and the peasants were seen to be ranged unquestioningly on one side and those of capital, domestic and international, on the other. Knowledge of the interests of the people was objective and available. In the period of authoritarianism these assumptions seemed hollow, and a democratic language was needed which would accommodate an agonizing reappraisal within the marxist tradition; the bill was filled by two writers whose unimpeachable credentials validated their transition, namely Ernesto Laclau and the Catalan/French sociologist Manuel Castells.

Argentine view of the country's history and its failures, the sexual repressiveness and patriarchal family organization, the repressive character of its education system. The account is more a *cri de coeur* than an analysis, but the change of emphasis, compared with the essays of the mid-1970s – is clear enough. The theme is taken up again in his contribution to the Hirschman *festschrift* (1986), which reflects on different styles of social relations in Argentina and Brazil – or to be more, exact, in Buenos Aires and Rio de Janeiro.
17 See for example the pages of the journal published by CLASCO, the Latin American Council for Social Sciences, *Crítica y Utopía*, and the two volumes published by them entitled, significantly, *Etica y Democracia*, (Ansaldi, 1986).

Both Laclau and Castells, like their contemporaries in Latin America, went through an 'Althusserian' phase, in which the concept of mode of production was given pride of place and capitalism was an all-embracing, over-determining machine dictating politics, ideology, law and state formations. But Laclau's dogged attempts to come to terms with Peronism drew him closer to Gramsci and led him to write first about populism and later about socialism in an increasingly confident and iconoclastic manner (Laclau, 1977, 1985). Living in England from 1969, Laclau broke new ground when he brought his Argentine background to bear on the Gramscian heritage: a confluence which had already been developing in the Argentine journal *Pasado y Presente*. In his work on populism Laclau turned on its head the old Argentine theme of the exceptional character of colonial and dependent formations and the need to adapt marxism to place it at the service of national liberation, by stating, if not in so many words, that the modifications proposed by the 'national left' in Argentina should be applied to marxism in general. Were not nationalism and populism universal features of political mobilization? (Laclau, 1977). Shorn of much jargon the message is that 'pure' invocations of class interests do not mobilize the masses – or even the working class. The invocations which 'work' are those which invoke identity and belonging-ness rather than interests, 'masses' rather than 'classes', and which do not place the 'proletarian tasks corresponding to this stage of history' on a pedestal guarded by the political leadership which arraigns to itself the exclusive knowledge of those tasks. The conferment of respectability on populism – decried by marxists as an illusion or worse ever since Lenin's famous polemics with the narodniks in the 1890s[18] – was a watershed.

In a later book, written with Chantal Mouffe, Laclau's 'post-marxist'[19] project becomes even clearer: it is to excise from marxism most of the canon, while preserving the Gramscian concept of hegemony. This concept is radically different from that of class domination because it refers to two inseparable faces of domination – the one denoting political and economic power, the other 'intellectual and moral leadership' – and Gramsci's view is generally held to be that a stable social order cannot exist unless the ruling class, or classes, wield both power and 'leadership'. At first blush, this might seem a mere variant on the standard marxist opposition of base and superstructure. But Gramscians claim more than that for it: 'through the concepts of historical bloc and of ideology as organic cement, a new totalizing category takes us beyond the old base/superstructure distinction' (Laclau and Mouffe, 1985, p. 67). Furthermore, they deny that there is any such thing as an idea necessarily

18 Out of which grew his *Development of capitalism in Russia*, 1899.
19 The book, they say, is both *post*-marxist and post-*marxist*.

connected to the desires or interests of a class; nor, on the basis of Gramsci, can it be stated that classes are agents in any sense of the word. Rather, an organic (dominant) ideology is formed through the articulation of elements which considered in themselves, do not have any class belonging (Gramsci, 1975, vol. 2, p. 68). Laclau and Mouffe quote Gramsci as follows:

> An historical act can only be performed by 'collective man', and this presupposes the attainment of a cultural–social unity through which a multiplicity of dispersed wills with heterogenous aims, are welded together with a single aim on the basis of an equal and common conception of the world. (Gramsci, 1975, vol. 2, p. 349)

Gramsci was a revolutionary, a founder of the Communist Party during the heady days after World War One. He was a leading protagonist of the split between Communists and Socialists, the heyday of sectarianism, of the Third International dominated by Stalin. But later he wrote of a process both slower and more profound than the Leninist strategy of a revolutionary seizure of power, describing a combination of 'war of position' and 'war of manoeuvre' – military metaphors which should not be confused with their modern connotation opposing conventional to guerrilla warfare.

By war of position Gramsci refers to a process whereby the proletariat gradually penetrates the cultural and social interstices of society, achieving ideological hegemony before embarking on a political war of position to seize power. The post-marxists elaborate further: social classes' interests are not monolithic or homogeneous; they are not agents on their own behalf and should not be instrumentalized by an all-powerful party; false consciousness is therefore an invalid concept; history does not proceed in stages; politics is not merely the interaction of 'class representatives'; power is not 'there' in the state, to be seized; the course of history is not a truth to be grasped and applied.

Political struggle involves not the remorseless pursuit by the working class of predetermined objectives, but 'articulating' (a favourite term) a variety of alliances and issues on a variety of fronts in accordance with a very general democratic principle.[20] Certainly, the attack on bourgeois democracy is off the agenda: indeed, the very term 'bourgeois democracy' is rejected by Laclau, on the grounds that democracy is the creation of the masses as much as of the bourgeoisie.

Although this sounds very similar to conventional social democratic politics – that very politics of 'reformism' which has failed so miserably in

---

20 All this is spelt out, sometimes in rather obscure language, in Laclau and Mouffe (1985). A much clearer summary is found in their response to the attack of Norman Geras, in *New Left Review*, 166, 1987.

Latin America – it also leads directly to the theme of social movements: for the claim of post-marxism is that they are a particularly appropriate form of politics in societies where identities have proliferated as against the unifying identities of 'worker' or 'peasant', and where the multiplicity of fronts of social conflict place a unified assault on a unified state power beyond the realms of the 'political imaginary'.

> The radically democratic potential of the new social movements lies precisely in . . . their implicit demand for a radically open and indeterminate view of society, in so far as every 'global' social arrangement is only the contingent result of bargaining between a plurality of spaces and not a foundational category, which would determine the limits and meaning of each of these spaces.[21]

In other words: a worker may be politically active as a local leader, a consumer, a member of an ethnic or religious group, as a union member, as a human rights activist, and so on, and all these identities and interests combine in unpredictable ways – whereas the traditional marxist and sociological assumption would have been that all these political involvements hinge on identities forged in production. The next step, then, is to formulate a theory and a programme which take account of these social movements, to fill the void left by the followers of Gramsci in Argentina and Chile who justify full co-operation in democratic political institutions and have abandoned the critique of democracy as 'bourgeois' – despite the evident biases of the state in these countries. They do not ignore social movements, but they have difficulty incorporating them into their theory or their programmes. Do not social movements, like Gramsci's war of position, pursue 'the progressive disaggregation of a civilization and the construction of another around a new class core', as Laclau and Mouffe describe it?[22]

The most influential post-marxist to engage with this theme is Manuel Castells. A Catalan whose formative period as a sociologist coincided with the May 1968 events in France, he has worked in various Latin American countries, but writes predominantly for a North American and European audience, and has held successive appointments in North American universities since the late 1970s. His early work was a strenuous attempt to synthesize urban conflicts and urban systems, in an overdetermined all-encompassing Althusserian model in which the rule of capital was supreme. But his most influential book (1983) switches attention away from the systems imposed by capital or the state to social

---

21 Laclau (1985, p. 39). Laclau is not necessarily persuaded, though, that social movements have a 'progressive' effect.
22 Laclau and Mouffe (1985, p. 70). It is not clear whether they are quoting, paraphrasing or summarizing Gramsci in this phrase.

movements as ways in which collectivities try to create identities and worlds of their own making:

> by definition, the concept of social movement as an agent of transformation is strictly unthinkable in Marxist theory. There are social struggles and mass organizations that revolt in defense of their own interests, but there cannot [in Marxist theory] be conscious collective actors able to liberate themselves. (Castells, 1983, p. 299)

Whatever Marx himself may have thought, the marxist–leninist tradition is marked at its 'very core' by its use as an instrument of ideological manipulation, by devotion to 'a programmed historical development'.

This is not a purely intellectual turnabout. Castells was evidently deeply affected by his experiences in Chile during the Allende years. Almost alone among foreign sympathizers, he found the settlements controlled by the revolutionary organization, MIR (Movimiento de la Izquierda Revolucionaria: Left Revolutionary Movement), so overpoliticized that they became an 'amplifier of ideological divisions', and he also found that the dominant party apparatuses made the autonomous definition of the goals of social movements impossible. The experience initiated his turning away from the formalism and ultra-determinism of Althusserian marxism.

Castells depicts social movements as the quintessential expression of popular will in complex urban societies: they may rise and fall, they may undergo institutionalization and lose their identity as movements, but so long as the state and civil society are driven apart, so long as the political system is closed to new pressures, so long as the state centralizes power over urban space, 'a massive appeal for local autonomy and urban self-management' will oppose it (1983, p. 318). They may not be 'new historical actors creating social change, nor the pivotal source of alternative urban social forms ... but ... they bear, in their structure and goals, the stigmas and projects of all great historical conflicts of our time' (1983, p. 319). Which, being interpreted, means that they are the last recourse of democratic initiative: labour movements have become sclerotic and institutionalized; political parties unresponsive; above all the issues at stake in social conflict and the 'fronts' on which conflict occurs, are not what marxist theory says they are, and perhaps never were. In the place of trade unions struggling across the barricades of the relations of production, we have 'collective consumption trade unionism' – groups pressing for transport, health systems, urban infrastructure and the like; in the place of class struggle we have 'the search for cultural identity, for the maintenance or creation of autonomous local culture, ethnically based or historically originated'; and in place of the virtues of centralized power, these movements pursue decentralization and urban self-management.

They are united by urban themes, and cut across the class structure, deriving components from 'a variety of social, gender and ethnic situations'. 'Between times', people continue to 'speak their languages, pray to their saints, celebrate their traditions, enjoy their bodies and refuse just to be labour or consumers' (1983, p. 330).

In Castells the expressive dimension risks overwhelming the instrumental purposes. Social movements and their goals and the level of participation of the 'grassroots' within them are their own justification, to the extent that:

> They are successful when they connect all the repressed aspects of the new, emerging life because this is their specificity.... When the vocabulary becomes too restricted (a single focus on rent control for instance) the movements lose their appeal and become yet another interest group in a pluralist society. When they try to impose their programme, they become a counter-society, and collapse under the combined pressure of multinational capital, a mass media system and the bureaucratic state. (1983, p. 331)

One might wonder, in response, how in Latin America the practice of democracy which Laclau regards as a central feature of a socialist project can proceed without institutionalization, and likewise Castells's social movements can hardly operate in an institutional void, especially if they are pressing for collective consumption. Unable to get around the problem of the state and its biases, he has withdrawn into civil society, calling the social movements up as an alternative, but also perhaps as a sign of despair. Since justice is unobtainable, will the people have to content themselves with expressive, rather than instrumental, politics? Is it significant that the notion of social justice, like that of 'interests' has almost vanished from this post-marxist discourse? The other line of defence, namely that social movements, though they may not be a solution, do at least constitute a corrective, is only persuasive if we return once again to the superstructures of the state that they must correct and recall that support for social movements does not and should not exclude efforts to improve the efficiency and responsiveness of institutions.

Ghosts of the past: the costs of consensus versus the costs of change

In this section we look at the more direct expressions of post-marxism in political life. The parties and opinion-forming publications we shall refer to take different stances in each of the three countries, but they have in common a generational phenomenon, namely the return to political activity of many figures who were prominent in marxist debates of the late 1960s and early 1970s, and some new names. As we shall see, with the exception of the Brazilian Workers' Party, they tend to miss the dimension of social mobilization which Laclau and Castells especially, look to as an agent of 'radical democracy' or 'liberation'. On the other hand, their interventions have an open-ended quality and democratic commitment which certainly leaves the way open for a wide range of initiatives. If the name of Marx still figures in their pantheon, it is because they do not wish to deny their inheritance, or to betray the spirit of revolt and generosity which impelled them in their youth.

Chile

In Chile, the post-marxists have a breakaway social-democratic Socialist Party more or less to themselves – known after their leader as the 'Nuñez' Socialists, in contrast to the more numerous 'Almeyda Socialists'[23] who still value a preferential alliance with the Communist Party. This party's membership brings together more or less the entire marxist intelligentsia of the Frei and Allende period: they have converged from the old Socialist Party, from the Christian left, and from the 'independent left', and the party has joined the Socialist International – the international social democratic club.

One of the leading figures of this party has written of his generation: 'only yesterday we were gods'.[24] Another recalls with some distaste the numerous gestures whereby the 'generation of '68' had proclaimed its break with the past and with institutions: by rejecting their families, by making and unmaking marriages, by abandoning their studies to devote themselves to the cause of structural change; by iconoclastically inverting the consecrated slogans of the day. Those had been the times when modernization meant impoverishment, development became underdevelopment, democracy a farce, and the nation's culture a mere foreign transplantation (Salazar, 1986). Now, in contrast, they see politics as the piecemeal engineering of social and political deals in the name of political coexistence, between classes and between parties. The aim is to provide secure guarantees for citizenship and human and civil rights, and to create institutional mechanisms for the resolution by compromise of the inevitable continuing class conflict. If this means pushing back the frontiers of the state, if it means making concessions to liberal individualist political theory, so be it. Like Laclau, he insists that the ideals of liberal democracy form an integral part of the socialist tradition, and do not stand in contradiction to it. The collapse of the old political system, and

23 Known after their leader Clodomiro Almeyda, who was Foreign Minister in the Unidad Popular government.
24 The title of one of the essays in Eugenio Tironi (1984).

fifteen years under Pinochet of erosion of the economic and welfare apparatus of the state, of disintegrating class structures and loyalties, in an environment moulded by modern markets and modern technologies, have made it impossible to rebuild the 'democratic, national and popular' consensus ironically described as 'elections *plus* industrial trade unions, *plus* the provision of state education, *plus* Neruda, *plus* civil engineers, *plus* Latin American integration, *plus* Land Reform etc. etc.'.[25]

In enumerating those elements of that consensus, Tironi denotes not an ideology, but a sensibility which he consigns firmly to the past. Neruda, the poet who was once the idol of any educated Chilean, is today almost forgotten: his effusive, uncontrolled, gushing imagery, his evocation of a cultural continuity from pre-Columbian times to the present day seems vacuous to a generation which has seen only ruptures with the past. Tironi takes his offensive further by attacking the idea that 'everything is politics'.[26] Chile has been an overpoliticized country and this has been exacerbated by the dictatorship.[27] What is now needed is a break with the tradition which embodies the belief that all social change is the work of the state, with its implication that the prime task is the seizure of power, that the prime organization is the party, and that a life of virtue is the life of a militant: 'the evident failure of "revolutions from above" . . . should sow doubts concerning even the *efficacy* of such a politics and concerning the true power of the state' (Tironi, 1984, p. 66). The 'pursuit of an ideological utopia' leads to authoritarianism and violence, as actors overstep established institutional boundaries (which are 'not mere for-

25 Eugenio Tironi: 'No todo es política', in Tironi (1984).
26 viz. the title of the paper cited in footnote 25.
27 It is very striking to observe this in contemporary Chile: the closed and secret character of the government and the prohibition of open political activity have indeed had the effect Tironi refers to. The population is constantly on the alert for signs and indications of shifts, attitudes and intentions within the government, and also for uncontrolled spaces where they can express their own views, for example in the theatre. After benefiting from its status as an area of 'permissiveness' dramatists are said to be worried that they 'have' to write protest theatre. Plays like David Benavente's *Tres Marias y una rosa*, which in 1977 depicted how popular culture provides crutches for survival on the margins of society, were a great success. Another striking example of this search for 'space' was the visit of the Pope in 1987, which drew vast numbers of people who either saw in the gatherings an opportunity to express their hostility to the government – and not exclusively by throwing stones at the police – or because they waited to pick up gobbets of the Pope's words which could be interpreted as attacks on – or indeed defences of – Pinochet. The Pope's speeches were thus ceaselessly interrupted by applause – and sometimes expressions of disapproval – which were directed not at him but at the international media, and at Pinochet. In other times the Pope would have drawn smaller crowds – as was the case in the visit he made to a now-peaceful Argentina on leaving Chile. These are all illustrations of the hyper-politicization of daily life under a dictatorship which purports to achieve precisely the opposite effect.

malities' without substance) and cast aside any commitment to the fate of the community.[28]

But the problem of meeting accumulated social pressures after a long period of dictatorship and economic polarization remains. In response, Tironi takes up the proposal of *concertación*, the social pact, in which a post-authoritarian government would create 'increasingly formal areas of intermediation between the government and the trade unions, professional organizations, and other middle-class and business groupings' so as to include these in its decision-making process (Tironi, 1986, p. 161). Like many others, this expresses the fear of a resurgence of worker militancy and seeks an institutional formula which would channel rational men towards rational agreement: there are hints here of a return to corporatism, and one might wonder whether that would not signify a return to the problems associated with it.

The Christian Democrats, with a far broader popular base, do not disagree. The economist and politician Alejandro Foxley invokes precisely this 'new socialist perspective' which emphasizes 'decentralization and the development of intermediary social organizations' and 'free and responsible self-management' (Foxley, 1985, p. 39). Decentralization should at least dilute or defuse conflict, and should also operate in such a way as to prevent the superimposition of conflicts and the resulting polarization (1985, p. 61). Foxley does also refer to social movements, advocating 'active community participation in the administration of daily life' and 'solidarity in dealing with the immediate issues of life' such as the management and use of public spaces and of local infrastructure and urban services (1985, p. 62). In addition, evoking now a different perspective, he argues for the transcendence of the 'suffocating and bureaucratic intervention of the state' – while defending its strengthening in certain strategic areas such as the regulation of foreign trade, and basic investment in priority areas, in regulating speculation and environmental degradation, and in achieving a redistribution of income and opportunity (1985, p. 40).

This 'strategic list' is not so short, on closer inspection, and Pinochet has surely done much to remove the 'suffocating' state from economic activity in any case. But the underlying concern reflected in these proposals is that centralized control leads to the superimposition and exacerbation of pressures on the state and thus, in an elective political system, to inflation followed by political vulnerability. But they also

---

28 Eugenio Tironi (1986). The title 'real liberalism' is an ironic reference to the phrase 'real socialism' which is intended to remind socialists of the reality of communism; likewise, Tironi is reminding the audience that real liberalism – à la Pinochet – is not what the theory promised.

draw from the new social movements the idea that civil society should be trusted more, with both economic tasks – be it in self-managed enterprises or co-operatives or in private business – and with democratization: from post-marxism they have drawn the idea that new instances of participation and new mechanisms of control over the state should develop in civil society, and also that new forms of self-government and self-management should arise. But they remain defensive in tone and intent, wrestling with ghosts from the past, just as their opponents on the right conjure up the fantasma of a repeat of Popular Unity.

Argentina

In Argentina the ghosts of the past are several: the charismatic figure of Perón himself; the militaristic Montoneros with the ecstatic hordes of young – and largely middle-class – followers mobilized in his name, though eventually excommunicated by him; the traumatic experience of state terror which seemed to encounter so little resistance from a timorous civil society. These legacies unite the intelligentsia around the theme of democracy, but they remain divided in their evaluations of the populist heritage, and over the relative importance of mass movements as against the less exuberant formal institutions of liberal democracy. Social movements à la Castells are not at issue.

The group who are deeply aware of the pathos of populism are the 'post-Peronists' (my label, not theirs). Peronism as a political force in the late 1980s is definitely not what it was in either 1945 or 1972; its contemporary expressions are the *renovadores* – who are trying to transform Peronism into a modern party of labour. But in the process have they lost the unique inspiration and devotion generated by Perón's charisma and the myth of his leadership and return? The editor of *Unidos*, the intellectual organ of the *renovadores*, expresses these suspicions in what amounts to a *cri de coeur* published in 1986: Alfonsín, with his rhetoric of 'modernization' is trying to undo the populist and corporatist past, encouraged by his post-marxist speechwriters;[29] political activity is becoming a matter of marketing; social policy denies solidarity, places people in a queue as if they were at the grocer's shop, a queue in which even neighbours do not speak to each other; he has even modernized the clientele politics which was the trademark of the Radical Party's traditional politicians. The (short-lived) proposal to build a new capital city in

29 Alvarez uses the term 'portantierismo' to refer to the Gramscian intellectual and former marxist theorist Juan Carlos Portantiero, who he presumes to have contributed to a key Alfonsín speech on the theme of modernization. 'Post-marxist' is my label, but it states what Alvarez is alluding to in the word 'portantierismo' in a manner understandable to those unfamiliar with the intellectual–political milieu of Buenos Aires.

Patagonia at Viedma – a windswept Brasilia – is regarded as a device whereby the apostles of modernization can remove the centre of political activity from a city whose avenues and squares reverberate to the echoes of the great epic struggles of Peronism.

Yet how, he asks, can Peronism respond?

> Our keywords are sick and degraded, they have become obsessions, because they served an all-knowing pretension. Doctrine, the National Project, the Organized Community, the People, Liberation, have lost any operative effectiveness, and have themselves taken the place of the things they were intended to denote. Mirror-like, they have become blind and blinding. (Alvarez, 1986)

There is no overarching Peronist alternative to Alfonsín's call to cement the guarantee of citizenship, to create something 'new', to place the individual and the modern above the community and tradition. The renovating force in Peronism must recreate a movement-like party if it is not to become a party of mere marketing skills with a careerist membership. Conjuring up dream tickets with the correct balance of women, class membership and ideology merely produces 'computerized decadence'.

As befits a *cri de coeur*, the article has no concrete proposals; but its call is, clearly enough, to assimilate modernity, democracy, the rules of the game, and at the same time to recapture and renew the solidarities and historical memories, the political culture, which made Peronism what it was.[30] He does not say – though he may in his innermost thoughts suspect – that this may need a style of leadership which truly no longer fits Argentine political culture.

There is a large and weighty body of intellectual opinion which has either not given these matters much thought or else states more or less directly that the worst thing which could happen for stable democracy would be a return to what it regards as emotive themes with too high a combustible content. Juan Carlos Portantiero, one of the most quintessentially post-marxist political theorists of all, attacks both the corporatism which places reason at the heart of the state ('the State as Reason') and the worship of substantive council-style or 'direct' democracy – *consejismo*, from the word *consejo*, a council. This he rejects because it is founded on a critique of the formal character of democracy: in reaction to a consecrated marxist view, Portantiero defends the formal, procedural, character of democratic institutions and attacks the idea that democracy is exclusively identified with a liberal (i.e. individualist) state. The central

---

30 It is Alvarez who has defined Peronism succinctly as a sequence of historical memories and a style of leadership. As a definition not only of Peronism but also of populism it is the best I have seen.

issue in the replacement of dictatorship by a viable democracy is – how to create consensus? Instead of searching for a new populist interpellation, or in everyday terminology, a new emotional discourse, he looks towards a foundational change, a change of hearts and minds (Portantiero, 1984).

Such sentiments are frequently reiterated in the Buenos Aires publication *Punto de Vista*, which began to appear, as an island of humane exchange, in the darkest days of the dictatorship, in 1978, and has blossomed into the meeting place of the post-marxist democratic intelligentsia, and others of less-defined political origin. It can be described as both post-marxist and post-Peronist in the sense that, although by no means all the authors have in the past identified with marxism or Peronism, their formative experience was one in which it was *de rigueur* for an intellectual to take a stand with respect to those two banners; they now look forward to a time when these pressures will have disappeared.

The editor of *Punto de Vista*, Beatriz Sarlo, pleads for the uncoupling of the 'national' and the 'popular', and for an end to the guilt-provoking barb that the intellectual élite is necessarily estranged from those two dimensions of culture (Sarlo, 1983). She rebels against a conception of Argentine culture as a 'homogenizing enterprise undertaken in the name of national identity, of the working class or of the people', or as a permanent battle between those who were 'for' the nation and those who by their attitudes betrayed it, or between the 'progressives' and the 'reactionaries'; and behind these attitudes she denounces a 'missionary' temptation which is determined to save the popular classes from the dangers of 'high' or 'cosmopolitan' culture, in the name of a respect for factitious regional or local 'folk' culture (Sarlo, 1984a). She rebels against the historic Argentine practice of politicization of themes which properly belong to the realm of private life, enlisting the less public, more personal dramas of death, torture, the elimination of individuals and their individuality, as a basis for human rights, citizenship, democracy. The personal accounts produced before the Commission on Disappeared Persons, which sat in Buenos Aires in 1984, are valued for their dispassionate, almost clinical nakedness, which places them beyond the polluting reach of political manipulation (Sarlo, 1984b).

The theme of human rights is indeed central to post-marxism, and converges with the Alfonsinista call for a respect for the private realm which goes with modernization. In the place of the appeals of traditional Peronism to the nation as a solidary collectivity, the post-marxist and liberal intelligentsia appeal to this more personal drama which is almost impossible to translate into a collectively externalized emotional experience: the politics of human rights, as the Mothers of the Plaza de Mayo in their heroism showed, is a politics of witness, and not one of mass mobilization in the name of a collective destiny. That is why it is entirely appropriate that the Church should be in the forefront of the defence of human rights – and entirely scandalous that in Argentina it was not.

The only remaining overreaching project is that of modernization, proclaimed by Alfonsín and shared by many prominent Peronists too, but it does not constitute much more than a call to dismantle some state enterprises and to reduce the foci of pressure on the state's reduced budget. It is not a strategy for development or economic stability. Unlike their Chilean or Brazilian counterparts the post-Peronists have not developed either a theory or a practice of grassroots politics, and therefore offer not even the glimmerings of an alternative in that direction. The experience of Peronismo de Base, active at the grass roots during the leader's exile and distinct from the official unions as well as from those who chose guerrilla warfare, has not been resuscitated. The idea of a pact does not appeal to Argentinians either, for their experience has been that it is little more than a short-lived façade behind which one interest or the other – usually either the unions or the state – takes all the benefits, and since 1983 repeated attempts to pact with the trade-union movement have failed (Portantiero, 1987).

Brazil

In Brazil the space for a new party of the left emerged in the wake of the São Paulo strikes of 1978 and 1979 which reflected the rise of a very large industrial proletariat, at a time when Chile and Argentina were undergoing severe deindustrialization, with a concomitant decline in the numbers and concentration of their industrial labour force. The party, formed in 1979 (Keck, 1986–7) as the Workers' Party (PT: Partido dos Trabalhadores), described itself as a completely new phenomenon in Brazil – a party advocating a socialist transformation, but free of the shackles of the international communist movement, in a society with a young and new industrial proletariat possessing no political culture at all (Oliveira, 1986). The PT is the only party in Brazil which takes ideology seriously; it has a disproportionate representation of professional intellectuals in its central bodies – and a shortage of the professional politicians so necessary to compete in Brazilian elections. It lacks a central unifying doctrine but some of its intellectual spokespersons pride themselves on this: according to one of them it is the 'indeterminacy of the proposals' coming from the workers themselves which constitutes their 'novelty', and to label them would be to 'deprive those proposals of that which places them in the tide of history. Politics is not a science, but action which is constantly reinventing itself.'[31]

31 Chaui, 1986, p. 73. Chaui is a philosopher and, like Oliveira, a prominent PT intellectual. Her writings combine a strong liberation element with a belief in the

Having been founded by the successful and popular trade–union leader Lula, the party was born with an enviable inheritance of working-class sympathy if not active support, and at first this enabled it to perform creditably, gaining over 20 per cent in the São Paulo mayoral election in 1985, and over 5 per cent in 11 other state capitals;[32] but thereafter came a decline, due at least in part to the wranglings of a leadership whose social composition has already been indicated. The party has suffered on account of its aversion to the clientelism and personalism which dominate Brazilian political practice. However in the municipal elections of 1988 the PT scored notable victories in São Paulo and several other state capitals, reflecting the division of the centrist and right-wing politicians and the discrete but pervasive support of Catholic groups, especially the base communities.

The PT line in daily politics places heavy emphasis on land reform, on debt moratorium, on income redistribution, on shaking off foreign monopolies; it looks like the traditional programme of the left, but as so often in politics, the true societal penetration of a party depends on something other than the specifics of the programme. In this case it depends on the party's relations with and indeed origins in the São Paulo trade-union movement, and on its congruence with social movements and Church-sponsored networks, in the São Paulo working-class 'periphery' and in the country as a whole.[33] The Archbishop of São Paulo has barely concealed his support for the PT, and priests involved in social mobiliza-tion tend to support it, especially in the countryside. But this is more an alliance than an organized co-operation: the secularized intellectuals who inspire PT ideology have difficulty attuning themselves to the discourse addressed to and used by the social movements, and when they write of social movements they tend to refer to the unions rather than the grassroots organizations.[34] The social movements, for their part, are

---

applicability of basic marxist concepts such as social class: for her, the 'workers' really do have an existence as a class and a historical force. In São Paulo, where the industrial proletariat has both grown in numbers vertiginously and also, in the last ten years, in the autonomy of their organizations, this may provoke fewer doubts than in London.

32 Keck op. cit.

33 Except in Rio, where the PT is a sui generis coalition of environmentalist groups, cultural contestation and middle-class aestheticism: cf. the surprisingly successful candidacy of Fernando Gabeira, novelist, environmentalist and former *guerrilhero*, in the 1986 gubernatorial elections, though he was not elected.

34 See for example the essays by Jose Alvaro Moises in Moises, 1982. Moises writes as if in general about social movements, but in fact keeps to the trade unions. Likewise, Chauí emphasizes the 'working class' rather than the 'people'. The usages are not accidental but mark out frontiers.

ideologically defined by their distrust of official politics, and therefore cannot be expected to offer unconditional support.

The PT is clearly something new in Brazilian politics, and although its real impact is limited for the time being, if it can produce a more coherent leadership with more professional politicians and fewer intellectuals and academics, it has several features which could serve it well in the long run: it is the natural political ally of the grassroots movements; it is the only party which consistently advocates structural change; it is the only party in the post-marxist area of influence in the whole continent which has a working-class base, and it has distanced itself from the traditional left – both populist and stalinist. It has the luck – illustrated by the 1988 municipal elections – to be confronted by a divided centre and right whose victory in the 1989 Presidential election is far from assured. It has the potential to become the region's first post-marxist party with any significant political weight.

It is therefore all the more ironic that the Brazilian who can properly claim to have been the first post-marxist of them all, the sociologist and Senator, Fernando Henrique Cardoso, is not in the PT at all, but in the Social Democratic Party, a breakaway formed in 1987 from the ideologically diverse centre-right PMDB (Partido do Movimento Democrático Brasileiro) and is deeply suspicious of *basismo*.

Cardoso's book *Dependency and development in Latin America*, written while he was working in Santiago at CEPAL in about 1966, (Cardoso and Faletto, 1970) is often thought of as the original text of dependency theory, yet in fact it was a polemic against it; did its title not speak of dependency *and development*, rather than *under*development? The book argued that class structures and alliances are conditioned, but not determined by, the mode of insertion of different social formations in the world economy (hence the term 'dependency'), and had also argued strongly for the autonomy of politics from its economic underpinnings. It introduced the themes dear to post-marxism, of social movements and the process whereby 'purely economic influences are filtered by the tensions between groups with differing economic, social and political interests' (ibid., p. 22). Although broadly within a marxist tradition, the book is littered with hedging phrases: for example, class relations were not precisely rooted in the mode of production – as an orthodox marxist would at that time have claimed without any second thoughts – but should be studied 'through . . . structures of domination'. Already at that time, Cardoso differed from the dependency theorists on almost every point of substance, and in so doing showed remarkable foresight on some issues: military governments (by which he meant the then new Brazilian one) ruled over a 'techno–bureaucratic corporation' more autonomous and more entrepreneurial than the populist state they had overthrown, and were anything but pawns in the hands of foreign capitalist interests. Even those factions of the dominant class which were linked to world centres of economic power, decried by the *dependentistas*, were seen as a positive force by Cardoso since, precisely for that reason, they could 'take advantage of new conditions or new opportunities for growth' (ibid., pp. 28–9). For a short time, in the late 1960s, when dictatorship and economic growth were both at their height in Brazil, Cardoso did take a pessimistic, dependency-style view, describing the country as engaged in an 'associated dependent' process of capitalist development, but even this was a dissident opinion at a time when few had recognized the industrialization spurt under way in Brazil (Cardoso, 1973). Thereafter his main concern has been the state: as a political manoeuvrer he was able to link the economic protests of the São Paulo business community against the 'dirigisme' of the military with the more political democratic protests of opposition politicians and intellectuals, and thus helped to create an important bridge in the liberalization process between 1977 and 1984. To the businessmen who spoke of reducing the presence of the state in the economy he responded positively, even while saying to the intelligentsia on more academic occasions, that the need was to democratize the state, not to dismantle it.

By democratization Cardoso means that those in charge of it should be subjected to periodic election – not that the apparatus should be democratized in its methods of operation by pressure from below. Whereas the *basistas* see social movements outside the institutions as essential to achieving citizenship, he interprets the grassroots movements dismissively as a demand for citizenship, saying that the way to achieve it is to consolidate citizenship in the official political framework and not to lead the people to conduct their struggles outside it. In his view 'direct democracy' and *basismo* (a pejorative term in his usage) may well be attractive when formal, party-based participation is frustrating, slow or merely impossible, but democracy depends on the confidence of the people in institutions (Cardoso, 1985).[35]

This analysis has been pursued further by his wife Ruth Cardoso, who, in a widely-quoted paper, dissects the three major claims made on behalf of social movements. Do they force the authoritarian state to democratize? No, that is the task of political parties; although movements force the state to recognize them as valid spokesmen for local communities, the state in its turn has the flexibility to respond, often favourably, to their demands and even to co-opt them. Do they force the state to recognize the 'Presence of the oppressed'? Yes, but this is a neat mechanism

---

35 I gained the impression that his views on this matter might if anything be somewhat stronger (in personal conversation in 1986).

whereby the state (then still controlled by the military) can avoid dealing with political forces proper – i.e. political parties – choosing to negotiate with small-scale movements from a position of strength. The parties, unlike the movements, can redirect the functioning of the state as a whole, instead of concentrating on local issues. Can the movements have a renovating effect on established parties and unions? Yes, by reducing the excessively hierarchical character of these organizations, but not by replacing them (Ruth Cardoso, 1983).

All of this is reasonable on the assumption that political parties can change the way in which the state functions – but the experience of Brazil's 'New Republic' holds out little hope on that score so far. The problem is whether the requisite popular confidence in political institutions can be built up in a society characterized by extreme inequality, and widespread abuse of power, and whether attempts from without to reform these features would lead to an interruption of the New Republic.

The modernizing – and modernist – conception of political development espoused by the Cardoso family is, to quote a famous article, an example of 'ideas out of place' (Schwarz, 1973): the slave-owners were liberals, the bringers of foreign capital were nationalists, and now the modernizers wish to bring citizenship under the aegis of a political system which guarantees rights only to those endowed with wealth and power. Argentina and Chile are countries where citizenship could probably be guaranteed by reforms of the state, but in Brazil such guarantees require structural changes in society. In those countries the mass of the people can be assumed to know what citizenship rights are whereas in Brazil it is likely that vast numbers do not know, except in a very localistic and context-dependent sense.[36] In Brazil levels of education are much lower among the poor,[37] the more or less direct purchase of votes is standard practice in elections; the integrity of the police is far more seriously in doubt; and lastly, but most intangibly and thus speculatively, the language of rights is not a feature of daily political discourse. The New Republic reproduces on a grander scale than ever, the political habits of the old days before 1964 – habits, it should be recalled, which the military government of the intervening period did little to eradicate and much to

36 It is interesting in this respect to read the study by Lygia Sigaud of the concept of 'rights' among sugar workers in the north east. The book shows that the workers think of rights as a set of personal obligations binding landlord to peasant, or dependent on a continuing dyadic transaction between worker and union, rather than in a universal sense. 'Rights', originally a 'gift from a reforming politician', can only be sustained by regular payments of the union quota; non-members do not have them. See Sigaud, 1979, ch. 9.

37 According to the World Bank Development Report, 1987, although all three countries had more or less 10 per cent of the relevant age group enrolled in primary school, in Brazil this proportion fell to 35 per cent at secondary level, compared to 65 per cent and 66 per cent for the other two countries.

encourage, as if contaminated by its civilian predecessors and the machine it inherited from them. In Argentina and in Chile, in short, the state may impose authoritarianism on a democratic political culture; but in Brazil the lack of democracy is embedded in the culture and the social structure and citizenship cannot, therefore, be so easily ensured.

Neo-conservative politics and neo-liberal economics

This period of reappraisal or revisionism among the generation whose ideas inspired the struggle for reform and revolution, has also been a period of revisionism on the right. Conservative thought has cast off its corporatist, organicist mould and has become enamoured of the market; it has set aside a concern for Latin American identity or uniqueness and has espoused the region's cultural and economic integration with the world market.

Like structuralist reformism, conservative ideology has been heavily influenced by economists, and has been moulded by the struggle against economic volatility. What was at first known as 'monetarism' became a policy of thoroughgoing structural change. This is most clearly visible in Chile, where the 1973 military government, coming to power in circumstances verging on hyperinflation, after an initial attempt to achieve disinflation by orthodox but gradual means, turned to shock treatment. The policy was more than a short-term attack on inflation. In addition to the standard recipe of devaluation, deregulation of prices, withdrawal of subsidies, reduction of fiscal deficits, the stabilization was an integral part of an entirely new philosophy of the state. It started from a thorough-going critique of the model of ISI: the source of all Chile's suffering was in state intervention in the economy. This had favoured only those able to exercise effective political pressure to obtain a favourable exchange rate, a cheap credit, a fixed price, a subsidy and so on.[38] Pinochet's economic team took the view that wealth had been the reward of politicking and not of producing, and tried to put an end to this. The pursuit of social justice by or through the state had merely created opportunities or rents for some at the expense of others – unionized workers at the expense of the non-unionized, for those enjoying legal protection at the expense of the rest; for importers at the expense of exporters and so on. In dismantling the system, they have proved themselves the true structuralists.

The arguments are by now well known, though the metaphors betray an interesting angle on this ultra-individualistic and highly moralistic

38 See statements made by Sergio de Castro – who, together with Pablo Baraona and Alvaro Bardon – composed this 'team', in Vergara (1985, p. 96). The account which follows draws extensively on pp. 89–101 of this book.

view: the market offers an order of 'toughness' as against the cissiness or 'blandness' of the political pursuit of social justice. Inflation is the work of spineless or merely corrupt governments in a world where all politics is a corrupt affair. It is not merely a pessimistic view of human nature – it is a macho one, in which we are all lone rangers in the rough and tumble of the market. The market ensures the success of the best-endowed individuals, 'stimulates creative effort and rewards self-improvement, thus giving a true meaning to the morality of effort and the fulfilment of one's duty' (Vergara, 1985, p. 96, quoting Baraona). Social justice is the 'socialism which levels down' (*mediocratizante*), it 'holds back the strong and rewards the weak, the inefficient and the ignorant who, fearing the market, run to the state and political favouritism to protect them'. The ideas may be American, having nothing in common with any politically significant discourse in Latin American history, but their expression bears not a little of the 'macho' imprint.[39]

Neo-conservative political economy teaches that once the state intervenes in economic matters the way is open for unbridled corruption, usually called rent-seeking.[40] To the neo-conservative, the task of the state is not to provide the resources facilitating the settlement of social conflicts – although it may provide the forum. The state – or those in government – cannot know which is the fair distribution, and no settlement involving discretionary decisions taken by politicians and officials can under any circumstances guarantee efficient returns to everybody's efforts – which usually means to 'everybody's' tax payment – not can it be immune to biases within the state. According to this view, politics in most modern states is all about rent-seeking, introducing biases in the state but paradoxically operating to the net cost of almost everyone. 'Almost everyone' then reacts by organizing to compensate for these biases, but this only makes matters worse, as the scale and the real incidence of the cost of special provisions becomes ever more obscure.

Indeed, for some theorists within this broad current, the very process of organizing interest groups has embedded within it an undemocratic element. In a thesis first developed twenty years ago, Mancur Olson argued that special-interest lobbies can only gain members – and thus the money to function – if they either coerce them or if they offer them

39 The original monetarists had come from the Economics Department of the Catholic University where, since 1955, under a scheme funded by the Ford and Rockefeller Foundations, a regular flow of people went to and came from the sister Department at Chicago, where monetarism was gospel. But this second generation had clearly shifted towards the (then) new and kindred political doctrine of 'neo-conservative', 'constitutionalist' or 'libertarian political economy, of which more below.

40 The neo-conservatives' concept of rent-seeking rests ultimately on a counter-factual – namely a hypothetical but possible other world in which there is no state intervention.

selective personal benefits – such as cut-rate insurance for members of a trade association, or a free subscription to an information fact sheet. The notion that the members would act in common exclusively for their own personal interest in the enjoyment of a collective resource, or good, is mistaken: no rational individual would do so, because the return to the effort is uncertain and not worth it. Lobbying except perhaps by very large-scale 'encompassing' groups reduces overall efficiency and productivity.[41] Unfortunately, the drawback of those encompassing groups is that lobbies have to organize within them, reproducing at one remove the same imperfections Olson observes of collective action in general.

So the modern state is fundamentally a 'pork-barrel' state: for James Buchanan, 'the faith in politics exhibited by twentieth-century man, at least until the 1960s, stems ultimately from his loss of faith in God, (Buchanan, 1975, p. 170). Buchanan, like Olson, is a 'rational choice' theorist; that is, they start out, whatever the question they ask, from the presumption that individuals ask not what they can do for society, but what society – or at least the state – can do for them; and they presume that if individuals do something which they – or others – describe as 'for society' that is at best because they want to increase their own moral gratification, as in the standard and despised case of socialist or even mildly liberal politicians. But the paradox, in the view of these two writers – and others in the neo-conservative or, alternatively, strangely denominated, libertarian, camp – is that by trying to do good we fail in that stated objective, and usually compound the failure by doing bad, especially if the vehicle for our 'do-gooding' is politics and public expenditure. Generally speaking, there is more loss than gain to society from public expenditure.

Two basic reasons for this paradox are that (1) the state taxes in an undifferentiated manner, but spends in a differentially directed manner, and (2) the state itself is not the neutral conveyor of collective choices, but rather – through the ideological or self-interested activities of the politicians and bureaucrats whose powers and numbers no eighteenth-century thinker could ever have imagined – creates an irresistible momentum driving society and politics to ever-higher levels of immorality, dissipation and exploitation of the citizenry. This momentum passes without substantial objection from the voters as a collectivity because the cost to each one of them of a hike in taxes – or the benefit of a tax cut – is

41 The original, and brilliant, work was *The logic of collective action* (1965). His *Rise and decline of nations*, (1982), is an application of those ideas rather than a further extension. It is probably only under quite restrictive conditions that Olson would even approve of encompassing groups, since so often their size precludes effective internal debate and participation (1982, p. 52).

minuscule compared to the possible benefits of a differential spending programme – like medical care for the old, or cheap credit for farmers, or a dam in your district. Lobbies don't fight to cut taxes for everyone; they fight to increase expenditure for particular groups. It is from here that proposals for constitutional reform in the US have come, recommending a constitutionally binding balanced budget (Buchanan et al., 1980).

The Pinochet dictatorship offered an unprecedented opportunity for the application of these ideas, but it also raised very serious questions: if their authors believe so deeply in liberty, how can they conciliate this belief with their faith in a dictatorship? And if they defend the dictatorship on the grounds that it is a necessary evil for a transitional period only, how can they be sure that once democracy returns the old habits will not also return? And finally, are there no special interest groups in a dictatorship? Neo-conservatives believe that constitution can be drawn up which will offer no special advantage to any individual or social group – but since we live in a world of lobbies and interests and innumerable other political struggles, it is hard to see 'what incentive anyone has to introduce the necessary constitutional limits'.[42]

The underlying message of these ideas is that democracy is an enemy of freedom – perhaps not the worst enemy, but an enemy nonetheless. Freedom in this school of thought is a concept intimately bound up with the concept of a property-owning person, whose rights are part of his property; yet the complex and tangled transactions concealed in the web of the democratic struggle deprive the person of property, both material and legal. Majority rule deprives minorities of their property systematically (Buchanan, 1975). Measures to redistribute income, therefore, are not only attacks on property – they are also, more emotively, attacks on rights, unless incorporated into a new constitutional contract which, so to speak, creates a *tabula rasa*.

The illiberal instincts of this 'libertarian' doctrine find their most evident expression in the macho language already quoted from the Chileans, and in Buchanan's own examples and incidental language; side by side with dispassionate dissections of two-person and multi-person exchanges and the distribution of gains and costs therefrom, Buchanan drops remarks about the collapse of moral values in the 1960s, the implied need to punish criminals more severely (instead of rewarding their riots with improved facilities as he sarcastically remarks) (Buchanan, 1975, p. 173) and the 'activist judiciary' with its 'widespread departures from any protective state limits', (1975, p. 172). For Buchanan only a near-

---

42 David Miller, reviewing Norman P. Barry: 'The new right' in *The Times Literary Supplement*, December 4–10, 1987. Gordon Tullock, who with Buchanan is the leading figure in neo-conservative/libertarian circles, attended a conference organized by supporters of Pinochet and his economic team in Santiago in 1980. See Foxley (1985, p. 99).

unanimity rule is acceptable. From there to the kinship of his ideas with the more ruthless of South American dictatorships is but a short step, since he does not seem to believe there is much difference between the violations of rights which occur under a majoritarian system with a licence to print money and the violations which occur under a military regime with a licence to kill and torture people.

All these writings raise the question 'what is a state for?'. For they show state apparatuses in which neither officials not politicians nor indeed the citizenry have any sense of mutual obligation or common belongingness. Far from the Hobbesian world in which the natural condition of civil society is a war of all against all until sovereignty is handed over to the state, here the war of all against all prevails in the state – a situation reminiscent of O'Donnell's account of Argentina.[43]

The ultra-pessimism of Buchanan is founded on the notion that almost all the resources appropriated from individuals by the state would, if left unappropriated, be used by the individuals in such a way as to benefit themselves and others more; and also on the notion that the state is not necessarily the appropriate intermediary even in the provision of such commonplace public goods as street lighting, the police, or nuclear missiles. In both cases the same objection can be made as is made to violent marxist revolution, namely that to pursue his objections consistently one would have to conduct a process the outcome of which is more uncertain than most people would wish to contemplate (Dunn, 1972). In both cases, also, we are being asked to believe that the very pure competitive conditions which underpin these assumptions could ever be brought about – even while the Buchanans of this world are proving daily that men, as political animals, are far too corruptible to allow anything of the sort to occur! In the end we return to one of our own two central themes: the modernization of the state, a slow, correctable, incremental strategy – and one which can be held to account in a democratic process.

A populist neo-conservatism

The most striking recent proposal for deregulation is that of the Peruvian Hernando de Soto, in his book *El otro sendero*. Published in late 1986, complete with unprecedented pre-launch TV advertising campaigns and a Preface by novelist and Presidential candidate Mario Vargas Llosa the book had gone through five editions and printed 50,000 copies within six months. It has been on best-seller lists in Colombia and Brazil as well. In

43 The writings of Robert Bates on Africa (1981) are particularly relevant in this regard. Although also placing himself in the rational choice school, Bates seems to believe that the organization of interest groups outside the political élite can be of benefit to their members.

September 1987 President Reagan recommended the book to his audience at the United Nations General Assembly. In January 1988 the *New York Times* devoted an editorial to it.[44]

Soto proceeds by a vivid description of the potential 'economic' dynamism exhibited by the informal sector. His subject is Lima, the 'Calcutta of Latin America'. His heroes are the innumerable petty entrepreneurs whose energies are suffocated and dissipated by the morass of laws passed by governments of every political colour; his villain is a redistributive system in which the state takes a role of redistributing wealth rather than providing conditions appropriate to its creation. This is a standard and unoriginal statement; but Soto goes on to describe in graphic detail the effects of this on 'economic' activity which, he says, is to create a rent-seeking society, in which individuals devote more time and energy to politics, to obtaining favours and exemptions, or simply to obtaining necessary permits, than would otherwise be required. Ever since colonial times, rent-seeking, and the fulfilment or evasion of rules and regulations, have been a central feature of economic activity, creating an informal sector of income opportunities for those who do not or cannot meet the impossible requirements of documented economic activity.

Unlike some economists, Soto does not regard the informal sector as efficient; on the contrary, he provides a vast array of stories and data illustrating the very high costs of entering markets, of obtaining and preserving the recognition of ownership rights, and of enforcing contracts in this extra-legal world. If the informal sector is more efficient than the formal sector in certain specific areas – such as selling prepared food to the public – that is for very special reasons.[45] The informal sector pays far more in bribery, for example – 10 to 15 per cent of gross receipts as compared with 1 per cent spent by small formal-sector businesses – and street sellers pay fees well in excess of what shopkeepers pay in rent per square metre.

The accounts of informality and co-operation in housing, retail trade (street selling) and transport in the book are graphic and illustrative. In each case Soto sings the praises of an activity which the defenders of

44 *International Herald Tribune*, 17 January 1988; President Reagan's reference was in his speech of 21 September 1987.
45 For example, the tax on value added operates to encourage the informal sector to keep to either the point at which a product reaches the final consumer, or to the point where it is processed as raw material. Since the final consumer pays value-added tax to neither a formal nor an informal outlet, there is no special advantage to the formal outlet at that stage since it cannot reclaim tax paid. Likewise, the processor of raw material is not charged value-added tax and neither formal nor informal sectors in that activity need reclaim it. In all the links which fall between the two extremes, formal sector businesses, which are registered and pay taxes, are at an advantage.

private property usually condemn, namely *invasiones*, that is seizures of land, of street space and of transport routes. These are the only recourse possible for people excluded by labyrinthine regulations from purchasing land, renting selling space, building covered markets, or applying for rights of transit for their buses. For example, there is no mechanism available for obtaining the right to ply one's trade as owner of a bus on a route through the vast expanse of Lima's streets. The rules say the authorities should provide all transport. In practice they provide perhaps 10 per cent of the buses on the roads.

Land invasions too are very carefully organized; to get several thousand people to act together at the same place and the same time requires something approaching military planning. Their leaders are dealmakers and organizers of great skill and sophistication. They search out appropriate sites, and suitable groups of people to settle there; they raise finance for initial operations, such as feeding the children while the parents stand guard against the police or counter-invasions. They set up an elected committee to administer the numerous common interests of the settlers, including keeping a register of houses and their owners. A range of elected bodies are established designed to press the authorities to recognize the settlement, to provide basic services such as street lighting, sewage and so on, and even to administer justice. In contrast to the elitism of the official legal system which does not trust the people to pass judgement on their peers, informal justice operates on a jury system.

To deal with the authorities, and their repeated and usually unsuccessful efforts to 'clear the streets', all sorts of devices are used, including bribery and physical resistance. The street sellers confront them with a gamut of organizations ranging from the small informal group who use a particular stretch of pavement to the large pressure groups whose leaders are for ever doing deals chameleon-like with the 'government of the day' at local or even national level, under the watchful and opportunistic eye of a capricious rank-and-file. They also manage to build covered markets, although these are rarely fully completed, so that, despite all the legal and financial obstacles, we are told that by 1984 there were 274 markets in Lima built by the street sellers and only 57 built by the state (Soto, 1986, p. 101). Likewise, in transport there is a gamut of organizations, from the small group of 'invaders' opening up a route by stealth in order later to obtain official recognition, to the highly politicized federation. The small committee manages a route rather like a co-operative in which membership can be purchased or inherited, or members can sell out to the committee itself who then look for a suitable new member.

Despite his enthusiasm for individualist economics and political theory, Soto's accounts of invasions show that a high degree of complexity is involved as well as a high degree of co-operation. While he chooses to emphasize the entrepreneurial flair of the informal operators, another reading of his material would also emphasize the robustness of co-operation when it is generated by individuals with clear objectives and without any governmental involvement at all.

Soto uses his evidence to develop an orthodox neo-conservative programme. He insists on the costs to society of regulation in general, not merely of inefficient or corrupt regulation. He believes that the state must pull out of all direct regulation and involvement in production, limiting itself to a strong judicial role as guarantor of institutions of property, and of the enforceability of contracts. If the legal system were reformed there would follow a radical reallocation of resources which would release entrepreneurial animal spirits and promote economic development. The rest is to be left to the market. Yet the evidence presented reinforces the argument that co-operation is a central feature of economic life, although the only viable co-operation is that which emerges from bargains struck among people with clearly defined private rights and interests.

Soto does confess great admiration for the high degree of self-management achieved in the informal sector, but he regards it as a makeshift solution which wastes a lot of time and will become unnecessary once the state puts an end to all the useless rules and regulations. He does not share the *basista* enthusiasm for grassroots organization as a form of people's power, as a mechanism for autonomy and communal self-determination.

The intellectual reaction, at least among supporters of the left, has been very hostile: *El otro sendero* is described as a 'return to the 19th century', to a free-enterprise capitalism which is not appropriate to the present day, as an attack on all forms of state intervention in the economy, and as a political programme to organize a base for Vargas Llosa and the right among the mass of petty entrepreneurs who make up the informal sector. The intelligentsia of the left feel threatened above all because they themselves believe that state dirigisme has on the whole failed miserably, and have therefore provided Soto with his main plank. But they can also learn from Soto that collective action can arise from economic calculation, and is compatible with accumulation as well as with marginality.

They can also argue against him on several important grounds. One simple one is that Soto's proposals to sack tens of thousands of public employees, however well-founded, would generate a massive depression in the economy. A more fundamental analytical objection concerns the claim that the removal of regulation will release the entrepreneurial initiative of the informal sector into the economy as a whole. This involves a misunderstanding by Soto of his own evidence: for the informal entrepreneurs themselves live in the interstices created by regulation, and if the regulation was removed they would lose their current competitive advantage. They are rent-seekers as much as anyone else; they exist because they evade regulations which raise costs excessively high for more formally established enterprises. Remove the regulations and those enterprises will expand into new areas hitherto occupied by the informal sector if they can pay lower wages, or few charges. This is especially relevant in the light of the great emphasis placed by Soto and by orthodox economics on deregulation in labour markets, and especially on the abolition of minimum wages. The experience of Chile – with its deregulation under Pinochet – is illustrative, for there deregulation has been accompanied by a shift of jobs from the informal to the formal sector and by a massive increase in open (formal) unemployment as a share of total underutilization of labour (which includes underemployment, most characteristic of the informal sector).[46]

Is this Pinochet with a human face? To say that would be to avert the real ideological challenge issued by Soto. The challenge to the left is both theoretical and practical: to recognize that market calculation is compatible with *basismo*, and thus to construct a populism which will appeal to the mass of informal-sector workers without mortgaging the revenue of the state for generations to come. Secondly, the left – the post-marxist generation – must find a way of creating out of grassroots social movements a force for purposeful, but not centrally directed, social transformation. Soto thinks he is a good neo-conservative, and refers frequently to writers in that school, but the ideas he proposes also contain a double challenge to the neo-conservatives: firstly, to recognize that public goods and co-operation from below have a central function to play in economic life, and cannot be dismissed by labelling them opportunities for rent-seeking. Secondly, they must bring distributional issues back into mainstream development economics, rather than consigning them to an appendage of remedial efforts.[47] In the final analysis, the task of theory is to break down the state–society dichotomy, to understand – as O'Donnell began to understand – the uselessness of confronting those

---

46 Chile's open unemployment rose from 4.1 per cent in 1970 to 11.7 per cent in 1980 and 18.5 per cent in 1984, while the Latin American average during the same period went from 6.6 per cent to 5.8 per cent to 7.9 per cent. The increase in Chile's open unemployment accounts for almost all the increase in total under-utilization of labour from 14.9 per cent to 19.7 per cent between 1970 and 1980. The informal non-agricultural share of employment rose by less than 1 per cent while in comparable middle-income countries – Argentina and Uruguay – it rose by 5 per cent. Thus labour markets began to function more transparently and competitively, but the employment performance was dismal all the same (figures from García and Tokman, 1985).

47 The Chilean government's policy is to take only very limited and carefully targeted steps to relieve extreme poverty; the result is to reduce the infant mortality rate but also to keep alive individuals in a state of chronic malnourishment. See Grupo de Investigaciones Agrarias (GIA), 1987. This is a detailed report using a vast range of macro- and micro-data.

two categories as homogeneously opposed blocks, and then to seek out forms of interaction between them which are transparent and open, not interstitial and corrupt.

Conclusion

The theoretical–ideological discourses we have surveyed – be they of the right or of the left – have in common a schematic, inflexible comprehension of the relationship between state and society. For structuralists rational planning could provide the basis for development, the dynamic of class conflict and its intertwining with state structures could be wished away. For the generation of political activists reared on dependency theory, the conquest of state power by parties enjoying massive popular support could create a society in which conflict had no material basis, and therefore no reason to exist at all. In both cases, state and society were presumed to move in harmony, but neither gave consideration to the existence of their relation with one another. Maybe those reformists and the revolutionaries among them who expected political change to follow on changes in the relations of production did so more out of despair than conviction, subconsciously suspecting that the power to transform society was not within their grasp and that it depended on forces beyond the control of the open political process. But on the surface at least they seemed to believe that power is power to transform entire social structures, that it is 'there', in the state, to be seized and used to that end. The problem of simply managing the state itself, with all its incoherence and its multiplicity of interlinked conflicts and alliances, is forgotten, for it seems so routine; instead, programmes, projects and structural changes are announced and the complexities of bringing them to fruition ignored. These are the means to achieve the ends and need to be managed. Latin American politics are deeply resistant to this because of the centrifugal patterns described earlier, the myriad of semi-independent fiefdoms which Fernando Cardoso called bureaucratic rings (*aneis burocraticos*). The only regime which has brought them under control is the dictatorship of Pinochet, by radically transforming the entire model of public administration, sacking thousands of civil servants,[48] devolving management to regional bodies, and stripping away those bodies of the state which attracted collective pressures, such as public health, public education and social security, and placing first a prohibition and later strict restrictions on trade-union freedoms.

---

48 The fiscal defecit was reduced by 34 per cent in 1974 and a further 68 per cent the following year (Corbo, 1985).

Pinochet may have succeeded in disciplining the machine, but the much more murderous Argentine counterpart achieved nothing of that kind at all. So violence is not the secret. And although Pinochet may have eliminated rent-seeking in some areas, it has created far more grandiose opportunities for a more restricted range of operations than existed before: this can be seen in the re-purchase of foreign debt to subsidize foreign investment,[49] but above all in the monopolies which grew up in the wake of the bankruptcies and privatization programme that accompanied the orthodox shock of the mid-1970s. In addition, a variety of manipulations created opportunities for dubious activities in capital markets subject to very weak regulation, leading to a financial crash in 1982, with bank failures and company bankruptcies on a spectacular scale (Corbo, 1985).[50]

If we speak of deregulation we must distinguish between the effects of regulation itself and the effects of the lack of transparency in its application, as well as of the distributional effects of different types of deregulation. By rendering regulation more transparent one could reduce time-wasting and market imperfection without engendering the large-scale dislocations which deregulation might provoke. In other words, the quality of bureaucracy matters more than its quantity. The task of improving management in the public sector may be long and hard, but the alternative of privatization, accompanied by higher levels of unemployment, deteriorating income distribution and loss of productive capacity, is better avoided. If in addition it is admitted both that monopoly may actually increase in the wake of such distortion, and that rent-seeking will persist in other forms, then the benefits of drastic deregulation may appear less attractive.

For their part the militants of Unidad Popular and of the second Peronist government would, to bring about the massive changes they

49 The mechanism is as follows: the Chilean government buys back its own debt at a discount on the secondary market in New York; it then sells it for dollars at the same discount to foreign or Chilean investors who acquire the *face* value in Chilean currency so long as they use that amount for investment in Chile. They therefore buy $100 of investment for, say, $60. After a specified number of years they can take out their profits in dollars at the going rate, and later the entire initial investment. But the crucial subsidy is at the first stage. The question is: does this mechanism attract investment which would not have been made anyhow?

50 This criticism does not take into account the argument that even if a total abolition of rent-seeking is impossible, second-best solutions are available which would at least improve resource allocations and lead entrepreneurs to devote less of their energies to rent-seeking. That is the argument of Krueger who would advocate restricting access to, say, import licences, to a few monopolists rather than opening it up to larger numbers competing for uneconomically tiny allocations (Krueger, 1974). Even so, the resistance from those affected would be very strong. Krueger later advocated a much more radical approach, though, when she became a vice-president of the World Bank.

proclaimed, have had to harness civil society with ruthlessness, hierarchy, concerted action, whereas acting *as if* they had that power enabled them to truly pursue the ideal, and thus to strain their discourse towards an ever-receding, ever-more-perfect ideal. For all Perón's obsession with organization, he only operated through the murky shadows of his court, with its hangers-on, its gunmen, its often macabre manipulations.[51] For all the Montoneros' militaristic obsessions, they relied on the mass spontaneity of middle-class youth. For all Chile's honeycombed matrix of left-wing parties, Allende could exercise no orchestrated mass mobilization capable of coming anywhere near protecting his authority.[52] The experience of power, or rather of office, acted like a drug on an entire generation.

These two experiences, and on a less dramatic scale that of Brazil in 1961–4, were accompanied by a popular mobilization more expressive than instrumental, by acts of presence rather than strategic actions undertaken in pursuit of the conquest of political power. The governments in power were frightened by the threat of radicalization that they represented, and allowed themselves to be hurled against the rocks by waves of pressure from their supporters. The idea that state power could be achieved by demonstrations, again reflected a supremely unsophisticated conception of the relations between state and civil society.

Clearly the neo-conservative attack on the state presents the survivors and descendants of the 'generation of 1968' with a severe challenge. Today, in the wake of so much agony, they need to think in a more open manner; institutions need to be created or reinvented, but they need to be institutions open to constant revisions of a piecemeal kind. There is a strand of thought which is open to this type of thinking in Latin America, both ideologically and practically, and in the next two chapters I will seek to document it.

51 For those who would doubt this, a reading of the extraordinary fictional biography, *La novella de Perón*, Martinez (1986), is recommended.

52 Allende was no *caudillo*; but Chilean political culture itself could bear no *caudillismo*. Even Pinochet is not really a *caudillo*: rather the refuge of the timorous who fear that the alternative is indeed *le déluge*. For an insight into Allende the man see the account by the US ambassador at that time (see Davis, 1985).

Three: The Church Returns to Centre Stage

Social advance and theological retrenchment in Europe

In the mid-nineteenth century, as the territories of the Papal States were overrun by the unification of Italy under the aegis of liberal nationalism, the Papacy was both physically and morally on the defensive; the response of Pope Pius IX (1846–78) was autocratic and centralist, culminating in the ratification of the doctrine of papal infallibility at the First Vatican Council of 1870. Pope Pius revived the cult of the Virgin Mary, proclaimed the Immaculate Conception, standardized liturgical usage throughout the world, and embarked on a process of bureaucratic centralization. The gradual disentanglement of Church and State as the latter renounced its role in episcopal appointments, and ceased subsidizing the Church, also brought centralization of power, as the Papacy gained control over the appointment of bishops in almost all countries. Ecclesiastical centralization, far from being a medieval inheritance, was a phenomenon of the late-nineteenth and early-twentieth centuries.

Nationalism involves both the creation of a myth of the primordial ties binding together a people and 'their' state, and the centralization of the state apparatus which that myth is designed to legitimate. Likewise the Church. During this period a myth of the past was created, of a middle ages when society was ordered and peaceful and the family intact, of a tradition of Papal centralization, of a theological wisdom unchanged since St Thomas Aquinas. Pius IX's successor, Leo XIII (1878–1903), transformed Thomism from an 'obscurantist relic of the Middle Ages' into official dogma, forbidding anyone who did not 'subscribe fully to the doctrine' from holding a chair at a Catholic institution, while at the same time welcoming workers' organizations and coming to terms with an industrial society in which the majority of Catholics would be urban dwellers (McSweeney, 1980, pp. 69, 73). It is only superficially paradoxical that this was the Pope who was the first to confront industrial society in other than utterly negative terms: indeed we shall see that the Church in the late-twentieth century is again combining openness to the world with internal retrenchment.

This openness can never be indiscriminate. The Church does not seek profits like a corporation, or votes like a political party and it is far from clear that it can preserve its identity and authority by adopting indiscriminate assimilation of the dominant values in civil society. The changes which have to be made in the adaptation process are more selective, such as the organizational modernization now under way, the sponsorship of lay movements which was initiated by Leo XIII, the liturgical changes initiated by the Second Vatican Council, the opening up of new areas of pastoral activity and so on. Likewise, the issue of world poverty has become a central theme, following in the tradition of the social doctrine, but while Popes Paul VI and John Paul II adopted the conventional wisdom of liberal opinion on many development issues, they steadfastly held their ground on birth control.[1] By now, also, the majority of Catholics were in the Third World.

The consideration of the 'social question' began with the most famous document of Leo's Papacy (1878–1903), his 1891 Encyclical *Rerum Novarum*, (literally 'Of New Things') which laid the foundations of Catholic Action, of corporatism and of Christian Democracy. The approach of that Encyclical remained dominant in the 'social doctrine of the Church' until the period immediately after Vatican II and it remains one of the most frequently quoted Papal documents even today.

The Encyclical's opening three sections are devoted to attacking socialism, thereafter condemning class conflict, and appealing to the charitable instincts of the rich to pay decent wages. Its hostility to liberal economics and espousal of the 'just wage' set it apart from the secular orthodoxies of the time, but fitted in with the Church's distrust of industrial society. Yet its support for workers' associations rendered it almost revolutionary in the eyes of its audience. In Georges Bernanos' *Journal d'un curé de campagne* (1936) an old priest recounts how when the encyclical was published:

> we felt the earth trembling under our feet. What enthusiasm! I was a priest . . . in a mining area. This simple idea that labour is not a commodity subject to the law of supply and demand, that it is not right to speculate with men's wages, with their lives, like you might speculate on the price of wheat, sugar or coffee, that idea really shook us. For explaining it . . . I was taken for a socialist and the peasants sent me off in disgrace. (1974, p. 75)

1 Pope John's Encyclicals *Mater et Magistra* (1961), *Pacem in Terris* (1963) and Pope Paul's *Populorum Progressio* (1967). The Encyclical dealing with contraception is, of course, *Humane Vitae* (1968).

Rerum Novarum sowed the seed of the idea of the solidary self-action of the poor, if not as a class, then at least as a collectivity. Pius XI, on its fortieth anniversary in 1931, published an Encyclical (therefore entitled *Quadragesimo anno*) which added 'a fundamental principle of social philosophy', known as the 'principle of subsidiary function'. According to this principle:

> Just as it is wrong to withdraw from the individual and commit to a group what private enterprise and industry can accomplish, so too its is an injustice, a grave evil and a disturbance of right order, for a larger and higher association to arrogate to itself functions which can be performed efficiently by smaller and lower societies. Of its very nature the true aim of all social activity should be to help members of the social body, but never to destroy or absorb them.

The limits of state intervention seemed quite tightly drawn; but modern ideas about grassroots organization and its potential are also foreshadowed.[2]

This philosophy opened a space in which a Christian inspiration could be invoked in the name of a variety of political and social activisms. Pope Leo, having encouraged a corporatist conception of society, had to distance himself from those who thought that the problems of industrial society could be resolved by a revival of a medieval guild system – or rather, as is so common in such cases, of their idealized version of that system (Camp, 1969). Later, Pius XI had to repudiate the views of Austrian corporatists who denied that capitalists had any right to a share of wealth which – doubtless inspired by marxism – they saw as being exclusively produced by labour. And in Italy in the early years of the

2 Leo's conception of society as an organism, 'as natural as the human organism', and the Church's profound distaste for class struggle, had a strong affinity with corporatist doctrines of the state: 'The Church teaches that the different social classes remain as they are because it is obvious that nature demands it'. And his successor, Pius X (1903): 'It is in conformity with the order established by God in human society that there should be princes and subjects, employers and proletariat, rich and poor, instructed and ignorant'. (McSweeney, 1980, p. 83). His successors hesitated initially to condemn both Mussolini and the French integrist movement Action Française, led by Charles Maurras, despite their dislike of both. In addition, conflict with Mussolini was dampened by the arrangement offered to the Papacy in the Lateran Treaty of 1929 and the resulting Concordat of 1931, which recognized the Vatican mini-state and made Catholicism the state religion of Italy (Noel, 1980, p. 33ff). But the Church's own sponsored unions and associations were still victimized by the Duce's shock troops (Poggi, 1967). In 1931 the Concordat with Mussolini placed severe limitations on the freedom of the church-sponsored political forces – expressly forbidding 'those who have belonged in the past to parties opposing the regime' – which included the Catholic Party – from being chosen as leaders of Catholic Action, and even forbidding the Church from organizing 'any kind of sport activity'! (Poggi, 1967, pp. 24–5). Eventually Action Française was also condemned, by Pius XI, (1922–39) but only in a 1914 declaration whose publication was delayed until 1926!

century, Catholic Action was spawning a left-wing faction which had to be suppressed. For wherever Catholicism was a cultural force, the meta-political character of its social teaching meant that it provided strands which could be woven either into a contestatory message or into a conservative one. The Church has on the whole preferred discrete political pressure to the formal sponsorship of political parties, and the mass movements and trade union organizations which it has promoted have either not been very successful, or else have become highly independent – as in the case of the French trade-union confederation, the CFDT, which in the 1970s adopted positions somewhat more radical than that of its Communist-led rival, the CGT.

Of more direct interest to us are the mass movements, known generically as Catholic Action, which developed first in Europe and later in Latin America. The Italian version was founded originally as a youth association in 1867, and rapidly gained the approval of Leo XIII, spawning a large number of 'economic, labour and welfare groups' after its first major Congress in 1874, to confront the rise of socialism. However, its left wing was suppressed by Pius X shortly after Leo's death in 1903, and by 1904 the elected national executive was also suppressed, after which the whole organization was brought under the direct control of bishops and clergy. It was sacrificed in the interests of the Concordat of 1931, and in 1940 Pius XII practically eliminated the participation of the laiety in its co-ordinating organs (Poggi, 1967, p. 26). Although the number of members appears very high (1.7 million in 1946, 2.8 million in 1957), they tended to be very young, and to be principally involved in the routine of the parish, while their indoctrination concentrated on self-denial, sexual and personal morality, petty apologetic themes and narrow devotional practices,[3] rather than on the tasks of spreading the gospel or the social doctrine of the Church. The experience in other European countries, was different, and foreshadowed that of Brazil and Chile. A Belgian priest, Fr Cardijn initiated the 'See–Judge–Act' method, still popular in Brazil today, in his organizational work with industrial workers, and this was adopted by the French Jeunesse Ouvrière Catholique, founded in 1926 (Fogarty, 1957, p. 272). After World War Two the tradition was taken up by the French worker-priest movement, but this became too radical and was 'recalled' by Pius XII in 1953 (Camp, 1969, p. 129). But if these movements did not prove very strong, despite the numbers involved, the same tradition did provide an ideological basis for the rise of Christian Democratic parties after World War Two in Italy and Germany.

3 These phrases are Poggi's.

Lay involvements in Latin America

Catholic Action was not much more successful in Latin America, except as a breeding ground for subsequently radicalized intellectuals. In Argentina the hierarchy began, during the Papacy of Pius XI (1922–39, by sponsoring a Unión Popular Católica, which was intended to improve welfare and encourage labour organizations, but concentrated on women and home workers. It did not get very far, and was supplanted by Acción Católica Argentina in 1928 (Kennedy, 1958, p. 143). In the 1930s the dominant Catholic currents of opinion – that is, the élite intellectuals who propounded a message couched in Christian terms, not the mass of the faithful – were deeply anti-democratic as well as nationalistic and unconcerned with the sort of mass intervention which Catholic Action envisaged, so that when Peronism arrived on the scene, from 1943 onwards, as a potential mass movement, the Church was drawn towards it, implicitly calling on the faithful to vote for Perón in the 1946 elections. The dominant discourse in Argentine Catholicism has not centred on the social question, as in Chile and Brazil, but rather emphasized the Catholic identity of the people, successively and even contemporaneously lending support to Peronism and to the authoritarian right. The most active spokesmen of lay Catholicism were anti-Peronist, but in the early post-war years Perón sponsored a law protecting religious instruction in schools and proclaimed the inspiration of his social policies in the social doctrine of the Church. Catholic lay militancy had achieved little in the way of evangelization in popular sectors, and this rapprochement was very much an affair between Perón and the hierarchy.

During the early 1950s relations between Perón and the Church hierarchy were nevertheless strained because of Perón's perceived bias towards the working class; more seriously the opposition to Perón began to carry religious banners and symbols, and the repression of that opposition came to be seen as repression of the Church. In response, laws were passed suppressing religious instruction in schools, withdrawing the Church's exemption from taxation, and legalizing divorce. Eventually, in 1955, Perón was excommunicated and overthrown, but during the subsequent years of Peronist proscription, leading Catholic lay militants and their clerical supervisors revised their attitude to the movement. If they wanted to work with the people, and build a democratic system, how could they reject the movement which the overwhelming majority supported? The Christian Democratic Party, founded in 1955 to under-mine Perón could not create a mass base and was perpetually divided over the correct attitude to adopt towards Peronism after the leader's fall. Eventually some activists embraced Peronism and even its revolutionary wing, while others, disillusioned after their collaboration in the 'gathering together of the nation' proclaimed at the start of the military government of 1966–73, withdrew into obscurity.[4] The hierarchy, for its part, continued to encourage Peronism as an expression of national identity and popular culture, while distrusting its evident working-class bias.

The relationship between Church and State in colonial and post-colonial Brazil was one of subordination and patronage. This meant subordination to a government which, from independence (1822) until the overthrow of the monarchy in 1889, did not permit its indifference to Catholicism to prevent it from exercising considerable prerogatives over the appointment of Bishops and priests, and controlled their communications with Rome.[5] The military and political elite which replaced the empire in 1891 did not improve relations, for they were mostly liberals and positivists, rather than true Christian believers.

By the end of the nineteenth century the Church had become a decadent and decentralized institution facing a struggle for survival. True, Catholicism was deeply rooted in the nation's popular culture, but in the hinterland the writ of the hierarchy scarcely ran at all. This detachment had its roots in the colonial conquest itself, in which, compared with Spanish America, the Church had a minor and dependent role with respect to the Crown. The hierarchy's distance from popular religion was most vividly and tragically illustrated in the military suppression – at the third attempt – of the millenarian settlement of Canudos in 1896, led by a holy man (*beato*) carrying a highly unorthodox Christianity to the people of the interior. There were several messianic movements inspired by Portuguese legends of Charlemagne and St Sebastian, crusading legends and legends of medieval heroism.[6]

In 1889 in Juazeiro, another town of the north-eastern hinterland, a priest called Father Cicero became a folk hero and consummate politician – though not a millenarian leader – continuing to function as a priest even while banned by the hierarchy, presiding over pilgrimages to a shrine where a miracle had purportedly taken place (Della Cava, 1970, 1968). These cases are the most famous, and they were symptomatic of the detachment of the official hierarchy from the masses.

4 Forni (1987). See below the account of the Movimiento de Sacerdotes del Tercer Mundo.
5 The Emperor Pedro II (1840–89) refused to allow the publication in Brazil of Pius IX's celebrated (and notorious) 'Syllabus of Errors' in 1864 (Bruneau, 1974, p. 26).
6 Da Cunha (1944) [orig., 1902]. The book is also a chronicle of the discovery of 'another' Brazil, a Brazil of the interland, in some sense the 'real' Brazil, by an urban intellectual. On the Sebastianist and Charlemagne cults see Vinhas de Queiroz (1977), and Teixeira (1974). Both these books recount a millenarian movement in the southern state of Paranå which organized itself after a version of the 'twelve peers' ['pairs'] of France and adopted idealized medieval images taken from the legend of the African wars of Dom Sebastian, King of Portugal. The 'twelve peers', of course, appear already in the eleventh-century epic of medieval chivalry, the *Chanson de Roland*.

In the light of this background, the quantitative and qualitative growth of the Brazilian Church in the past hundred years is quite remarkable: where once it was a client of the state it became, for a period during the 1970s, the government's principal opposition force; where once it had less than 3,000 priests and 17 diocesan sees, by 1965 there were over 12,000 priests and 241 dioceses, and the number of the latter has increased even further in the 1980s. Although the structure remains dependent on a supply of European priests and its coverage remains inadequate for such a large country, the growth is still impressive.[7]

During the inter-war period, coinciding with the Papacy of Pius XI, the Brazilian Church embarked on a process of renewal, under the leadership of Dom Leme, the Church's first dynamic modern leader, Archbishop of Olinda in the north east, from 1916 to 1921, and later of Rio de Janeiro until 1942. Dom Leme concentrated his efforts in the field of religious education, creating the Centro Dom Vital[8] which inspired and co-ordinated the Church's work in promoting Catholic Action in the University (Açao Católica Universitaria), founding what was to become the Catholic University of Rio, and an ill-fated attempt to form a Confederation of Catholic Workers. It is to the Centro that one can trace the diffusion among the intellectual elite of the social doctrine of the Church. Leme also promoted Catholic Action on a broader front but again with little success. He opposed the idea of a Catholic party but formed what would nowadays be called a 'political action group', the Liga Eleitoral Catolica (Catholic Electoral League), most of whose favoured candidates were elected in the 1933 elections.

Leme's main achievement was a tacit unwritten understanding with Getulio Vargas, President of Brazil from 1930 to 1945 and again from 1950 until his suicide in 1954. Vargas remains the dominant figure in twentieth-century Brazil, the creator of a corporatist apparatus which is still a fundamental element in the Brazilian state structure. Unlike his predecessors, influenced as they were by the liberalism and positivism which dominated Brazilian political thought in the late nineteenth and early twentieth century, Vargas saw little merit in conflict with the Church, but much advantage in making common cause with it against Communism and integrism. Leme, for his part, reflecting the policy of the Church world-wide, was opposed to the integrist idea of a state dominated by religion or by the Church. In the Church's perspective the best way to protect the Church's interests is to keep a distance from party-political activity, and to proclaim the Thomist doctrine of due

7 Bruneau, 1974, ch. 1.
8 It was called Centro Dom Vital, after a Bishop who resisted the Emperor Pedro II's instructions to cease suppressing freemasonry in the Church and was imprisoned for it (Bruneau, 1974, p. 29).

obedience to the established authorities (democratic or not) while seeking guarantees over fundamental moral issues such as divorce, religious freedom and freedom for religious education (if possible with subsidies.) On this basis, Leme obtained guarantees on marriage, divorce and education, from Vargas, in exchange for which Vargas received tacit political support and ritual legitimacy (Bruneau, 1974, ch. 2; Mainwaring, 1986).

The ideological projection of the Church remained weak in Brazilian society, until, during the late 1950s and early 1960s the bishops in the north east of the country undertook a variety of initiatives to stimulate peasant literacy and organization, while in the south, also in the name of Catholicism, integrist or at least extreme right-wing forces, in league with some bishops, dynamized a massive middle-class revolt against the 'Communist threat' of President Goulart's proposed 'basic reforms', culminating in the coup of 1964. This was the final fling of frankly reactionary Catholicism. The Bishops' Conference supported the military coup of 1964, but by the end of the decade had become the military régime's sole effective political opponent.

In contrast the Argentine church to this day has never completely distanced itself from an integrist project – that is, a project based on a triumphal historicist and anti-democratic conception of the common destiny of people, Church and State. The Argentine Church sees its mission more in terms guarding the Catholic identity of the people than of social reform, and has rarely even been pressured to call for reform in the way that became the hallmark of the Brazilian Church, in the 1970s and 1980s.

Before that time, the lay movements' relations with the Brazilian hierarchy underwent crisis and rupture, as political tension grew in the early 1960s. The lay movements' ideological problem was that, in the face of powerful vested interests, they could not see how the ideals of a Christian society and of the Church's social doctrine, could be anything but socialist. Thus the student branch of Catholic Action eventually joined the Communist Party and the Catholic Workers' Youth movement (JOC: Juventude Operaria Catolica), shifted away from an apolitical but routinely anti-communist position and an exclusive concern with evangelization, to a defence of basic reforms and conflict first with the hierachy and then with the military. By 1968 JOC as well as Catholic Workers' Action, (ACO: Ação Católica Operaria) its 'adult' sister organization, were openly marxist (Muraro 1985). All these Christian organizations which had become involved in political agitation in support of either reform or revolution were the victims of severe repression in the aftermath of the coup (Lima and Arantes, 1984; Muraro, 1985).

The most enduring legacy of this activity was its gradual transfer to grassroots organizations protected – but not sponsored in the traditional style – by the Church, which by 1968 began to take a far more committed stance on human rights and later on social issues. In Brazil the Church was the first to encourage the rural poor to organize on their own and for themselves, before the left joined in. Perhaps this was only to be expected in a country whose culture is reputed to be deeply permeated by clientelism and paternalism.[9] The hierarchy then gave up control of some of the movements it encouraged, but even after that the Christian origins of their activism remained a bond among a generation of intellectual activists and local leaders, and thus left a mark on popular movements and political parties. In 1962, on instructions from Pope John, the Bishops established an Emergency Plan. Their social base was thinning out and they saw little hope in a gradual spread among the middle classes: they had to become involved in the defence of the poor if they were to meet a perceived desperate need for renewal.

In shifting from a charitable concern for the poor to a concern for their rights and their organization, the Church opened a space which has never since been closed off. The space thus opened was not only a political space – that is, protection for organizational activities among the poor; it was also in discourse, the possibility that a non-marxist language of political agitation could develop. The most enduring ideological expression of this legacy of ecclesiastical involvements in the early 1960s is the educational revolution of Paulo Freire, while its most famous political figure is Dom Helder Camara.

Paulo Freire and the origins of *basismo*

In the early 1960s, Freire was a Professor of Social Work in the north-eastern city of Recife, and he was involved in both research and education in the popular sectors of the city which led him to a revaluation of popular culture. During the Goulart government, he was called in by the Governor of the neighbouring state of Rio Grande do Norte, Aluisio Alves, to conduct a literacy campaign in the Governor's own birthplace and political fiefdom, financed by an agreement between the state

9 During the period under discussion there was a lively debate – mostly among foreign social scientists working in Brazil – about the relative importance of clientelism and class consciousness in the rural union movement. See Galjart (1964) and a response, against the straightforwardly clientelist view, from Huizer (1965); see de Kadt (1970, ch. 1) for a summary. It must be said that although the view that Brazilian political loyalties have nothing to do with ideology is neither original nor inspiring, the impossibility of understanding alignments in ideological terms is evident as much today as twenty-five years ago, and indeed perhaps to a greater extent now.

government and USAID. This agreement was part of a strategy to bypass the institution which was appointed to orchestrate the overall development of the north-eastern region as a whole, namely SUDENE (the Superintendencia do Desenvolvimento do Nordeste: the Northeast Development Superintendency) whose President was none other than Celso Furtado. Furtado was regarded by AID, together with his organization, as harbouring Communist sympathizers and generally being too radical and nationalistic (Roett, 1972). Freire, on account of his uneasy relationships with the left, was trusted both by AID and by the conservative Alves.[10]

This initiative, though, must be seen as part of an even broader educational effort in which the Church was deeply involved and which included the famous Basic Education Movement (MEB: Movimento de Educaçao de Base) perhaps the original use of the word 'base' in a context of popular mobilization. MEB was the result of an agreement between the Church and Goulart's Ministry of Education, and provided for radio stations as the medium of teaching, using local people as group 'monitors' and 'animators'. Eventually MEB controlled 53 stations, and 7,353 radio schools and in 1963 the movement claimed that 111,000 people were learning to read and write through its system, of whom almost 100,000 were in the north east (De Kadt, 1970, pp. 128, 133): it was a potentially subversive method, and was certainly regarded as such by the landed elite, not so much because it offered the chance to learn the basic skills of literacy, but because it did so through new channels that they did not control. The content of the educational material was described in the movement's 1961 annual report:

> basic education must confer three benefits on man: a conception of life, making him conscious of his own physical, spiritual, moral and civic worth; a style of life, which guides behaviour in the personal, family and social spheres; and finally a mystique of life, which acts as an inner force ensuring dynamism and enthusiasm in the fulfilment of duties and the exercise of rights. Basic education must teach the peasant about the human condition, social behaviour, work, the family, and civic and political organization. (De Kadt, 1970, pp. 151–2)

But the report also went further, signalling a radicalization of previous positions and reflecting the struggles within the various branches of Catholic Action:

10 Freire's relations with the marxist left had been tense when he was working on popular culture in Recife; the reason, I suspect, is simply that Freire wanted to listen while the left were trying to force upon him – and upon the people – a ready-made version of popular culture and class consciousness. But this is pure speculation. Later, Freire carved out a space for himself which overlapped with some of the marxist tradition; see below.

to contribute in a decisive mode to the integral development of the Brazilian people, taking into account the full dimensions of man and using all the authentic processes of *conscientizaçao*. This should be undertaken from a perspective of self-promotion and lead to a decisive transformation of mentalities and structures. (1970, p. 154)

The English term 'consciousness-raising' probably has its origins here, and the Brazilian radical Catholics in their turn had been inspired to use it by their reading of the French Catholic philosopher Emmanuel Mounier, whose 'personalist' philosophy represented the socialist wing of modern European Catholic thought, as contrasted, for example, with Maritain's Christian humanism, of which more below.[11] There were other sources too, such as the French West African experiences baptized 'animation rurale',[12] a phrase which reappears in Brazil as *animaçao popular*.

The elision of 'consciousness' in Freire's original sense with 'class consciousness' in the sociological sense was probably inevitable, just as Mounier's use of the term 'solidarity' was easily elided with socialism. Freire's inspirations were various and maybe it is precisely their variety which ensured his originality and impact. As with other ideological innovations documented in this book – such as those of CEPAL and dependencia – Freire's thought derived from an amalgam of schools which either did not know of each other's existence or else considered themselves mutually incompatible. There was the thought of the Instituto Superior de Estudos Brasileiros (ISEB) in Rio de Janeiro, established during the 1950s as a think-tank for developmental nationalism; there was Maritain, though Mounier probably became more important to him; there was the cultural sociology of Karl Mannheim and, in the wings, the effervescence of radical Catholicism.[13] From ISEB – and thus indirectly from orthodox modern sociological theory in the tradition of Weber and Durkheim – Freire drew the idea that the country was in a process of transition from a traditional to a modern society, and that it required a political culture, or consciousness, which would enable the masses to participate rationally in the democratic system which best fitted a developed society. In the absence of cultural change there was a risk of 'massification' in the sense meant by the Spanish philosopher Ortega y Gasset, author of the celebrated *Rebellion of the Masses*.[14] For Freire, in

11 Mounier was the founder and editor of the influential publication *Esprit*.
12 Associated with an organization known as IRAM, closely connected with the French overseas aid programme, and which has also operated in Latin America.
13 Much of what I have to say on this subject is inspired by Paiva (1980).
14 Ortega y Gasset (1929). Ortega y Gasset, expressing the horror of the rise of mass society and the ease with which the 'rootless' masses can be lead by the most superficial and empty ideas: 'never as now have these weightless and rootless lives – *deracinées* in their destiny – allowed themselves to be led on by the most lightweight of ideas' (35th edn, 1961, p. 159).

his writings of the early 1960s – later the emphasis was to change somewhat – 'massification' could be overcome only by a fundamental democratization of society, to which the democratization of education could contribute. This term, was already being used in a different sense by the radical Catholics in MEB to denote the political manipulation of the 'mass' by populist leaders, paving the way for a convergence with Freire. To avoid this massification and promote rational participation, the people had to be educated, but in such a way that they would recognize what Freire called the 'value of each person', and also in a way which would recognize the validity of their own culture (Paiva, 1980, p. 117). Traditional culture had produced men who were not free, 'who did not recognize themselves as persons'. The transitional phase had questioned the beliefs on which traditional society was based and it was now time 'to refashion beliefs in a manner compatible with the new cultural phase' (1980, p. 115). There was also a nationalist message, very much in the style of ISEB, reflecting this time the inheritance of Brazilian corporatist thought of the inter-war period, but with a humanist, as opposed to a political or institutionalist content: the old, closed society had been a 'reflex' or 'object' society, lacking a sense of nationhood. It was colonial, backward, illiterate and 'anti-dialogical' – that is, lacking the conditions for rational, unemotive, non-sectarian communication. 'We imported the structure of the national democratic state without first considering our own context, unaware that the inauthenticity of superimposed solutions dooms them to failure' (Freire, 1974, p. 28). Indeed, Freire praises ISEB specifically for its thinking of Brazil in terms of the country's own reality,[15] rather than as 'not Europe' or 'not the USA' in the manner of previous thinkers. For Freire the term 'radicalization' had a meaning far removed from its customary connotations: 'radicalization is predominantly critical, loving, humble and communicative' (Freire, 1974, pp. 8–10). A radical does not try to impose his own choice on others, and he is deeply non-violent, but he has 'the duty, imposed by love itself, to react against the violence of those who try to silence him – of those who, in the name of freedom, kill his freedom and their own' (1974, p. 10). Although he retains sympathy for the sectarians of the left, who at least wish to change the prevailing order of things, he nevertheless condemns sectarians of all colours as 'emotional ... arrogant, anti-dialogical and thus anti-communicative' whose sloganizing remains at the level of 'myths' and 'half-truths'. The transition through which Brazil is passing should, ideally, lead to a type

---

15 This usage of the word 'reality' comes uneasily in English; the emphasis in its use in this context, in both Spanish and Portuguese, is on the opposition between an image of the facts built around a misguided conception of the ideal, and a confrontation of the facts in their social and cultural context.

of consciousness (i.e. awareness)[16] in which science replaces magic and thus irrationality has no place. He is by no means opposed to technological progress, but he does ask that it remain under man's control. The word 'man' crops up over and over again.

Thus Freire was led to a revaluation of popular culture, but also to a concept of education which had the merit of appealing to a wide range of political opinion while at the same time lending itself to a strategy of reform from below. For him *concientizaçao* meant not promoting class consciousness, which at least at that time, in the early 1960s, he probably distrusted somewhat, but 'the integration of man with the spirit of his epoch and his society' in order that he might thereby 'discover his basic tasks'; this was only possible if he was freed from the domination of myths, and if reason was to prevail over emotion' (1974, p. 133).

Freire first formulated these ideas systematically in a thesis written in 1959, but revised for publication in prison in 1964 and then published in 1967 as *Education: the practice of liberty* (1967). In exile he went to Chile, where his work in the agrarian reform was extremely influential, and subsequently taught at Harvard, where the *Harvard Education Review* published a monograph devoted to his work.[17] In the early 1970s he worked, crucially, with Ivan Illich, whose critique of conventional education was influenced by Freire, and who in his turn probably influenced Freire himself, encouraging him to generalize his educational method into a much wider-ranging social criticism. Subsequently Freire worked with the World Council of Churches in Geneva before returning to Brazil in 1979. It was after his period in Chile that he became a guru and a saint of anti-capitalist *basismo*. So much so that Vanilda Paiva was persuaded to hold up her book for publication because it showed that the origins of his thought, far from *basista*, were in what for *basismo* was a highly undesirable philosophy of development, namely the search for an *étatiste*, nationalist capitalist development.

Freire's thought would never have gained the popularity which it did if his method of education had been simply a method of stimulating class consciousness. It is later, when he became an international figure and grasped the broader political significance of his message, that he produced *Pedagogy of the oppressed*, with its more combative message. To compare *Education: the practice of liberty* with his later *Pedagogy of the oppressed* (Freire, 1972) is to compare two books with essentially the same message but a radically different set of footnotes: suddenly, in the second book, the names of Marx, Engels, Lenin, Lukacs, Marcuse, Régis Debray make their appearance. Nor would Freire's ideas have gained popularity if they

16 Paiva makes the point that his use of the term is probably more akin to Mannheim's 'awareness' than to 'consciousness' in its political acceptance.
17 *Harvard Educational Review*, monograph no. 1, 1970.

had not arisen at a moment when the Brazilian government – under Quadros – was interested in supporting the activism of lay Catholic groups 'going to the people' to teach them to read and write, and when those groups themselves were undergoing a process of radicalization. The Goulart government, which succeeded that of Quadros and was on the face of it more radical, sought to outflank these efforts because it wanted to control the process through its own Ministry of Education. This led the activists to insist on their critique of populist manipulation, and their distrust of reformism, sometimes dismissing Goulart's project as that of the 'national bourgeoisie'. Freire's ideas gained their special appeal from the fact that they cut across the conventional ideological barriers of the time: they emerged from technocratic developmentalism – the search for a critical culture which would facilitate the development process; they appealed to the lay Catholic movements active in the north east of Brazil; they appealed to Conservative politicians sponsored by USAID; and above all they carried a clear message for practical activity.

Freire himself was of course a Catholic and in these early writings expressed a belief in the importance of religion as a binding force in a society whose values were threatened by fundamental social changes. But he was not a Catholic militant; his identification with Catholic radicalism derives from the elective affinity of his ideas with those of the groups mentioned in Brazil and with those of Christian Democracy in Chile. The unabashed use of words like 'love' and 'dialogue' was bound to make his thinking attractive to all sorts of Christians, both in the Church hierarchy and among lay activists.

His method of teaching has an organizational dimension as well as a substantive one. It trains people from a community to be the teachers, rather than relying on professional personnel shipped in from without (hence the affinity with Illich's critique of educational professionalism). In effect this means training community leaders, an aspect taken up with some success by MEB. Substantively, the important element is the use of the social and physical environment of the students – usually adult illiterates learning to read and write – as the subject matter, and the orientation of the students towards a critical view of that environment. As in the case of the term 'consciousness', this word 'critical' lent itself to crucial modulations: it was probably intended more in the sense of 'objective' or 'placing it in context', but the term 'critical consciousness' could be modulated to mean 'revolutionary' or at least 'socially critical'.[18]

18 In Chile, it was said that President Frei became worried that Freire's method was provoking growing class consciousness among rural people, and that he sought to have its use stopped or at least moderated. There is no evidence for the effects but the institution which used it with most enthusiasm was the one responsible for the promotion of rural

The Church in Brazil in the late 1950s and early 1960s, then, provided a framework in which lay groups which it could not fully control were able, at least initially, to go to the people and invite them to join in a project of social transformation under the aegis of a highly respectable institution. This marked the beginning of an estrangement between the Church and the rural élite especially, which has never been repaired. Certain Bishops in the north east created organizations to promote the formation of agricultural unions among the peasantry and appointed priests to do the job, rather than relying on Catholic Action and similar lay organizations. In the highly conflictive state of Pernambuco there was serious competition between Church-sponsored unionism, led by Father Crespo, and the Peasant Leagues. The leagues made more noise and more radical noise creating an international political scandal which contributed a lot to the climate of destabilization leading up to the 1964 coup – a climate fomented by the political establishment without doubt – but it is not clear which of the two had more adherents. Certainly, after the coup the repression did not distinguish between them, labelling both Communist subversion. Twenty-two years later, in 1986, Father Crespo, was still involved in pastoral activity of a similar kind, while his rival Francisco Julião, the notorious firebrand whose name was a byword for Communist subversion in the early 1960s, was standing as a candidate for the very conservative Frente Liberal.

A similar experiment was the Movimento de Natal, a movement sponsored by the Archbishop of Natal Dom Eugenio Sales,[19] which began in the 1950s as a drought relief operation but which ended up in the early 1960s stimulating popular organization and workers' unions. The movement explained that charitable works do not exempt an individual from observing the principles of justice, or from the legal obligations of a labour contract; its educational work tried to change violent behaviour within the family, and also produced a new generation of community leaders (Camargo, 1971). Like MEB and the rural unions of neighbouring Pernambuco state, it was suppressed in 1964, but all this activity left traces which later reappeared when the Church, towards the end of the

---

unionization (INDAP – the Instituto de Desarrollo Agropecuario, or Institute for Agricultural Development) which was a very large organization concerned with organizing the peasantry in unions and – in the case of smallholders – committees and credit co-operatives. For this purpose INDAP ran numerous training courses for cadres of these organizations and the formation of unions and their membership did grow at a dizzy pace between 1965 and 1970 in that country. In 1968 Frei imposed a moderation of its work. (INDAP's first Director under Frei was Jacques Chonchol. Like him, many prominent INDAP officials later became members and leaders of the left-wing party formed by the breakaway left of the Christian Democratic Party from which they sprang).

19 Although today Dom Eugenio is regarded as a conservative, at that time he was denounced as a Communist by the landowners of the north east.

1960s, returned with its pastoral agencies and to organize Basic Christian Communities.

Unlike Ireland, Poland or Mexico, whose populations also identify overwhelmingly with Catholicism, the countries we are studying have low levels of Church attendance. And, again unlike those three foci of peasant nationalism, they are countries where the Church has not in modern times, or even earlier, made its presence felt in politics as the institutional representative of a popular force. The Church has political influence, but that is not the same thing. In this century, in all three countries, the social doctrine of the Church has nevertheless had far more influence on the state than in Ireland, Poland or Mexico, and this influence has operated through a variety of organizations, institutions and individuals not directly controlled by the Church. The organizations created by the Church in order to promote the social doctrine – Catholic Action in various disguises – were short-lived, and their most committed members migrated to the ranks of Peronism, socialism and Christian Democracy. In the 1920s in Chile, in response to the 'social question', in the 1930s in Brazil, with the corporatist state, and in the 1940s in Argentina with Peronism, the influence of the social thought of the Church on corporatist thought was clear enough, but the Church had played only a small role in its transmittal. The hierarchy, then, may have been conservative, as in Argentina, or reformist as in Chile and Brazil: but they could not control the effect of their 'own' doctrines in these countries. These doctrines had a stabilizing effect in the inter-war years, when the emphasis was on building the institutions of the corporate state, but in the 1960s, when the emphasis was on social reform, they were to be one of several springboards of radicalization. The Christian identity of reformist ideas endowed them with a legitimacy in crucial social groups whose social and educational background made them hostile to socialism and class conflict: yet when they pursued those ideas and experienced setbacks they thought again, and were often then convinced by marxism or, in Argentina, Peronism.

A simple, if cynical, conclusion would be that the social doctrine is potentially subversive and that in countries where the Church has greatest and deepest influence it can prevent it from realizing that potential. In other countries, the Church's relative weakness, and its lack of influence over public opinion on most issues, allows secular elites to develop ideas which, stemming from Catholic origins, enjoy some popular legitimacy, without regard for the censorious eye of the hierarchy. In short, it is where the Church is institutionally weak but the people overwhelmingly Catholic, that the social doctrine of the Church has contributed most to legitimizing reformism, and even revolution. In the next section we move on to consider Christian Democracy, a tradition which, though derived from the social doctrine, has been developed by lay persons who believed that Christian political action independent of church control was possible and necessary in a plural society.

Christian Democracy

Whereas in Brazil the social doctrine of the Church came to be applied predominantly by lay Catholic organizations in direct contact with the people, and engaged in a broadly educational strategy, in Chile it was applied by a political party looking for votes and power. Christian Democracy, did not prosper politically in Argentina or Brazil, but in Chile it has consistently been the largest party in the country, in terms of votes, since 1963.

Chilean Christian Democracy stands in contrast to its Western European counterparts because it is not a conservative but a reforming party. It has many ideological factions and has in its time made many alliances with conservative political forces, but reformism remained a central plank of the party's doctrine in a way which clearly distinguished it from its counterparts in West Germany and Italy, as well as El Salvador and Venezuela.

The distinctive character of Christian Democracy as it developed after the mid-1930s can be judged from the philosophy of its founding father, the French philosopher Jacques Maritain as expressed in his writings of the 1930s and in particular the book which has strongly influenced many senior Christian Democratic politicians, *Integral humanism* (1936). Maritain was for long distrusted in the upper reaches of the Church hierarchy because of his support for pluralism and tolerance. His work can be described as a long and arduous campaign to persuade Catholics that religious values could be brought into secular politics without the direct control of the bishops – that there could be a 'distinction of planes' between the religious and the secular.

Yet Maritain was traditionalist to the point of arcadianism. He idealized the Middle Ages as a time when the state possessed a 'qualitatively maximal organic unity', and was employed for the 'spiritual unity of men and of the social body itself' (p. 462). He likened medieval society to a family in which the monarch was consecrated as father of the 'multitude',[20] the organization of work was an extension of the family and the guild was a kind of second-level family; it was, he believed, a period when authority relations had a family-like quality which, 'for all its occasional brutality' was 'preferable to indifference and contempt'

20 'Le sacre du roi le constitue père de la multitude' (Maritain, 1984, p. 462).

(Maritain, 1984, p. 464). Finally, the legal and social structure, as he saw it in this highly idealized retrospective vision, was 'placed at the service of the Redeemer' through the baptism of man and of politics (1984, p. 464).

Maritain's critique of contemporary society was heavily charged with this retrospective utopia. He gladly recognized Marx's 'flash of truth' (1984, p. 347) in perceiving the alienation and dehumanization of capitalist society, and he saw communism and atheism as the outcome of the mentality of 'bourgeois man'. In place of an unbridled materialism which foreshadowed the destruction of Christianity,[21] he sketched out a 'historic [ideal] deal', a society based on communitarian and personalist values, in which 'civilization would tend towards a common good distinct from the mere sum of individuals' wellbeing and higher than the interests of the individual' (1984, p. 433) and in which the 'supra-temporal ends of the human person' would be respected.

Maritain took up the theme of the social function of property which figured prominently in the Church's social doctrine.[22] Invoking Aquinas, he envisages the 'purification and ennoblement' of private property and a form of co-ownership which would give workers 'a share in labour' (*titre de travail*) – as opposed, implicitly, to the 'shares' (*titres*) of the capitalists (1984, p. 505). In politics Maritain insists on pluralism, on the legitimacy of Christian participation in parties of differing ideological orientation, and, quoting Aquinas again, on the absolute requirement of tolerance towards other faiths. He is thus profoundly opposed to integrism or ultramontanism. The cité pluralisté is a cité laïque vitalement chrétienne – based on Christian principles but in no way imposing Christianity. No wonder he had a hard time in Buenos Aires, in 1926, when he was the butt of vicious attacks for his participation in the movement for peace in Spain.[23]

Christian Democracy is based on Maritain's thought, combined with the social doctrine of the Church and a liberal democratic version of corporatism. The Chilean Christian Democratic party originated in the mid-1930s in a society enjoying a stable electoral system of government –

21 'un matérialisme sans frein qui ... proclamait, dans l'existence, la ruine de l'esprit chrétien' (Maritain, 1984, p. 422).

22 'whoever has been generously supplied by God with either corporal and external goods or those of the spirit, possesses them for this purpose – to apply them equally to his own perfection and, in his role as a steward of divine providence, to the benefit of others' (*Rerum Novarum*, 1891, para. 19).

23 *Oeuvres Complètes* (1984, pp. 805 and 1071). The editor of the Argentine integralist nationalist publication *Criterio*, Julio Meinvielle, attacked Maritain as the 'advocate of the Spanish reds', provoking a furious and pained response from Maritain (see *Criterio*, 8 July 1937). These activities almost cost him the Ambassadorship to the Vatican to which De Gaulle nominated him in the 1940s (Hebblethwaite, 1984).

interrupted between 1925–7[24] and 1931 by a military regime which was overthrown by popular protest – and which differed then, and even differs now, from other Latin American societies in the extraordinary depth and spread of political and civic organization. Already in 1935 the Christian Democrats could muster a National Convention with 2,000 delegates from all over Chile, and in 1938 they claimed 20,000 members in 250 different places distributed throughout the country (Grayson, 1968, pp. 129, 144).

The growth of Christian Democracy as a developmentalist and reformist mass party is consistent with other features of Chilean ideology and politics which distinguish them markedly from neighbouring countries. The content of Chilean nationalism is sharply different from that in Argentina, and Chilean political culture seems highly resistant to the appeal of charismatic leadership as well as invocations of national destiny. The Chilean intellectuals of the 1920s and 1930s did, like their Argentine colleagues, have before them a nationalist tradition, yet it was not taken up by any significant political force.[25] Writers in Christian Democratic, conservative and 'developmentalist' camps, for example, may have admired the achievements of Diego Portales, Minister of the Interior from 1829–52 and President from 1831–33, who laid the foundations of South America's earliest centralized state apparatus, but those who invoked Portales in support of an authoritarian state were, until Pinochet, uninfluential politically.[26] For the Argentine anti-liberal right in the inter-war period, in contrast, the cruel caudillo Rosas, the 'Caligula of the River Plate', who came to the capital from the hinterland in 1829 and imposed twenty years of iron, but hardly bureaucratic, rule, was the symbol of an authoritarian undemocratic state embodying their country's nationhood; and the Argentine left regarded him no less as a popular anti-oligarchic caudillo (Halperín Donghi, 1984). In Chile, the figure of Portales has been used to support a strong, centralized bureaucratic rule, whereas the invocations of Rosas emphasize the leader's intuitive contact with destiny and the people, at the expense of law and institutions.

Chilean Christian Democracy produced unusually detailed policies and programmes. The '24 Points' adopted in 1939, when they still called themselves the Falange, were firm on the separation of Church and

24 A two-year period during which government was constrained by a military figure, General Ibañez, who did not take over power formally until 1927 and was overthrown in 1931.

25 Gazmuri (1984). The main text in the Chilean nationalist tradition is Eyzaguirre (1973) [first edn 1957].

26 Although the classic condemnation of the 'politicking' which took over Chilean politics after Portales' influence had waned is strongly critical of the way politicians behaved, it could not be called anti-democratic (see Edwards, 1984, [first edn 1928]).

politics, and yet sustained emphatically the Christian inspiration of their political activity, describing it as a 'crusade'. Capitalism, they said, perpetuates the 'moral and economic slavery of the masses'. Inspired by the social doctrine of the Church they proposed a corporate state, a 'just wage', profit-sharing with workers, trade union freedom, and measures opening up access to property. Production must grow as fast as possible, but the resulting wealth should be distributed in a spirit of social justice. Measures to improve the performance of agriculture and the lot of the peasantry were emphasized, though they did not (yet) include land reform.

The tension between revolution and freedom – the two mottoes of their 1964 campaign – was resolved by the Maritainian notion of 'communitarianism', which purported to offer all the benefits of socialism, such as income and land redistribution, workers' power, the socialization of capital, planning, and popular participation, without the dictatorship of the proletariat. And all this in the short period of one government! It was bound to generate frustration (Lehmann, 1971, pp. 365–95).

After Frei's 1964 electoral victory the 'left' exploited[27] these ambiguities: for them the 'revolution in freedom' really had to be a revolution; the social function of property really meant expropriation when necessary; the communitarian society meant worker-managed socialism. These struggles led to a split and the formation of a new Movement for United Popular Action – the MAPU (Movimiento de Acción Popular Unificada). MAPU was a small party, but it represented a disproportionately large number of intellectuals from the Christian Democratic fold, and it therefore acted as a bridge in the encounter between Christian and marxist thought.

There was an additional element. In the early 1960s families were already torn apart by the migration of their children to Christian Democracy and their proclamation of revolutionary change. In 1959 the Christian Democrats first won the elections in the Student Union at the élite Catholic University in Santiago. Thereafter the student movement became a hothouse of reformist and Christian ideas: students went to spend their summer holidays raising their own – and the workers' and peasants' – consciousness in mines, fields and factories; they participated actively in Frei's 1964 election campaign, giving their appalled parents the sense that they were taking over the country with their triumphalist songs; the ideology of the movement became ever more committed both

27 In retrospect it has become clear that the struggle between left and right was a tightly organized affair involving the penetration and takeover of the Christian Democrat Youth wing by a well organized faction. However, they could hardly have succeeded if had there not been an underlying dissatisfaction with the Frei government among the student and youth of the party in 1968.

to change in society and to change within the university. In June 1967 the leader of the student union appeared before the Rector (a Bishop) and the Council of the Catholic University – all appointees of the Vatican – and told them that the students wanted a university which would 'perceive and incarnate the contemporary existential experience of Chile and Latin America', which was truly Catholic, and which was authentically 'communitarian'. The students received the tacit support of Frei's government and after a series of high-level interventions in Santiago and in Rome, the Archbishop of Santiago, Cardinal Silva Henriquez – was commissioned to solve the conflict. He did so by giving in to the demands and creating a system of full student participation in the government of the university. There were people in the upper classes who never forgot this and never forgave the Rector who was subsequently elected, Fernando Castillo.[28]

Medellín and Puebla

We have now gathered together several elements of the ideological watershed of the late 1960s in the region: the renewal of marxism, the rise of dependency theories, their attack on developmentalist economics and reformist politics, and the attack on mainstream bearers of Catholic social and political thought from a dissident Christian left. To complete the picture, we need to recall the earthquake in the life of the Church and especially the priesthood, provoked by Vatican II. The Council, which sat for three sessions between 1962 and 1965, had brought about a variety of changes in the Mass, in formal features of Church life, and in certain institutional arrangements, but above all it had brought about a change in the atmosphere within the Church: debate was now tolerated, and the doors were now open to the influence of secular thought. This spirit filtered rapidly down to the educational institutions in which Jesuits, among others, taught the sons and daughters of Latin America's elite. This 'up-dating', or *aggiornamento* as Pope John called it, must also have been demoralizing: the supply of novices dried up, seminaries all but closed down, so that the post-conciliar Church seemed to have even less appeal than before the Council, even though one of the central themes of the Council had been the involvement of the laity, and the opening up of the Church to the influences of the modern world.

28 Garretón and Martínez (1986, pp. 24ff). Contrast the equivalent Argentine mobilization of the young middle classes, which produced the Montoneros. Years later, Fernando Castillo was still remembered as the man who had started the process which led from Frei to Allende and then to Pinochet. It was as if the students imposed a total transformation of the system of government at Harvard and in so doing were supported by the Archbishop of Boston and a prominent member of the Kennedy family.

In this unfamiliar climate, the Latin American bishops prepared for their own 'mini-Vatican Council' – the 1968 meeting of the Latin American Episcopal Conference (CELAM) in Medellín, Colombia. They had before them drafts of a concluding document drawn up by, among others, Gustavo Gutierrez, who was to become a major figure in the Theology of Liberation. The final document became the charter of (official) Radical Christianity.

The Medellín document came in the year following the encyclical *Populroum Progressio*, in which Pope Paul espoused what was then received liberal doctrine on development, denouncing the widening gap between rich and poor nations, the inequalities of trade, and the selfishness of rich nations. Pope Paul had not said anything of substance in that document about the inequities within the poor nations, but Medellín took up that theme with a vengeance: the problem of peace in the region was one of inequality of all kinds which reflected a 'rejection of God's peace and of God himself'. There could be no peace until this institutionalized violence had been overcome. The bishops also opened a way for lay involvement by recommending the creation of Base Communities (Comunidades de Base) 'Christian base communities' as the first and fundamental nucleus of the Church which should become a focus of evangelization, and the prime mover in development.[29] Others saw their role as one of assisting in Church services, catechism and the like. Little did they know that this term was to become the banner of a whole project of Church renewal and of challenges to episcopal authority. Above all, Medellín proclaimed the Church's 'preferential option for the poor', though it appears innocently enough in a practical section concerned with the ways in which the Church's resources are deployed. The poor were, in a phrase revived by Pope John XXIII, the people of God: they needed the Church most, and to help them achieve a life of dignity was to rescue social structures from their sinful state. They were, as it implied, also more deserving of God's grace than the (unrepentant) rich. Christ, the document stated, 'did not only love the poor but "being rich, became poor", lived in poverty, concentrated his mission on the announcement of the liberation of the poor'.[30] Of course, the document did not proclaim a total revolution in society, but it did provide enough denunciatory material to legitimate the nascent Theology of Liberation.

But in the following ten years the factions who believed that the Church was going 'too far' or that Medellín had been a mistake from the beginning, regrouped, and succeeded in gaining control of the Secretariat of CELAM (Conferencia Episcopal Latinoamericana: the Latin Amer-

29 CELAM, 1985, ch. 5, para. 10. Ch. 1, para. 20 speaks more guardedly of 'sociological base communities'.
30 CELAM, 1985, ch. 14, para. 7.

ican Episcopal Conference) in Bogotá, under the leadership of the Colombian Bishop López Trujillo. There was a ferocious struggle in the preparations for the subsequent 1979 General Assembly at Puebla in Mexico. The outcome was certainly not the text first proposed by the secretariat, but it was a very different document from that of Medellín. The emphasis at Puebla was on evangelization and on culture, on impregnating social life and culture with Christian values, on the struggle against secularization, and also on consolidating the internal life of the Church. And the text is full of warnings – warnings of politicization in base communities – much as these were welcomed; warnings against mistaken conceptions of liberation – much as liberation, as defined by the Church, is to be sought after, in principle. Even so, the change in direction marked by Medellín was irreversible in its broad outlines, and this was in part due to the experience of the Church in the defence of human rights under the authoritarian governments in power during the 1970s.

The Church under authoritarian regimes

In the 1950s and 1960s, years leading up to Vatican II and Medellín, the Church in Chile was a supporter of reform, but its influence in society was limited. There was nothing to compare with the initiatives taken in the north east of Brazil, although there were some initiatives in the field of rural education, rural unionization and in redistribution of the Church's own land. The existence of a Christian Democrat party meant that the party rather than the Church itself took up the ideas of progressive Catholicism. Membership of Catholic Action and its various branches was tiny (Smith, 1982, p. 96). The Church's initiatives in social organization were fast overtaken by those of the Christian Democrat party, which became influential in the union movement in both industry and agriculture.

As political conflict deepened in Chile neither the Church nor lay Catholic organizations became as deeply involved as in Brazil: the extreme right-wing groups who fanned the flames of fear in 1972 and 1973 did not (with minor exceptions) claim a specifically Christian obeisance, and there was only limited activity linking religion with the defence of private property and the struggle against communism, as there had been in Brazil in 1964 and in Argentina in 1955. The Church leadership maintained a good relationship with Allende until the last few months when the government – astonishingly, given its rapidly weakening political and economic position – proposed a radical reform of education. The proposals took inadequate account of the views of the hierarchy, even though the bishops found some things to agree with in them, and the Bishops' Conference for the first time took a clear public position against a policy of the Popular Unity government.[31]

After the Allende government was overthrown and the country subjected to a regime of terror, the Church did establish organizations to help both political prisoners and the poor, but it took over a year and a half for the Bishops in Chile to take up the cause of human rights in a militant fashion. In Brazil it also took several years, during which Dom Helder Camara was a voice almost literally crying in the wilderness – for his name and his statements were banned from radio and the press for several years after 1968. In both countries the bishops only started to speak out in a wholehearted and 'prophetic' way[32] when priests or bishops, were physically attacked, tortured or killed.[33] These incidents, coming on top of numerous physical attacks against priests or religious working with the poor, marked a turning-point, for what began as a protest eventually ballooned into first a generalized defence of human rights and attacks on governments which were regarded as systematic violators of those rights, and later, more profoundly, a generalized attack on a model of development which led to and even required this organized state terrorism.

The Bishops' Conferences became, for a time, in both Chile and Brazil, almost the only opposition force. In Brazil the Pastoral Land Commission was created to support the defence of Indians and poor farmers, as well as numerous other Pastoral organizations. In Chile the Archbishop of Santiago had started an interdenominational Peace Committee in 1973 which initiated legal actions on behalf of thousands of prisoners and sued for compensation for workers sacked for political reasons; the committee then started a programme of support for health clinics and some 400 soup kitchens in 1974 and 1975. This was a massive operation employing over 300 full-time lawyers, social workers and medical personnel. In January 1976 after pressure from the government and also from other bishops, the Archbishop closed the Committee and opened a new Vicariate of Solidarity placed directly under his control, which expanded operations

31 The Church controlled almost the entire private education system, which accounted for 25 per cent of primary and secondary school enrolments. (Smith, 1982, p. 198)

32 Smith's term (1982). The word should be taken to mean 'standing up and being counted for justice' – in reference to the Old Testament prophets. It is a word which has become common currency in Latin America; it does not seem to get a mention in Vatican II.

33 Smith puts it thus: 'The hierarchy as a group was coming to realize that the abuses of power by the Chilean security forces were not isolated, transitory or unavoidable mistakes. They were part of a whole system of repressive state power present in Chile and several other Latin American countries in the mid-1970s. It took, however, a direct attack on themselves and prominent laity in the PDC [Christian Democratic Party] to open their eyes to the fact' (1982, p. 307).

previously conducted by the Peace Committee. He also created the Academia de Humanismo Cristiano which acts as an umbrella for a large number of independent research centres.

In Brazil there is less centralization, and less direct involvement by Church institutions in projects and organizations on the ground. Instead we find the Church acting as sponsor or protector of smaller, more independent organizations, or semi-independent ones like the Pastoral Commissions. If we compare the accounts of two North American political scientists – Scott Mainwaring on Brazil (1986) and Brian Smith on Chile (1982) – we obtain the impression that whereas in Chile differences are ironed out in an orderly way in Bishops' Conference meetings, and priests for the most part remain respectful of the principle of unity within the hierarchy, in Brazil there is a continual struggle for power taking place at many levels, and through many channels and media, within the Church and for the minds of the faithful.

The difference between the Churches no doubt reflects differences between the two societies; as we shall see in the chapter on social movements, the urban movements in Chile, though they owe much to the Church's protection, do not seem to have as strong a religious charge as in Brazil. In Brazil there is a far more abundant literature explaining the lessons of the Bible for today in the light of the struggle of the people; such a literature would not find a ready audience in Chile. In Brazil the Bishops have used a far more apocalyptic – or as they would say, prophetic – language in denouncing the government, the social structure, the international system; in Chile they are more cautious. Where Cardinal Silva would speak against 'fratricidal hatred', would denounce violations of human rights, describing them as the tearing apart of a family, the Bishops of the north east of Brazil would denounce the oppressive structures of dependent capitalism and insist that these were matters of structure, deeply embedded in the society and in the world order, and would say so in a document entitled 'I heard the cry of my people'.[34]

Also, in Chile, there is now a fifty-year-old tradition of independent secular Christian politics occupying the political space corresponding to the Church. And the country has a much deeper tradition of political organization at all levels of urban – and more recently rural – society spread across the full breadth of the ideological spectrum. The Church finds itself now replacing the dismantled welfare state, channelling funds from international charitable bodies to self-help organizations, support-ing essentially secular initiatives. It has been much less open to influences from without and from below than its Brazilian counterpart; its language

34 The sermon of the Cardinal referred to was given in April 1974; the declaration of the north-eastern Bishops is from May 1973.

remains that of pleas for love and understanding and peace. It is more difficult in Chile for the Church to infuse its evangelization into grassroots mobilizations since that space is already occupied.

Argentina: Repression and decay

In Argentina the process has been radically different, marked by glacial change in the Church, by deep conflicts and internal repression, and by a close relationship with the military regime of 1976–83.

After the conflict between Peronism and the Church which presaged the collapse of Perón's first government in 1955, the Church lapsed into its customary somnolence, almost managing to avoid taking any notice of the Vatican Council. Yet it was in Argentina that the first call for revolutionary change in the name of Christian ideals was heard.

Initially the Christian Democrats were anti-Peronist, but in Argentina between 1955 and 1972 anti-Peronism meant supporting military intervention and suppressing electoral freedom, so they shifted towards alliances with Peronism and with the Peronist trade unions. In addition, the liberal and internationalist economic doctrines of the anti-Peronists prevented even the more conservative Catholic nationalists from joining them – except briefly at the beginning of Onganía's military government in 1966 when calls for a gathering together of all social forces were in vogue – and thus propelled some of them toward Peronism (Forni, 1987).

Peronism was thus once again proving its capacity to act as an agglutinator of a wide variety of political tendencies under a 'national and popular' banner; in addition to these lay Christian groups, both liberal and organicist, it also became a focus of attraction for dissident priests, who came into more serious conflict with their hierarchy in Argentina than anywhere else in Latin America. A series of conflicts culminated in the resignation of 30 priests in Rosario in 1969 (Mayol, Habegger and Armada, 1970). Many of these were inspired by the declaration of the Bishops of the Third World, drawn up in Rome in August 1967 by a group led by Helder Camara, to create the Third World Priests Movement (Sacerdotes del Tercer Mundo), with some 355 members in 1969. They were to become fervent Peronists and in some cases supporters of the Montoneros. They complained of the lack of any assimilation by the Argentine hierarchy of the spirit, lessons or teaching of Vatican II, its insensitivity to social justice and to the 'signs of the times'. There were conflicts over the alignment of the hierarchy with the military government, and one bishop was even removed from his see because he protested about this. In October 1966 Helder Camara was due to attend a CELAM meeting in Argentina; the Argentine bishops tried to persuade him to stay away but he came anyhow. During his stay, he was prevented from speaking in public, and a seminar at which he was scheduled to appear was stopped by the police. There were repeated other instances of the close relations between the hierarchy and the military government.

As Argentine politics polarized, and as violence became a recourse both within Peronism, in the struggle between revolutionaries and neo-fascists, and between the Peronist left and the army, the police and the paramilitary commandos (who themselves were linked to the neo-fascist factions within Peronism) so priests and lay Christians were sucked into the vortex. The Third World priests first became fervent supporters of Peronism, because their primary commitment to the poor led them to join the only political force which seemed to oppose the rich and which clearly had mass support among the poor. In addition, right up to 1972 Perón welcomed support from anyone and issued appropriately delphic statements consistent with that policy. So they felt wanted.

It ended badly: many Third World priests – and others who had taken up an option for the poor or had supported trade-union activity and worker dissidence – were murdered, others had to flee during the violent struggles which developed after about 1972 and which became blanket repression after 1976. One of the most famous of them all, Carlos Mugica, mentor of Montonero leaders when they were still at school and drifting away from the integrist right, fervent supporter of Perón, hero of the shanty-towns, was gunned down as he left his church in May 1974, when the 'wave of assassinations' within Peronism and against its youth wing, was at its height: some blamed the Montoneros, others blamed the 'Triple A'.[35]

Argentina produced the most lucid – if also the most cruel – dissections of the condition of the Church at this time. If elsewhere priests resigned privately and individually – in Argentina they resigned, on at least one occasion, en masse; rarely elsewhere did priests resign because they disagreed with their superiors or with the Church as a whole – rather they gave reasons concerned with their private life, with their psychological disposition, or with a crisis of faith. Not so in Argentina. Nowhere else in Latin America, did priests and lay people – but especially priests – make such clear and public pronouncements on the stultified, inward-looking posture of a hierarchy; but also nowhere else did the hierarchy so doggedly refuse to enter into dialogue, to go to the poor, or to reconsider its close relationship with the holders of political or economic power.

Among the most influential of these analyses were those of Lucio Gera,

35 The 'Argentine Anticommunist Alliance', a shadowy organization operating under the protection of the then Minister of Social Security Lopez Rega, and staffed presumably by off-duty policemen, with innumerable deaths to its 'credit'. The 'Triple A' emblem was derived from Lopez Rega's involvement in the occult.

Dean of the Theology Faculty of the University of Buenos Aires in the late 1960s and early 1970s. In 1966 he was a leading figure pleading for a renewal of the Church, and in 1970 he published an analysis of the Church in Argentina which is noteworthy both for its measured tone and also for the frankness with which he wrote of the contradictions within the Church and among the Catholic community.[36]

Gera's thesis – drawing on the tradition of Argentine nationalist thought – was that the Church was deeply divided, and that its dominant sectors were 'liberal' and 'developmentalist', concerned to apply European and universalistic ideas to Argentina without taking into account the country's distinctive culture: they issued statements of principle in accordance with the spirit of the Council, but did not apply them. The Church's style was secretive and defensive; it had been reorganized by Rome in the nineteenth century and the resulting concentration on the norms and practices of its own institutional life placed it on a collision course with 'a charismatic reawakening and an identification with the national historical process' which seeks to make of the Church 'more an experience of life and of history than a means to an end'. The institutional instinct of the Church implies the 'temptation to the exercise of power and to identify with civil power', rather than protesting against that power and aligning itself with the poor (Gera and Melgarejo, 1970, p. 70).

The Argentine Church was divided by Gera into three currents of opinion: one, preconciliar and almost integrist; another liberal, progressive but of European inspiration, centring its attention on questions of liturgy and spirituality; and finally one he describes as 'social protest' which was slowly shaking off its European and marxist inheritance and adopting the positions of the 'national revolutionary left'. 'Popular Catholicism' – Catholicism as practised by the people – was a purifying agent which made of the social protest tendency an authentically Argentine movement.

Gera's analysis was in line with that of the 'national' intellectuals, and indeed with certain statements of principle of the Argentine Bishops

---

36 Gera and Melgarejo (1970). The article was first published in the Montevideo review *Víspera*, whose director was Alberto Methol Ferré (see below). The article – and no doubt his involvement in various initiatives designed to prod the hierarchy into action and into commitment – cost Gera what might have been an extremely promising career, not to speak of unwelcome attentions from the authorities and their agents. I interviewed Gera in Buenos Aires in 1986 and left with the sense that I had been speaking to a man who represented a broken generation, a man of great, but wounded, dignity. Yet by then he was also publishing numerous articles in a new journal edited by Methol Ferré, *Nexos*. He appears to have moved from a position consistent with that of Liberation Theology to one of implicit opposition to it. The contradiction is only apparent: both men stand in the Argentine anti-marxist and anti-liberal tradition of 'lo nacional', which argues that the people have a distinctive culture which the Church, as well as politicians, must interpret.

themselves: if the interaction between the Church and the world is to be concrete, historical and incarnate then it must arise from an interpretation of the history and consciousness of the Argentines; 'the People can be found where one finds the evangelical values of liberation, brotherhood, dignity, justice, creativity–originality and a certain magnanimity necessary for them to become an agent in the face of the challenges of history'; the concept of the people is not reducible to that of a social class such as the peasantry or the proletariat; and finally, in an allusion to the famous war cry of nineteenth-century Argentine liberalism, 'civilization or barbary', he states that the people do have their own rationality and the elite have no choice but to follow it as expressed in the 'national experiences of the People'.

These references to the people show a mystical dimension which sets the Argentine version of post-conciliar theological innovation apart from the early years of theology of liberation proper, just as Argentine left-wing thought is set apart from Left-wing thought in other countries by the special status it accorded to the national–popular experience. In the case of political thought the influence was crucial in producing a shift from orthodox marxist analyses of imperialism to dependency theory; in the case of theology, the theology of liberation as we shall see, was born under the sign of modernism and rationality and a distrust of superstition and thus of popular religion, and the theologians of liberation – among whom Gera and other Argentines hesitated to count themselves for precisely this reason – took some time to even attempt to come to terms with popular religion.

The future held little hope. The Third World priests were swept away in the whirlwind of armed revolution and the repression which followed. The dissidents who remained within the Church were either isolated and ignored by the hierarchy – or else silenced more violently by the military and their associates in a 'dirty war'. Even Bishops suffered – including the Bishop of La Rioja, Monsig. Angelelli, who was killed in August 1976. In stark contrast to Brazil and Chile, the murder of priests – 19 in all – and their arrest, torture or exile, did not move the hierarchy to action. With one or two isolated exceptions, the Bishops allowed the process of 'weeding out' of subversive elements to pass without comment, and indeed there is evidence of active collaboration by some of them, such as the Archbishop of La Plata and the military chaplains. The Church took no part of significance in the defence of human rights, even verbally (Mignone, 1986, p. 236 and passim.)

When electoral government was re-established in 1983 the Bishops returned to their favourite themes, as if nothing had happened: they accused the radical government of promulgating materialist education and supported the continuing yearnings of union leaders for national grandeur and an economy 'all of our own' (Portantiero, 1987). Bishops have again advised voters to support the Peronists, and have established an institution to liaise with the trade-union movement, with the support of international lay spiritual movements such as Communione e Liberazione[37] and Opus Dei. Even today the Church's position has in common with that of Gera and the Third World Priests an obsession with the unique role of the people as bearers of the destiny of the nation, expressed in their political activity but also in their own religious practice.

Modernity and tradition in the Theology of Liberation

The previous sections of this chapter have shown how after Vatican II the Catholic Church in Latin America, as in the rest of the world, went through a multiple crisis; the elements of this crisis included a disillusion-ment with Christian Democracy and Catholic Action as effective ways of bringing Christian values to bear on politics and on the shape of society; a growing commitment to some form of socialism and a tolerance of marxism among Catholic intellectuals; a sense that the doctrines of the Church, even after Vatican II, had to be moulded to the conditions of underdevelopment, injustice and dependence prevailing in the region; and finally the new roles acquired by or thrust upon the Church in some countries by the wave of authoritarian regimes which swept the continent in the 1960s and 1970s.

In the midst of this period the Medellín assembly of Latin American bishops (CELAM) produced a document unprecedented in its prophetic tone and content, in which the Bishops committed themselves to a leading role in changing the structures of oppression and injustice prevailing in the region. As an official document of a highly authoritative body of the Church, it left an indelible imprint.

Medellín marked the beginning of a new school of thought, namely the Theology of Liberation. Prominent members of this school, like Gustavo Gutierrez, who were still relatively unknown, had a hand in the drafting of its conclusions, and they caught a moment of openness – and perhaps also of confusion – among the bishops which would never again be repeated.

Since then, Latin America and the Theology of Liberation have come to be almost coterminous in Catholic discussion, because to outsiders this

37 An Italian organization with a substantial and committed following among the youth, which until recently was viewed as the creature of conservative Christianity. In 1988 however, CL took steps to distance itself from both the Christian Democratic Party and the Church hierarchy. The pattern of separation previously observed in Catholic Action seems to be repeating itself.

has been the region's distinctive and provocative contribution to Christian thought in modern times. Some see it as little better than marxist infiltration; others – often far from identifying themselves with revolutionary causes – see it as the great hope for the Catholic Church. In the pages that follow I shall give as clear an account as possible of the thought of the main theologians of liberation, and I shall also assess its real influence both within the Church and in society and politics as a whole.

As its name indicates, the Theology of Liberation has set out to break a mould, and to challenge received ideas in Christian thought and action, and in the world at large. The word combines a social and political usage – as in 'liberation movements', 'women's liberation' and so on – with a psychological connotation of freeing oneself from an inner captivity or repression. It was, when the term was first coined, very much a slogan of the 1960s.[38] Since then the idea of liberation has found its way even into official Catholic doctrine, as the Vatican tries to cope with dissident theology by creating its own approved version.[39]

By joining the words 'theology' and 'liberation' Gutierrez and those who followed in his wake were bound to shock, and no doubt knew it, for they were placing the word on their banner in order to carry out a revolution not only in Catholic theology, not only in the structures of the Catholic Church, but in the very idea of what it means to be a good Christian and of the meaning of a worthwhile human life even for non-Christians and atheists. The beliefs, actions and attitude to life encompassed by the slogan 'liberation', they were saying, did not belong on the fringe, and could not be consigned to a ghetto of dissident marginality: nor were they a totalizing historical rupture which could lay siege to the citadels of the pseudo-civilization of industrial capitalism and replace the world order. No, they were in fact very ancient dispositions towards the central questions of man, God and society, enshrined in the sacred texts of Judaeo-Christian tradition, and in the life of Jesus Christ himself. These texts, this life, and that tradition had been successively distorted and instrumentalized for oppressive purposes by feudalism, capitalism and now dependency and underdevelopment; the task was to recuperate them and turn them into the spiritual, ideological and practical basis for liberation. The new religious thought was radical in the strict sense that it proclaimed a return to the roots – to the roots, in this case, of Christianity.

But the consequences of digging deep into tradition may also be

38 The phrase was coined at a meeting in Chimbote, Peru, in July 1968. It was consecrated in the book which has become its flagship: Gustavo Gutierrez (1973).
39 See the Documents issued in the wake of the 'Boff affair': Instruction on certain aspects of 'Liberation Theology', 1984, and especially, Instruction on Christian freedom and liberation, 1986.

modernizing. One thesis of this book is, indeed, that the religious renewal proclaimed, though as yet far from achieved, by this theology, as well as its practical involvements, may have deeply modernizing consequences.

This can be appreciated if we compare their recourse to tradition with Catholic nationalism. Where Catholic nationalists emphasize cultural specificity and the unique melding of indigenous and Hispanic religion, the theologians of liberation emphasize the universal character of Christianity and draw their programme from their interpretation of its universal message. Catholic nationalists – by which I do not refer to integrists, who are explicitly reactionary – do not take a position, as do theologians of liberation, on the sinfulness of unjust social structures, or even on the application of Christian belief to political action. Rather they view Catholicism as culture and politics, as the enactment of a destiny, a destiny usually achieved by the emotional experience of populism, as in Perón's Argentina or in Vasconcelos' vision of Mexico.[40] They are self-consciously and proudly provincial, while the theologians of liberation, with their sophisticated European scholarly background and multilingual footnotes, and their appeal to universal values, are cosmopolitans. Even their nationalism, couched as it is in economic rather than culturalist terms, is universalistic in content and appeal.

This brings us to a second, and superficially paradoxical, feature of the Theology of Liberation. Its philosophical and theological sources are European, yet it proclaims itself – and is seen as – an autonomous Latin American phenomenon. It describes itself as born out of the concrete experience of poverty, injustice and dependence which is the daily lot of millions of Latin Americans, but it also draws on modern (especially German) theology, modern Christology and modern ecclesiology, all European products. Although it expresses many reservations about the 'liberal–bourgeois' content of modern European theology, it draws on its insights to conduct a critique rooted in 'praxis', in the 'concrete' and structural conditions in which its authors find themselves, in the Church, and in society. These three words – 'praxis', 'concrete' and 'structure' – appear again and again in Gutierrez' *Theology of Liberation* (1973), and reflect without doubt the influence of the social sciences and of the marxism then dominant in Latin American social sciences. For marxism teaches us to analyse thought in its social and political context, and to ask what interests lurk behind it, or, for the more sophisticated, in what ways its message reflects and refracts political and economic conflict in society: stated most simply, marxism invites even the theologian to ask how his or her ideas form part of continuing ideological arguments, and carries at its

40 For more on this tendency see the final section of this chapter.

heart a warning that no body of thought can escape the constraints and interests of time and place.

Hence Gutierrez' call to write not of poverty, or salvation, or love only as general principles, or indeed even as guides to our individual relationship with God, but as processes (not states) which are embodied in the dynamics of social change, occurring in real, as distinct from transhistorical, time. European theology has taken a defensive posture in the face of the materialism and atheism of bourgeois society: opening up, or as in Pope John's famous motto, getting up to date (*aggiornamento*). The theologians of liberation, like Pope John Paul, distrust this reaction, though the conclusions they draw are not his at all. For them, living in a continent where Catholicism is so deeply embedded in culture at all levels, the problem of modernization is not the threat it poses to religious belief, but the material impoverishment, social polarization and dependency which it brings, and the more or less explicit ideological support which an unreformed Church lends to it. They have followed dependency theory in turning the ideology of modernization on its head: whereas their European predecessors and mentors experienced modernity as secularization,[41] and secularization as a process to which the Church had to react either by coming to terms with it or by turning in upon itself, the theologians of liberation perceive the process of modernization as savage capitalism, creating injustices of all sorts. The remedy they propose is to place the Church at the service of the poor, to preach a reading of the Gospel from the viewpoint of the poor, whereas John Paul stands in the tradition which responds to modernity and secularization by retreating into the fortress-Church and reaffirming dogma and authority.

The ecclesiological implications of this – that is, the implications for the institutional structure of the Church – are, as we shall see, little short of revolutionary. To place the Church at the service of the poor is taken to mean placing it in the hands of the poor, with a hierarchy to serve it and them, not to dominate it or to pronounce on matters of dogma. It also means opening its structures up in a way which would contradict most of its modern history since it would undermine the idea that there is a dogmatic truth to be dictated by a human institution.

Much as they pillory the Church's structures, its authoritarianism, these writers are very much products of it and many of them clearly love, cherish and respect it. Although some liberation theologians have left the active priesthood, most have remained, even when subjected to severe

41 As Harvey Cox (1966), for example. Cox has, however, recently changed his position quite sharply and largely as a result of the influence of Liberation Theology. In his *Religion in the secular city: towards a post-modern theology*, (1984), he states his expectation that renewal in theology will come from the 'bottom' of society and from the 'periphery' of the world.

pressure, as in the case of Boff. Their writings may have a subversive intent with respect to the authority structures of the Church, but insofar as they carry forward a tradition, insofar as they invoke official Church documents and Papal Encyclicals, however opportunistically, they also contribute a perhaps essential dimension to a process which, with all its ups and downs, advances and retreats, has been an obvious feature of the Catholic Church in its survival: namely adaptation to a changing environment.

For the theologians of liberation are modernizers too, though they would not like to go by that name. They call for a penetration and transformation of popular religion which, despite protestations to the contrary, they regard as largely subordinate to the status quo, as permeated by superstitions which do not serve the people's true interests. Although they profess a respect, even wonderment, at this popular religion, the idea of founding – even refounding – the Church's organiza-tion on Base Communities must in fact imply that the unreflective impulses and rituals of popular religiosity will be channelled into a more goal-oriented, more organized, more settled routine. Whereas there is a complementarity between a 'top–down' organization of the Church and the proliferation of daily rituals, worship of saints and minor petitions to the Virgin which constitute popular religion, there is surely a contradic-tion between these practices and the organization of the people of God into base communities with regular meetings, with trained lay leaders, and with an explicit spiritual and ideological programme. The following pages will give an account of this programme and of the conception of the Church which accompanies it.

The message of the Theology of Liberation

The composition of the founding text of the Theology of Liberation, Gutierrez' book of that name, dates from the late 1960s.[42] It is thus marked by a moment of opportunity and disillusion. The opportunity was afforded by the intellectual climate arising in the wake of Vatican II, a climate of unique openness to debate within the Church, and the disillusion came from the fate of lay Catholic movements in the early 1960s, and the perceived 'failure' of Christian Democracy to achieve promised revolutionary change, especially in Chile after Frei's election in 1964. Gutierrez had personal experience of this, as adviser to the student

42 Although first published as a book in Spanish in 1971, the Preface states that it originated in the paper delivered in 1968 (again, 1968) in Peru. All quotations are my own translation from the 1985 Spanish edition. The English translation leaves much to be desired in accuracy as well as style, though a new version was published in 1989 by Orbis Books.

branch of Catholic Action in Peru, and during periods spent in Chile in the mid 1960s.

Transcending the limitations of lay Catholic movements

In the view of Gutierrez, the lay apostolic movements had 'exhausted their potential' (Gutierrez, 1985, p. 95). The superficial reasons for this lay in the radicalization of the movements and their estrangement from the ecclesiastical authorities. But there was a deeper reason in the 'crisis of the distinction of planes schema' – the title of Gutierrez's fifth chapter. The distinction, elaborated as we have seen by Maritain, separated the Church and the world into autonomous spheres in order to define a role for the Church in the world attuned to a pluralist, democratic society. The Church was 'not to interfere as an institution, in temporal matters, except . . . those of moral concern. The building of the earthly city, then, is an endeavour which exists in its own right' (1985, p. 89). The Church, in the words of Yves Congar – the foremost modernist authority on ecclesiology and the role of the laity – is, 'the soul of human society'; it both constitutes an 'order apart' of salvation and holiness and also fulfils its mission by the 'evangelization and the inspiration of the temporal sphere'. In practice, as Gutierrez says, this model worked less well in Latin America than in the more secularized environment of Western Europe. In any case, it is not a model which is ever consistently applied, or conceivably could be consistently applied. For Gutierrez, in Latin America the distinction of planes is a device which conceals and in effect legitimizes the support of the established (secular) order by a large sector of the Church. Indeed, although the voices calling for the Church to defend the poor and oppressed were the first to press for the distinction of planes, it was increasingly used to neutralize those very voices by pigeon-holing them in a separate category marked 'the World'. Thus the 'dominant groups, who have always used the Church to defend their interests . . . today – as they see "subversive" tendencies gaining ground in the heart of the Christian community – call for a return to the purely religious and spiritual function of the Church' (1985, p. 97). What had been a liberating idea was thus being used to prevent liberation.

In theology the distinction of planes, and the underlying dualisms of 'natural and supernatural', of human nature and divine grace have been transcended by a 'historical and existential' view, in which there is 'but one vocation: communion with God through grace. In reality there is no pure nature and never has been: there is no one who is not invited to communion with the Lord, no one who is not marked by grace' (1985, p.

104). In a manner which recalls earlier theologies,[43] Gutierrez writes that 'we know man only as actually called to meet God' and furthermore – and in a more revolutionary vein – that 'men are called to meet the Lord insofar as they constitute a community, a people' (1985, pp. 105–6). A people, not in the sense of an aggregation of individuals but of an organic collectivity with a common historical experience and joining, as the Children of Israel in the Wilderness, in a common search, a *caminhada*, an arduous journey in search of a goal. That goal is the kingdom of God, but it is not precisely known, nor can it really be known – and in this it differs from conventional populisms.

It is often thought that for the Theology of Liberation the task of a good Christian is to build the Kingdom of God on earth, and not wait for it to come in the after-life, and that it will be a socialist society. Perhaps in vulgar versions there is something of this.[44] But in Gutierrez the emphasis is on the *process* of liberation, the achieving or struggling to reach a 'just society', a 'new man'. Likewise conversion 'is a permanent process in which very often we encounter obstacles which force us to turn back and start anew' (1985, p. 268). The issue of what the goal, the kingdom, the state of liberation might *actually* consist of is implicitly not one which can be very usefully discussed. It leads to sterile speculation and serves little purpose.

Likewise, a discussion of 'who' is 'called to communion with God' is regarded as sterile. If there is but one convocation to salvation, if 'all men are in Christ efficaciously called to communion with God' (CELAM, 1985, p. 106), then not only non-Catholics but also non-Christians cannot be excluded. Vatican II was already moving in this direction, and Gutierrez quotes Medellín: God sent his Son, 'to liberate all men from *all* the enslavements to which sin has subjected them: hunger, misery, oppression and ignorance, in a word the injustice and hate which originate in human selfishness' (CELAM, 1985, p. 238).

In this perspective 'the frontiers between the life of faith and temporal works, between Church and world, become more fluid' (p. 107). Secularization, far from an obstacle to Christian fulfilment, may make

43 Gutierrez refers to 'the line of theological thinking until the rise of the doctrine of pure nature in the sixteenth century', but one might also mention the post-Enlightenment German philosopher Schleiermacher, who is one of the pillars of modern German Christology (see McGrath, 1986). Schleiermacher also posits the consciousness of God as a feature of life in community, presaging further aspects of Liberation Theology, which, given the erudition of its leading figures, is replete with such resonances.

44 See Ernesto Cardenal's delirious *En Cuba* (1974), a chronicle of a trip to Cuba in the mid-1970s. Cardenal is a religious and also one of the greatest living Spanish-language poets, whose *Salmos* (1973), for example, are wonderfully moving. Since 1979 he has been Minister of Culture in Nicaragua.

man aware that he is an 'agent of history, responsible for his own destiny' (1985, p. 99), thus bringing nearer such a fulfilment. Indeed, the assumption by man of this responsibility is a defining feature of liberation. Modern European theologians would not disagree, but the sharp end of the message is that in Latin America people are, Gutierrez says, rightly or wrongly, waking up to a revolutionary struggle and for them being master of their destiny means liberation, means building a just society, and to do so is 'already, in a certain sense, a salvific work' (p. 108).

This is not at all the same as saying, simplistically, that the kingdom of God can be built here on earth and it will be a socialist state. It is not the kingdom of God itself which is to be built, but a just, or at least more just, society, and the 'salvific work' consists of the process of building it.

Spiritual foundations

The Theology of Liberation, or the Church of the Poor, appear to the outsider to be exceedingly naive with respect to the world, but also exceedingly skilled, even machiavellian[45] within the Church. The naiveté we have already glimpsed: it is apparent from repeated professions of faith in the revolutionary awakening of the people, from the touching notion that an authentically Latin American socialism with freedom and without 'dogmatism' can be found.[46]

When it comes to the politics of the Church, to ecclesiastical intrigue, they are frequently active and sophisticated. They managed a successful campaign ahead of the Third Latin American Episcopal Conference (CELAM) at Puebla in 1978 which changed the conservative, 'ultra spiritualist' line proposed by the CELAM Secretariat led by the López Trujillo. In Central America they operate an extremely effective network, manned mostly by Jesuits and designed to orchestrate international support for the Sandinistas and for liberation movements in the area. In Brazil they have gained substantial influence in the planning and implementation of the Church's pastoral activities concerning the agrarian

45 Gutierrez' essay 'A retreat from commitment' is a strong attack on a draft prepared by the Secretariat of a Preparatory Document which was later substantially amended. The draft was criticized by him and many others because it played down questions of oppression and injustice, emphasizing instead the dangers of secularization. It has been reprinted as Chapter 5 of *The power of the poor in history* (1983).

46 See José Miguez Bonino (1977, pp. 65–7). Theologians of Liberation are particularly subject to a constraint frequently observed among Third World reformists and nationalists. This is an unwillingness to criticize socialist states openly because that criticism is the warhorse of conservative politicians and of the governments of the main capitalist powers. There is an underlying sense in these milieux that to show intolerance towards socialism would be to 'give in' to the pressures of what they see as their principal enemy.

question and base communities. In several countries they run research and documentation centres funded by international Catholic, non-Catholic and lay organizations.

Yet Gutierrez in particular, in his later work, has given ever more attention to spiritual themes. The very title of *We drink from our own wells: the spiritual journey of a people* (1983), hints at a criticism of those who might overemphasize the political and militant dimensions of Liberation Theology. The Introduction admonishes thus: 'It is a serious historical mistake to reduce what is happening among us today to a social or political problem. Consequently, one shows a lack of Christian insight if one thinks that the challenges to spirituality are simply those raised by the relationship between faith and the political order, by the defence of human rights, or by the struggle for justice.'[47] He could hardly be more emphatic in saying that the challenge to spirituality is also within ourselves.

But it is a collective 'self'. For Gutierrez and for Leonardo Boff the sacred texts are to be read by the people, and the theologian's task and skill is to interpret them in the light of the people's understanding. The objection that the people do not have the training to understand the context, the original meaning, does not take into account the very special character of all religious texts: it is of their nature to be open to innumerable interpretations, and they are written in a symbolic and often mysterious language which invites listeners to make of them what they can. The Old Testament prophets, the parables of Christ, while inviting the listener (rather than the reader) to confront himself as a moral being, are couched in an allusive, metaphorical language which does not always, if ever, offer very clear conclusions. If there is one joke in the Gospels, it comes when we are told that after Jesus had delivered a cascade of delphic answers to the questions addressed to him by the experts, 'no one dared ask any more questions'.[48]

Gutierrez, in his numerous Biblical commentaries, is presenting a literary version of the message that (he believes) gets through to the innocent untutored listener he calls the 'people'. He respects strongly the element of 'story' in these texts. 'The Samaritan approached the injured man on the side of the road not because of some cold religious obligation, but because "his heart was melting", a reading justified not only by general principles but also by the original Greek text (1985, p. 199). Matthew's account of the final judgement, in which those who *think* and claim they have been doing what it takes to love God have done nothing of the sort, while those who do not make the claim were in fact doing so,

47 Gutierrez (1984, p. 2). See also in Gutierrez (1985, p. 308): 'the kingdom is not equivalent to the establishment of a just society'.
48 Mt., 22,46.

is interpreted as a millenarian vision. The 'obvious sense of the text' stresses the 'universality of the judgment and the central and universal character of charity'.[49]

The Matthew vision is taken, with the Good Samaritan, to point to some very fundamental features of Gutierrez's theology or better, perhaps, his moral proclamation: 'the stress on communion and brother-hood as the ultimate meaning of human life; the insistence on a love which is expressed in concrete actions, reflecting the primacy of "doing" over "knowing"; and the revelation of the human mediation necessary to reach the Lord' (1985, p. 256). Thus we come back again to the breaking-down of the walls between Church and world, Christians and non-Christians, for in line with the Matthew vision, God is present not only among the followers of Christ, but 'in each man', and his 'temple is human history'; it is in history that men encounter 'God's Word made flesh'.

From theological debate to Church renewal (Ecclesiogenesis)

The poor and the People of God

In Liberation Theology the oppression of the poor is as much a result of the structures of capitalism as of the moral rapaciousness of the ruling class; they are the bearers of virtues and beliefs which are the outcome of their sufferings and will mark with their imprint the society of the future. But who are the poor? Are they the sum of actually existing poor, marginalized or insignificant individuals? Or are they a theoretical construct embodying already known values and ideals? Are they a historical abstraction with theoretically defined interests properly pursued only in approved parties and organizations? Should their real consciousness be matched up to an 'ideal' consciousness required in the construction of a new order?

These questions are particularly hazardous for a theologian because he risks excluding the 'rich' from the salvation to which his own theology invites not only all Christians but all mankind. The question of the 'false

---

49 Gutierrez (1985, p. 197). Coming to the text almost completely fresh, my own sense was that, like Mary's *Magnificat* (Luke, 1,47) its *first* impact is to stress the unexpected, counter-intuitive character of divine judgement and action: where an unreflecting person *thinks* it will go one way, it in fact goes the other. Likewise, Mary's song could be said to praise the capacity of God to turn the world upside-down. The second impact, though, is the awareness, in both texts, that the rich have been sent away empty, and have failed at the final judgement.

consciousness' of the people is likewise thorny because the theology of liberation is littered with remarks about the manipulated character of 'popular religiosity', seen as a bundle of customs and beliefs which tend to breed conformity and resignation or simply to distract the people from their real problems and thus from the call of liberation.

The Theology of Liberation situates itself in an 'alternative', but ancient, tradition, one that emphasizes community, marginality, dissent, protest, self-sacrifice, one that sees itself as an heir to the early Christian Church as it was before Constantine. 'The poor', in this perspective, are the bearers of a religious belief, an innocent wisdom, untainted by the corruption of wealth and of universal relevance. Poverty is both deplorable and admirable, both material and spiritual. In a revealing passage Gutierrez quotes Medellín, where the Church is invited to preach and live 'spiritual poverty as an attitude of spiritual childhood[50] and openness to the Lord' (Gutierrez, 1984, p. 127). This spiritual childhood is necessary both for entering the world of the poor and for entering the kingdom of heaven.

In his earlier book, Gutierrez had sharpened the polemical edge of this tradition, by insisting on the dangers of under-estimating the importance of material poverty, of separating the world, in which poverty was material, and faith, in which material poverty was even seen positively. This error outraged him, and he affirmed that to live in extreme poverty was inhuman and thus offensive to God.

According to Harvey Cox (1984, pp. 143–4), this is a biblical rather than a medieval view of poverty. Poverty is not an 'estate' but rather the 'result of oppression ... a result of the sin of the powerful, a cause for God's wrath'. For Gutierrez the term 'always carries with it a collective connotation, and takes into account a potential for social conflict' (1983, p. 119), as well as an 'evangelizing potential': the poor, in their struggles against oppression, undergo a conversion and ultimately have the potential to convert us all. If we agree that the rest of us – the 'rich' – could hardly be converted if the poor remained oppressed, then it follows that religious awakening is also a matter of social transformation, not because the rest of us are, each in our own lives, oppressive individuals, or any more oppressive than individual poor people, but because none of us, poor or not, lives outside society. The issue then, of whether a rich person can enter the Kingdom of Heaven, posed as a private problem, is irrelevant: the message is that no one, rich or poor, has an excuse for not working for the transformation of the structures which sustain material poverty, and embody spiritual poverty.

Even so, there is more; there is a growing awareness – to which we shall

---

50 A reference to the theologian Dietrich Bonhoeffer, who coined the phrase.

return – that the religion of the poor (*religiosidad popular*) has something to teach us all, that it is more than manipulated consciousness and ritual distraction. The politics of the grassroots then becomes a serious practical issue.

The *base* as the foundation for a rebirth of the Church[51]

European and North American observers are often heard to say that the growth of *Communidades Eclesiales de Base* (CEBs)[52] in Latin America is one of the brightest hopes for the future of the Catholic Church world-wide. The observation reflects an underlying sense that the Church must create an active role for the laity and also that straightforward numerical facts oblige it to find a way of responding to a shortage of priests.

The idea of a grassroots lay community has particular interest because it is both innovative and respectable, it is welcomed by all the interests and factions involved in the Church, each no doubt for different reasons, and thus constitutes a central theme which each would like to control, and none dares to denounce. It is an important bridge between even the most extremely opposed factions because it enables them to meet on at least apparently common ground. It offers to the advocates of rebirth (as opposed to mere renewal) a reason for hope and thus for not abandoning the Church.

The Medellín conference document of CELAM, in its section on *Pastoral de Conjunto*, or general pastoral[53] work (as opposed to the particular pastorals of the family, education, students, workers and so on) speaks of the Church as, 'above all, a mystery of Catholic communion', in

51 It would be best for the reader to think of the word in Portuguese or Spanish (pronounced 'ba-zi' or 'ba-seh'). The English word 'base' does not adequately convey the connotations of the word *base*, with its populist connotation, hence the frequent use of the word 'grassroots' in translation. The word 'rebirth' is used, in preference to 'renewal', to reflect Boff's term 'Ecclesiogenesis'.

52 This is the term as used in official Spanish and Portuguese documents, but it is not an 'official' consecrated term. It is interesting, in this context, to note that the official English translators of Pope Paul's 1975 Encyclical *Evangelio nuntiandi* had a similar difficulty, and use the French term *communauté de base* even in their English text, adding it to '"small communities"' (in quotes in the text itself) which they evidently considered inadequate. Note also that the word used is 'ecclesial', not 'ecclesiastical'; the reason for this is that, although the Greek root of both words meant 'assembly', the term 'ecclesiastical' has come to signify the structured, hierarchical dimension of the Church, with strong connotations of 'official'. The term 'ecclesial' is presumably designed to refer to the original meaning. Yves Congar confirms this interpretation, noting that the first modern usage of ecclesial in this sense was by Maritain in 1938 (Congar, 1985, p. 56).

53 The term has in recent years been adopted in the place of 'mission', now presumably felt to be too patronizing, and reminiscent of colonial missions.

which 'all should take part in the responsibility and effort needed to achieve a common mission to bear witness to God who saved them and made them brothers in Christ' (CELAM, 1985, pp. 15,6). Concretely, this means a series of institutional innovations, including the National Episcopal Councils whose status was enhanced by Vatican II, various other advisory bodies, and 'communidades de base'. It was conceived as a 'local community' of a size appropriate to the existence of 'brotherly' social relations among its members (ibid., pp. 15,10). The Church aimed to transform these communities into 'families of God', by making of them a germ of 'faith, hope and charity'. They should be responsible not only for the expansion of the faith, but also for religious rites, and therefore constitute the 'basic unit of Church structure' and the 'prime factor in human progress and development'.[54]

Their leaders could be priests or lay persons, male or female, whose training was of particular importance, emphasizing the 'acquisition of responsibilities in a climate of autonomy' (ibid., pp. 15,11). The document concludes the discussion by linking the resurgence of these communities to the role of Christian communities in the work of the first missionaries who brought Christianity to the New World.

Stated thus, the role of the communities does not appear revolutionary, and it is noteworthy that these passages are not linked in the Medellín document to others in the same document which denounce the prevailing social and political conditions in the region.[55]

But by 1975 the alarm bells were already ringing in the Vatican, and Paul VI, in *Evangelio nuntiandi* used very strong language to distinguish between those CEBs which remained 'firmly attached to the local Church' and 'do not allow themselves to be ensnared by political polarization or fashionable ideologies', and others which 'come together in a spirit of bitter criticism of the Church which they are quick to stigmatize as "institutional" and to which they set themselves up in opposition as charismatic communities, free from structures and inspired only by the Gospel' (*Evangelio nuntiandi*, 1975, para. 58).

The subsequent CELAM Conference in Puebla referred several times

---

54 The precise words of the first phrase are 'celula inicial de estruturaçao eclesial' (CELAM, 1985, pp. 15,10).

55 These official texts, much as their denunciations may be shrill and their call for change urgent, usually carry what might be a 'warning to the consumer' to the effect that to promise sudden, revolutionary transformation is to peddle illusions. Thus Medellín quotes Paul VI: Christians know that 'sudden or violent structural changes would be deceptive, ineffective in themselves, and not in accordance with the dignity of the people, which demands that necessary changes be brought about from within, that is through the appropriate growth of awareness, sufficient preparation and the effective participation of all – conditions which are prevented from coming about by ignorance and often subhuman living conditions' (CELAM, 1985, 2,15).

to these concerns, but also, quoting the same Encyclical, described the CEBs as 'the hope of the Church'. They contributed to the Church's traditional social concerns, in the world of the family, of work and of local communities, creating within them an 'acceptance of the word of God, a revision of life and a reflexion on reality' (CELAM, 1986, para. 629). But Puebla went further also – reflecting perhaps the negotiated character of these official documents – in stating that they 'contribute to the questioning of the egotistic and consumerist roots of society' and 'offer a valuable point of departure for the construction of a new society, the "civilization of love"' (para. 642). They express the Church's 'preferential love for ordinary people ... they emphasize and purify their religiosity and offer the concrete possibility of sharing in the tasks of the Church and in the commitment to transform the world' (paras 642 and 643).

The vision here is definitely one in which the CEBs act in harmony with, but also within boundaries defined by the Church hierarchy, but the concerns voiced by Paul VI show that the Church was experiencing serious difficulties – it had unleashed a tiger, or at least a potential tiger. For while some might regard the CEBs as a suitable auxiliary for overstretched parish priests, and for a Church unable to provide either full-time parish priests or missionaries or religious in innumerable remote and poor parishes, others saw them as the seed of a new Church which would recapture the spirit of community and true brotherhood, channelling the energies of popular religious feeling and belief and the solidarity of the poor into secular as well as ecclesial transformation. This is what the Brazilian Franciscan, Leonardo Boff, has advocated untiringly. In doing so he has touched upon some sensitive spots, though he would insist, at least in public, that nothing he says contradicts the teachings of the Church.

Ideological background to the idea of a CEB

The idea of a CEB has obvious affinities with, and differs in important respects from, the apostolic lay groups embodied in Catholic Action and its various specialized offshoots described earlier. Both are attempts, in different times and places, to find an appropriate role for the laity, and both face similar problems. Catholic Action was more tightly subordinated to the hierarchy, its task was apostolic, one of evangelization, and it was founded on a conception of the distinction between the Church, as the repository of sacramental tasks, and the laity who could propagate Christian values and ideas but in a separate, worldly sphere. This was not to deny the unity of the People of God, but it was to delineate clear and distinct functions for clergy and laity (Congar, 1985). In contrast, the

CEBS have begun to take over roles previously performed by the clergy and neglected by default because of the shortage of priests. There are now dioceses in which they are replacing the parish as the basic cellular organization. The conception of a small-scale group coming together in a spirit of fraternity, in some sense to act out their identity as the People of God, is different from that of a large-scale organization devoted to infusing Christian values in the institutions of secular society. The CEBs are more independent than Catholic Action at the local level, since they are not part of an authoritative nationwide organization. They can also not really be 'dissolved' because they were not 'founded' in the first place; they do not have official legal or religious status, remaining, significantly, informal bodies. Perhaps the hierarchy is wary of the conflicts which might ensue from a more formal relationship – while the CEB leaders and members themselves may see little benefit in abandoning an unofficial status.

The hierarchy and the CEBs, as concepts, can be said to represent one current form of the permanent tension between two poles – or 'aspects' as Congar would say – of the Church, or indeed of religious life in general. One pole is the Church as 'men's fellowship with God and with one another in Christ', the other is the Church as 'the totality of the means provided by the Lord to bring men to his fellowship' (Congar, 1985, pp. 28–9). Congar, by advocating a shift towards the latter pole, in the years prior to Vatican II, had been seeking to correct a 'one-sidedness', to bridge the chasm between 'an ecclesiastical machinery existing in itself, complete, in charge of the clergy ... and the human community'. He described the prevailing situation as 'a priesthood without people; a wonderful liturgy, but which had often ceased to be worshipped *by some person*, the prayer of a real community of people [emphasis in the original]' (Congar, 1985, p. 56).

The sociologist might translate this problem as an example of the permanent, irresolvable tension between hierarchy and community in innumerable religious contexts. Congar himself, having pointed out the opposed error of the Protestant view of the Church without hierarchy constituted by 'only the Holy Spirit and the faithful' (1985, p. 30) traces the various exaggerations in one direction or the other in writings on the Church and the laity since the earliest Christians. His idea of 'integration', by which he presumably means the achievement of a correct balance between the two elements, is belied by the mountain of evidence to which he refers showing that 'one-sidedness', tension and imbalance between them is the normal state of affairs.[56] Vatican II, like Congar and

---

56 It is noteworthy that Congar himself admits that 'Protestant communions ... are in practice almost as clericalized as the Catholic Church', (1985, p. 51).

under his influence,[57] was also concerned to redress the balance. Paragraphs 33 to 39 of the Council's most authoritative 'dogmatic' statement, the 'Dogmatic Constitution on the Church',[58] contains numerous statements giving them 'a share in [the] priestly function of offering spiritual worship' (para. 34), a role in co-operating in the 'apostolate of the hierarchy' (para. 33), in exercising certain church functions for a spiritual purpose, and so on. This was more important, perhaps, for its presence, at some length, in the document, than for its content which remained guarded and emphasized most of all their role as 'living testimony' or bearing witness, in their daily and above all their 'married and family life' (para, 34). As in so many other fields, the effect of the Council was above all to raise an issue, and to create a climate of debate, the consequence of which went far beyond its authoritative statements on the subject.

The concept of the CEB in Liberation Theology

The concept of the laity, and the formulation of the laity's role in the Catholic Church, has undergone a profound transformation during this century, especially since Vatican II, which pronounced on the subject thus:

> The Church has not yet been truly established, and is not yet fully alive, nor is it a perfect sign of Christ among men, unless there exists a laity worthy of the name working along with the hierarchy ... very many men can hear of the gospel and recognize Christ only by means of the laity who are their neighbours. In fact, wherever possible, the laity should be prepared, in more immediate cooperation with the hierarchy, to fulfill a special mission of proclaiming the gospel and communicating Christian teachings.[59]

But Leonardo Boff, the leading theologian of liberation in ecclesiological matters – that is in matters concerning Church organization – offers us a vision which goes much further than this: 'After centuries of silence, the People of God are beginning to speak. They are no longer just parishioners in their parish; they have their own ecclesiological value; they are recreating the Church of God' (Boff, 1985, p. 126). The model for this reborn Church is all but a complete inversion of that of the existing Church and is schematized by Boff, who himself writes that it 'inverts the relationships', in the following simple diagram:

57 Congar spent many years teaching at the Dominican study centre, Le Saulchoir, in Paris, but was removed for 'false irenicism' by Pius XII. Later John XXIII recalled him as an adviser to the Second Vatican Council.
58 Usually known as 'Lumen Gentium', after the opening words of the Latin text.
59 *Ad Gentes*, para. 21. (Decree on the Church's missionary activity), in Abbott, 1966, pp. 611–12).

God	Christ – Holy Spirit
Christ	Community – People of God
Apostles	Bishops – Priest – Co-ordinator
Bishops	
Priests	
Faithful	

On the left hand, he writes, 'the faithful have only the right to receive. The bishops 'receive all religious "capital", produce the religious "commodities" and the people consume them"'.[60] On the right, 'everything revolves around the People of God'. It is the same model as that envisaged by the Nicaraguan priests whose disagreement with Archbishop Ovando of Managua has as much to do with these 'domestic' issues of authority in the Church as it does with secular politics. Boff expresses this by saying that the functions of bishops and priests are those of 'unification, not sanctification'.[61] That is, sanctification does not require the co-operation of an ecclesiastical hierarchy: it is present already in the People of God.

Boff, at least in his earlier writings, does not for all that wish to do away with the hierarchy: the *bases* can bring about a true renovation in the Church's institutional structures, but this is not to say that the Church should lose its identity or stray from its 'historical essence': 'there is no change in the permanent coexistence of a more static, institutional and permanent aspect and another, more dynamic, charismatic and vital, (Boff, 1977, p. 17). The latter aspect is embodied in the base communities whose task is in part a political one, since without their corrective action there is a risk that the Church will remain tied to the service of the rich and powerful.

The tasks of the People of God, organized in their base communities, vary enormously, ranging from Bible study and prayer to the defence of

60 This is an example of Boff's propensity to use marxist terminology. I suspect that he does it to make a point, to provoke perhaps, for it does not serve much use here, and indeed I do not really believe that he conceives of religious sacraments as 'capital' in the economic sense. Other examples of his propensity for irony are his use of official ecclesiastical texts, like the documents of Puebla and Vatican II, in support of arguments which are patently not to the taste of the authors of those texts. (I have slightly altered the English translation, replacing 'goods' with 'commodities'.)

61 The right-hand schema, bears an uncomfortably close resemblance to Congar's depiction of the Protestant version: 'God transcendent in heaven ... the faithful ... Church, assembly of the faithful' (Congar, 1985, p. 30).

human rights and rights to land, and community development projects. But Boff's vision is a far from secular one; on the contrary he takes the Church to task for excessive post-Conciliar secularization. The Council may have brought about a change, symbolized by the generalization of the phrase 'People of God', but 'the change did not affect the people':

> The priest . . . became incarnated among the people. This process was one of secularization. The priest abandoned . . . his cassock and cloister; the liturgy was simplified and his house opened to the people. The question today is whether the priest has gone too far; the people are not nearly as secularized. The people value their own religiosity while the priest diminished his own piety and that of the Church. He conscientized the people; in the process he destroyed a great deal of popular religiosity.[62]

This criticism of the post-Conciliar Church is certainly not what one would have expected from a marxist.

Once again we find a dissent from the standard image of a Church attuning to its environment by being less 'ceremonial', less 'otherworldly'. This in turn is linked to a communitarian model of Christian experience as a face-to-face experience of small groups, which is equally anti-modern and anti-secular, insisting on personal relationships and experience rather than impersonal authority and complex organization. Boff invokes the early Church as the inspiration for this tradition, and opposes it to the conception which came to prevail of a Church in which one does not need to know who is the priest, so long as he says Mass correctly, nor need one have personal contact with the other members of the congregation.

So a CEB is not merely an interest group, or an organization for the pursuit of special causes: in Boff's conception, and that of large sections of the movement, it *is* the Church: 'a Church does not live by faith alone, but by the celebration of faith. To celebrate is not merely to conduct a ritual, but to make a rite of life before God and one's brothers' (Boff, 1986, p. 88). The struggle for change also needs its symbolism, which is not necessarily that of the established ritual.

In the CEBs communion – in the sense both of 'community feeling' and 'communion with Christ' – demands that the singer, the lay leader of the group, the poor worker, the farmer, even the 'rich man converted to the cause of justice' should take their place side by side with the bishop and the priest (1986, p. 88). All learn from all; no one has a monopoly of wisdom. And, in one of many ironic references the CEBs are described as being 'one . . . holy . . . catholic . . . and apostolic'. They are 'holy because

---

62 Boff (1977, p. 132). The ugly neologism 'concientize' is as it appears in this translation; it has been inducted into the English language courtesy of the followers of Paulo Freire. It is better rendered as 'raising the consciousness of'.

they are committed to justice and solidarity; they are catholic [with a small 'c'] because they address themselves to all men and to each man as a whole, and they are apostolic 'because they follow the faith, life and mission of the apostles and are in communion – often unreciprocated communion – with the shepherds of the church' (1986, p. 89). This is an unpredicted amalgam of elements of community and elements of social complexity, of the traditional and the modern, and a rejection of the divide which separates the secular and the profane. How does it work out in practice?

The real world of the CEBs

CEBs are numerous, decentralized and small; they sprout up, decay and disappear. Some meet to read and comment on the Bible with or without priestly guidance, others are involved in development work, organizing the provision of sewage disposal or a community health project; some may be involved in the struggle for land, in the countryside or the city, or in conflicts over wages; and very often they are involved in the defence of human rights, as when members are taken to prison because of their political or semi-political involvements or, in the countryside, when they are victimized by landowners.

The two important ranges of variation concern the degree of their independence from the bishops and the different aims pursued by bishops in collaborating with them – or not; and, secondly, the relationship between spiritual activities, such as Bible study and catechism, and social mobilization.

Although CEBs are not official bodies, they do receive recognition from the local Bishop, and are usually advised by a priest, religious or trained lay person. But the degree of formality of such a recognition, and the extent to which it is sought, remain unknown. In some places – notably São Paulo, Recife and Vitoria in Brazil – they form part of an elaborate apparatus of parish and diocesan committees and consultations.

The numbers involved are unknown, and since membership seems to be as informal as the status of the Communities themselves, probably unknowable: the figure usually cited for Brazil is 80,000 CEBs (della Cava, 1987); but this is not based on systematic data. Even when the CNBB (Conferencia Nacional de Bispos Brasileiros: the Episcopal Conference of Brazil) commissioned a study of CEBs in the 1970s the authors did not venture an overall figure, confining their observations to the returns they received from a sample of unknown significance, (CNBB, 1981). A 'Grand Evaluation' conducted by the Archdiocese of Vitoria, published in 1986 revealed some 1,200 CEBs each with about

250 families. Active individual members totalled some 50,000, or an average of some 40 for each community, which is by no means a low figure (Oliveira, 1986). In Recife, among the equivalent organizations, known as 'Meeting of Brothers (Encontro de Irmaos) 269 'evangelization groups' were counted, with some 70,000 participants, averaging 260, though the discrepancy between this and the Vitoria figure may be explained by the possibility that a 'participant' in Recife meant a whole family.[63]

In the Archdiocese of Vitoria the parish remains as a 'centre of religious and administrative services', but the CEBs have become the 'base' of Church organization (Oliveira, 1986). In São Paulo (Petrini, 1984, p. 121) we find an elaborate system of elected representatives and consultations whereby people from the communities are elected and sit on a variety of committees, together with priests, religious and trained laity appointed by the Bishop. The communities are 'enmeshed in an extremely intense organizational network which supports ... most of its activities, from liturgical chanting to Easter Week processions ... to material for the ... Cost of Living campaign (ibid., p. 122).

The communities in these places are encompassed in a pastoral plan which is elaborated and implemented by Bishops in co-operation and consultation with parish priests and a growing band of professional advisers, priestly and lay. It is above all in Brazil that this 'informal Church' has flourished, as a penumbra, not under the control of the Church, nor carrying out tasks precisely assigned to it by the hierarchy, but nevertheless enjoying a degree of ecclesiastical support.

There is another view, of course, which would seek to control CEB activity quite tightly through the parish priests, confining them to the teaching of the catechism by trained lay persons and to the performance of those rituals entrusted to them. We have evidence of how this operates in practice from Colombia (Levine, 1985). But for others they should be highly participatory and the role of the priest one of 'facilitator'. Thus a Brazilian Bishop[64] insists on avoiding ready-made forms of organization, on not making neat divisions on a street map and implanting a CEB mechanically in each, on not depending on outsiders, on not drawing up elaborate organigrams and on distributing tasks as quickly as possible. His ideal is a CEB born from an identifiable collective concern: a

---

63 do Passo Castro, 1987, p. 87. The title is an allusion to Dom Helder Camara, founder of the CNBB in 1952 and Archbishop of Recife and Olinda from 1964 until his retirement in 1985.

64 In a handbook entitled 'How to build up a Base Community' by Dom Luis Fernandes (1985, pp. 47–8). Dom Luis is Bishop of Campina Grande in the north east of Brazil. He was previously in Vitoria, where he may have been involved in creating the climate for the sort of CEB activity mentioned above.

shanty-town hears that the authorities are planning to clear it, people get together, and suddenly someone begins to pray. . . . Or, a newly arrived family initiates regular Sunday meetings without waiting for a church to be built or a priest to visit. As in Boff, the spiritual element is central to this conception, a sense of togetherness and a distrust of leadership, especially of any hint of 'personalism or clientelism'. Yet at the same time the insistence that 'every thought and every prayer is embedded in real life', that 'in the innumerable community meetings the thought of the Gospel is constantly reinforced by and leavened by the yeast of reality', means that political discussion –which is also part of life itself – cannot be excluded. Politicians have no business interfering, but neither should Bishops try to prevent CEB leaders from standing for political office. Likewise it is quite right that the CEBs should take part in the renewal of the trade-union movement, in the struggle to rid the unions of *peleguismo*[65] – that is, of leaders beholden to the employers or the state.

If Bible study, catechism, celebrations and ceremonies are the bread and butter of community life, will they dampen or exclude initiatives aiming to change social relations within the community or in the wider society, and will they change as the pattern of lay participation changes?

One writer who studied the changes attendant upon community participation found that participants began to petition saints less for their own personal needs (praying to pass an examination, or for a sick person to be cured) and more for their spiritual needs or for the needs of the community (Rolim, 1980, p. 127). But the author concedes that 'immediatist and individualist' practices remain in the CEBs, some of which 'drown themselves' in intensely sacramental activities (p. 128). He sees – or perhaps would like to see – these practices as a stage on the way to the development of a 'collective religious awareness' and thus of an understanding of the 'contradictions of capitalism'.

The evidence is mixed, and those who believe that this sort of class consciousness is an extraneous implantation can find support in a study of CEBs in São Paulo which showed that activities such as charitable works, Bible study and religious festivals were more important than 'consciousness-raising' or even community action programmes; it also claimed that 'innovative activities' such as community action programmes *never* occur without the presence of politically active priests and religious men and women. Unfortunately, the study concentrated too much on quantitative aspects and also seems to have drawn a very narrow sample.[66]

65 *Pelego* is the thick sheepskin rug used to soften the seat of a saddle. Hence the use of the term to describe corrupt union officials.
66 Hewitt, 1987. Overall, the study showed little difference in the pattern of activity of middle-class and lower-class CEBs. However it may have missed the poorest sectors, because even those defined as 'lower-class' earned '5 minimum wages or above'. This is also the only study to refer to 'middle-class' CEBs, and draws on a very small sample.

If radicalization is coming from without, we have some notion of where it is coming from. A survey carried out in São Paulo in 1982 found that younger priests (those under 35) were particularly prone to define the 'Brazilian people' as 'the poor', and to describe them as oppressed, exploited, undernourished and so on.[67] The author of this study scarcely conceals his distaste for the strong political priorities of the younger priests, and for their mistaken concept of a 'popular Catholicism 'always, always [sic] to be tirelessly and militantly inculcated in search of new converts to the cause and of an organized and politicized (Catholic) people', in utter ignorance of the actually existing popular religion practised by the people. Indeed, he even found some priests who agreed that it would under certain circumstances be legitimate to suppress the Church if it turned against the poor, and that this would be a matter for 'the people' to decide (Pierucci, 1984, p. 484). But he also found some who had been shocked when they found themselves being manipulated by parties of the marxist left in popular mobilizations in the early 1980s, and from one came the following outburst: the left-wing groups 'forget that the people also want to live . . . they don't want to die here and now to create a new life' (p. 356).

Our notions of what is spiritual and what is political are deeply imprinted with the ideological environment in which we live, as is our notion of 'popular religion'. Is personal morality a purely spiritual matter? Is it more spiritual than issues of public morality or social justice? The claim of Liberation Theology is that these dualisms are misleading, and indeed that they are ideological constructions whose effect is to distract us from the reality of our selves and society. What, for example, do we make of a group discussion about Christ healing the leper (Mt., 8, 1–5.)? After some discussion the group's co-ordinator asked participants what were the leprosies in their own community which would need to be cured by Christ; the answers poured our explosively: 'Egoism – hunger – disunity – a shortage of schools – and drinking' (Castro, 1987). When pressed the participants would go no further. Were they the prisoners of traditional morality and conservative Christianity? Who is to say that those who stress personal morality are 'conservative'?

The most challenging interpretation of popular religion in Brazilian culture is that of Carlos Rodriguez Brandão, but his account is in reality an elaborate – if coded – warning to those who would try to infuse religious symbols and beliefs with a secular revolutionary project.[68]

67 Pierucci, 1984. Some of the results were published in Novos Estudos CEBRAP, 16, December 1986. The survey analysed responses from 140 priests in the Archdiocese of São Paulo.
68 Brandão, 1980. That is, to an explanation of actions and beliefs in terms of the class membership of those who hold them.

Brandão conceives religious life in terms of a permanent tension between the 'erudite' and the 'popular', and applies the opposition to Catholicism, Pentecostalism and 'Spiritism'. In all religions, he says, there is a constant effort by the 'official' or 'erudite' institutions to control or co-opt the popular, but it never works. There always remains an uncodified and uncontrolled set of popular practices and beliefs which are in constant flux. The division between the 'erudite' and the 'popular' is far more fundamental than that which divides different formally constituted religions. In any case, he notes, there is frequent migration between religions, permanent and temporary. Popular religion is a constituent element and a defence of the identity of popular classes. Efforts at organizing the laity under a priest's supervision, such as Catholic Action, tend in his experience to be doomed to a short life, while networks of uncontrolled brotherhoods and 'agents of salvation' thrive. The implications of this position should be extremely troubling for the informal Church, but it is not clear that even Brandão himself has understood them. He describes the official 'post-conciliar Church' – ironically placed between quotes by him – as a modernization mechanism which, while appearing to allow lay participation, is in fact destroying the community spirit which it claims to defend. He uses the term 'modernization' in the ironic sense common among Latin American radicals of his generation, meaning a prolongation of the tentacles of erudite religion, a co-optation of the popular in defence of the erudite. But he does not ask whether the same 'erudite–popular' opposition will affect the informal Church of the Poor. For although the prophets of liberation may try to put their message in the language of the people, it remains in many ways a version of erudite religion, literate, aspiring to coherence, drawing on a self-aware philosophical tradition.

This erudition is transmitted through a set of institutions and networks which I call the 'informal Church', loosely related to the Church hierarchy, and organized principally to communicate the message of liberation. These include Pastoral Commissions[69] which in Brazil are sponsored – though not precisely controlled – by the CNBB (Brazilian National Episcopal Conference). For example, the Brazilian Comissão Pastoral da Terra, (CPT: Pastoral Land Commission, formed in 1975), created as a legally independent body has, in the words of one of its chief officials, 'a relationship of mutual collaboration and criticism' with the CNBB, (Poletto, 1985, p. 134) and is concerned with the advocacy of land reform and the mobilization of the peasantry in favour thereof. There is a Pastoral Social, concerned with social questions, a Pastoral da

69 The word *pastoral* is originally an adjective but has increasingly come to be used as a noun denoting pastoral activities in 'the world'.

Juventude em Meio Popular, devoted the young people of the peasantry and the working class. The CPT is a large organization with a central office in the city of Goiania at the edge of the Amazonian hinterland, and regional branches all over the country, which give legal advice and moral and political support to peasant and rural workers' organizations; it has incurred the wrath of the military government and also of landowners; its representatives have given strong support to Indian groups in the defence of their lands and in their attempts to recover lands usurped from them. The CPT has suffered much unwelcome attention from the police and secret services, as has the CIMI, its sister organization concerned with the fate of indigenous peoples.[70]

There is also what has become a vast network in Brazil of Centres for the Defence of Human Rights. These are separate from the more official Commission for Justice and Peace, established worldwide by Pope Paul VI and with local commissions composed of persons appointed by Bishops. In Recife the Centre for the Defence of Human Rights for the north east as a whole, had, in 1986, offices in the same building as the Archbishopric, and issues a vast number of pamphlets on subjects as varied as the rights of rural schoolteachers (who have no formal qualification) the Constituent Assembly, the exemplary struggles of a shanty-town to survive in the face of grandiose urban development projects, and the rights of sharecroppers and employees and how to enforce them (complete with model contracts). (Dom Helder's successor has, I understand, withdrawn his support.) Elsewhere local centres have for example provided indispensable documentation and legal assistance to farmers organizing to prevent the construction of a dam which would flood their fields and force them to move elsewhere (Pandolfi, 1986). These Centres have come to form a network of sources of information and legal advice for peasants' and workers' organizations, that is for the 'popular movement'. Like some of the Pastoral Commissions they receive funding from international non-governmental organizations, and are often helped by a relationship with the CNBB or with local Pastoral Commissions, or simply with a sympathetic local Bishop.

Like Brandão, the informal Church proclaims its hostility to modernization, which is seen as an adaptation of the power structure to a changing world, but it is also the bearer of a process of modernization among the poor. It resembles the author who finds himself astonished by the realization that the technical agents and progressive intermediaries who would promote indigenous knowledge, for example, on grounds of appropriateness, as against expensive and inappropriate modern technologies, are nonetheless, through their efforts, undertaking a task of

70 Conselho Indigenista Misionario, formed in the early 1970s.

modernization, because they are so to speak rewriting indigenous knowledge according to the methods of modern science, and they are therefore
open to the same charge of authoritarianism as the 'technicians' they
criticize (Lovisolo, 1986). The promoters of the Church of the Poor are
creating leadership roles by the hundreds and thousands, they are
promoting complex organizations with division of tasks at the local level,
building up little by little a rudimentary bureaucratic back-up, and
although they resist the creation of large-scale formal organizations, they
are fitting their activities and the organizations they promote into
national and international networks which make even the remotest
activists and participants aware of a movement which goes far beyond
their own communities. The promotion of 'popular education' on what is
becoming a vast scale (see next chapter), has similar modernizing effects
in the sociological sense of the term. A study of popular organizations in
non-religious spheres would probably reveal a very high proportion of
local leaders who had spent their adolescence working in Christian lay
organizations. The crucial difference between this modernization and that
which its promoters so dislike is that it is coming, slowly, from civil
society, and not from the state; its great weakness, of course, is that it has
no economic accompaniment.

The Bible according to the Church of the Poor

The message emanating from this informal Church is a translation into
popular language of the erudite contribution of the theologians of
liberation, with liberal use of the Bible as a source of inspiration and
exemplary stories. The writer or speaker draws the audience onto a level
of contemplation where the metaphorical mode which pervades the
biblical text seems not mysterious or impenetrable but utterly clear and
straightforward; the view of Carlos Mesters, a biblical scholar, is that the
exegetes, of whom he is one, with all their erudition, can go only so far,
and while their learning may be indispensable, it is of no use unless
integrated with an understanding of the 'spirit'. Modern exegesis[71] grew

71 Beginning in the later nineteenth century in Germany with Bultmann. In an interview
Mesters spoke of Bultmann, the pioneer of modern exegetics, as having 'opened a door in a
wall which had no doors'; but he then, fundamentally, tried to 'demythologize', even to
secularize. He also insisted on the insufficiency of rational categories in understanding
history and seemed to be saying that the poor, and in particular the poor of the countryside,
have a special affinity for the symbolic language of the Bible. Furthermore, it is the poor
who have forced the Church to take up their cause and even caused Cardinal Ratzinger some
embarrassment – presumably when he came to pass judgement on the Theology of
Liberation (interview, São Paulo, 16 September 1986). I heard Mesters give an address to a

up outside the Catholic Church and was considered a challenge to her, as received beliefs about the 'literal' correctness of what is told in the Bible were challenged. The Church responded with exegetes of its own. But this, Mesters is saying, was to go too far along a road mapped by others, and it led to a position in which the 'normative and exemplary' character of the Bible, its 'spiritual exegesis' became a mere appendage, and was left behind, fossilized in the methods of a bygone age. 'The growth of the scientist was not accompanied by the growth of the man of faith.'[72] The demand to integrate the two functions of Biblical interpretation arises from the people (p. 68). The people upset conventional wisdom – they 'disorganize everything'[73] – and thus pave the way for a new interpretation.

The informal Church seeks to make the Bible relevant to the poor and the oppressed, and there is no shortage of material appropriate to this. The story of the Exodus is interpreted as the liberation of an oppressed people ('I will bring you out from under the burdens of the Egyptians': Exodus, 6, 6) – but an oppressed people who first became aware that they were oppressed ('I have surely seen the affliction of my people . . . and have heard their cry by reason of their taskmasters': Exodus, 2, 7).

The children of Israel are likened to the migrant workers of the contemporary Brazilian countryside. The Pastoral Land Commission, from whose pamphlet 'The struggle for land in the Bible', these quotations are taken, (Comissão Pastoral da Terra, 1981) is particularly concerned to show the relevance of Mosaic land and labour legislation for contemporary Brazil: the jubilee law, the prohibition on harvesting the corners of the fields, laws against usury, and so on. But beyond these down-to-earth applications, there is a more emotive appeal: the children of Israel 'had a bond to the land similar to that which is found among the Indians of Brazil. They love the land, commune with it, feed themselves from it, and through it they are united with God and with their fellow-men'. The second chapter of Genesis ('And the Lord God formed man of the dust of the ground, and breathed into his nostrils the breath of

---

gathering in the Cathedral in São Paulo. The occasion was the closing meeting of a series concerned with 'The People of God and the city' (literally 'The people of God and urban land tenure'), presided over by the Archbishop, Cardinal Arns. Speaking of the theme of the city in the Bible, Mesters started by noting that there were two images: the City of God (Jerusalem), and also the city as a place of sin and immortality (Babel, Sodom, Babylon). The Bible, he said, was 'born from a people of farmers', who were oppressed by the Kings who ruled over them. From time to time, he would break into a song, and the several hundred people attending would join him in tunes reminiscent of Negro spirituals.

72 Mesters, 1984, p. 68. The title translated is: 'Defenceless flower', and refers to the idea of a flower which is without defence yet can transform its own blood into a seed or fertilizer.
73 The phrase used in the interview quoted above.

life': Genesis, 2,7) is referred to, leading up to the statement that the people had a 'devotion to the land, which formed so essential a part of their lives that it was a gift from God'.

Another instance of analogy between biblical times and the present is the account of Solomon, who incurred 'foreign debts' abroad in order to embellish his capital and maintain his prestige. To build his temple he had to pay vast sums to the King of Tyre, but to the '30,000 Israelites' who worked on it he paid nothing. He even gave the King of Tyre twenty cities 'where the poorest people lived, so they had no way of protesting'.[74] With the establishment of a 'Monarchy, the people of Israel saw their culture 'becoming ever more devalued', as a result of the modernization of their customs in the urbanization process, the growing importance of private property, and what is nowadays known as 'real-estate speculation'.

The reaction comes with the prophets, Isaiah, Amos and others, whose message provides a rich source for demonstrating the indivisibility of faith, social justice and morality, expressed in a language of extraordinary power. This emphasis placed on the Old Testament has not gone unnoticed in the Vatican.[75]

This pamphlet literature dwells on the life of Jesus rather than on the difficult questions of his death, resurrection, and the meaning of these. Jesus is a social reformer, a man of the people, a man who denounced the rich and powerful, above all a man. In some ways, the life of Jesus in the literature of the informal Church is the life of another saint. Faced with unfamiliar popular culture and religious beliefs and practices, yet aware that they must write for an illiterate or ill-educated audience, the authors choose a method which uses the Bible largely as a source of moral tales: the power of its language and even of the symbols – so appreciated by Mesters – is sacrificed by the pamphlets in favour of a transposition of Biblical situations into the contemporary world. The Children of Israel

74 1 Kings, 9,10. The text actually specifies that although he did use forced labour, he took care not to use that of his own people, but rather survivors of other tribes who had escaped annihilation by Israel! (v. 20).

75 See for example the fourth section of the *Instruction on certain aspects of the 'Theology of Liberation'*, published in the wake of the 'Boff affair' in 1984. Here the Vatican recalls the Exodus and the Prophets and, in veiled terms which none but the cognoscenti may fully understand, tries to redress the balance, by noting that the Exodus is not merely a political liberation, but rather a stage on the road to the covenant made at Sinai; likewise the document recalls that the call to justice of the Prophets is indissolubly linked to justice 'in relation to God'. The later and more definitive document on the subject, published in 1986, and entitled *Instruction on Christian Freedom and Liberation*, is less pointed. On the notorious occasion of the Pope's visit to Managua (1983) the Pope specifically criticized what he described as the 'so-called People's Church' for, among other things, its excessive emphasis on the Old Testament.

are migrant workers in Egypt; Solomon is a spendthrift authoritarian ruler, the tribes of Israel are like the states of Brazil and so on.

The popular religion which faces them in reality is one which gives much importance to the cult of the Virgin and devotion to saints, in which individuals are not afraid to shift between Christianity and spiritism as the 'spirit' moves them, in which religion is part of the daily business of life rather than a consciously acquired set of beliefs. Conceivably the informal Church is fighting an equivocal battle: its 'real' enemy – the enemy it understands – is official Catholicism and it is translating its own arguments against official religion into the language of the people in the belief that official Catholicism controls the beliefs and practices of the people, or manipulates them, and in the hope of riding the wave of a radicalized popular religion to transform both society and the Church, the upshot could be a tense but complimentary division of labour in which the official Church occupies the space of morality and collective identities while the informal Church gets on with modernization, its legitimacy ensured by its practical achievements.

Conclusions: Counter-attack and retrenchment in Rome

After the traumas which came in the wake of Vatican II, maybe any Pope would be impelled to reassert episcopal authority, even at the cost of losing some of the benefits of the commitment of the 'People's Church'. 'Better fewer, but better', as Lenin said.

This means devoting more attention to internal problems, such as the quality of the education and training of priests. Since the Vatican Council trainee priests have spent a lot of time 'in the community' and especially among the poor; in downtown Recife, the Theological Institute takes in young men who have not completed secondary school, of whom only a minority eventually become ordained. They live for one year together in a residence and then go and live in small groups in working-class communities. There are too few experienced people to look after them, and the students themselves complain that they feel insufficiently 'accompanied'. They are trained in a broad range of subjects in Philosophy, Theology and the Human Sciences, but not to a very high level. The building is a poorly equipped and ugly construction of the early 1960s. Yet it attracts some of the most distinguished Theologians of Liberation and counts among its staff Yvonne Gebara, one of the top exponents of the theology of women – in short its teaching is in touch with the vanguard.

Not far away, in colonial Olinda, the Benedictines run a rival establishment: it is a beautiful and peaceful monastery, whose ornate baroque Church and perfectly proportioned cloister symbolize those established and dignified traditions which the Theological Seminary's utilitarian building ignores. The training programme here is more rigorous and more erudite, and entry is more selective. Dom José Cardoso, successor to Archbishop Helder Camara, now sends his novices to the Benedictines instead of to the Theological Institute. We may expect a determined effort by the authorities to operate a rigorous selection system and to tighten up training, so as to avoid later defections and ensure a more orthodox adherence to doctrine.

A more inward-looking Church might not be entirely disagreeable to the Pope. When John Paul II went to Chile in 1987 he drew huge crowds on the expected scale, but it was difficult to know whether this was simply because of the political opportunities offered by such a visit during a time of dictatorship.[76] If the Pope can only attract big crowds for incidental political reasons, that does not bode well for the evangelical influence of the Church. A more inward-looking Church might be smaller and less influential, but it might also be more solid and enduring.

There are countries – Ireland, Poland, Mexico – where for varying reasons, although there may be conflict between religious and political forces, or even between Church and state, religious and political commitment are ideologically complementary. In Mexico the post-revolutionary state broke with the Church in the 1920s, as it implanted itself in the countryside, provoking a wave of violent uprisings throughout the south and centre of the country in which peasants and clergy rose up to demand land and the reopening of the Churches (Meyer, 1974). The repression was brutal, and although a sweeping land reform was implemented in the early 1930s and the Churches were allowed to reopen, for fifty years Mexican governments behaved outwardly as if the Church did not exist. The Church for its part, confined firmly to civil society, has avoided the crises brought about by commitment to social and political causes, and has lived comfortably with a popular religious practice embedded in the daily life of the people. The Pope's visits to Mexico have not been marred by a struggle for control of their significance and symbolic projection among Catholic or political factions: the possibility of ambiguity has simply not existed. The avoidance of politics seems to go hand in hand with religious consensus and a certain resistance to modernism. Unlike in Argentina, where there has never been a break between Church and state, and resistance to modernism takes the form of ill-concealed distrust of liberal democracy, integrist velleities, and continuing political intrigue.

76 The speeches given by selected representatives of the *bases* to mass meetings of the Pope with the poor of Santiago (the *pobladores*) and with the young people, had been vetted and cut by Church authorities in advance, but the delegates from the rank-and-file restored the cuts. One outcome was the summary dismissal by the Archbishop of Santiago of the head of the 'Youth Pastoral'.

The counter-attack against the Theology of Liberation has drawn selectively on these histories and on an intellectual strand of Catholic nationalism. Its principal organ is *Nexo*, edited by Alberto Methol Ferré[77] in Montevideo. For him Latin America occupies a very special place in the history of the church: the continent remains the sole repository of pre-Enlightenment Christian values and as such the great hope of a Church assailed by secularism. These values are embodied not in philosophy or theology, but in a popular religious culture which express-es a particular Indo-american heritage. While the Church as an institution was marginalized in the post-colonial period by liberalism and secular-ism, popular culture preserved the heritage of the colonial evangelical experience, and only in 1979 at Puebla did the Church embark properly on the recuperation of this culture.

The shape of this pattern of thought has many more surprises in store for us than the Theology of Liberation. The recuperation of a pre-Enlightenment consciousness is joined with the invocation of Latin America as one nation, and of the Argentine 'National Left' – of which Methol Ferré was an exponent in the 1950s. Lucio Gera, whom we have met as a ferocious critic of the Argentine Church in the 1960s, now reappears in the pages of *Nexo*. Twenty years ago he was attacking the hierarchy for their lack of awareness of the autochtonous, 'national' elements in Argentine society, calling on it to ward off extraneous ideologies. His distrust of liberal modernism is now expressed in a slightly different message: Latin American popular culture has never truly assimilated the individualist culture of capitalism: the Baroque style is 'passionate and dyonisiac'; in it 'the explosion of festivities, pleasure and good living coexists with repentance and mortification'. It is, he admits, ridiculous to deny to the people the technical and social skills and instruments of the modern age: unadulterated indigenism for example is an absurdity. But some sort of compromise or synthesis between this and modernity is the task of the evangelization of culture (Gera, 1986).

The most ambitious exponent of this school of thought, the Chilean Pedro Morandé, writes that in pre-Columbian societies work was a sacrifice, and that the idea of work as a commodity has never really taken root in the region. Secularism is a nineteenth-century phenomenon which gained a lot of ground at the level of the élites but not among the people. If the Church can take seriously the evangelization of culture then this substratum will return to a dominant position (Morandé, 1984). For him the Theology of Liberation shares with these authoritarian regimes the cultural bankruptcy of the worship of secularism and development. Far

77 Who, from his position as head of CELAM's Department for the Laity fought hard against the Theologians of Liberation in the lead-up to Puebla. Methol published the inside story, but unfortunately, I have been unable to trace the book.

from being an integrist, he takes the view that the Church has no business becoming involved in secular politics: the Church's world is that of culture.

The counterpart of these ideas is the movement to strengthen places of pilgrimage, popular shrines, and the Marian cult, sponsored by organizations such as the German Schoenstatt, the Italian Communione e Liberazione and Opus Dei. These activities offer a stylization of popular culture, controlled by the representatives of official, erudite religion – as distinct from the self-managed rituals of village fiestas and shrines, so common in Mexico and the Andean countries, each with its autochthonous and localized forms and mysteries, and where the priest's role is to be in attendance rather than in control. The organizers of these places, and the more active participants in the supporting organizations are drawn from the educated middle classes and private Catholic schools. The accompanying ideology of popular religion as national identity and as the core of culture fits well the Papal project of institutional consolidation because it proclaims no alteration of Church structures or philosophy.

Thus popular religion – so eagerly sought after by both these rival schools – remains elusive. Those who would seek to evangelize culture are unlikely to transform their stylized version of popular Catholicism into the standard-bearer of the continent's future common identity; the apostles of liberation, for their part, and despite much protestation to the contrary, will not be able to shake off the modernity and the suspicion of popular religious culture which is an inherent part of their world view.

The Theology of Liberation may not (yet) have transformed the institutional Church as fundamentally as its protagonists would have liked. In the wider world, however, its influence has been enormous. The informal Church has provided an institutional and ideological framework for popular movements after the decline, or repression, of marxism. Even if the 'Church of the Poor' inhabits a different world from the popular religion it has come optimistically to invoke, this does not necessarily mean that it holds no appeal for the rank and file: it simply means that the rank and file will look to it as much for practical advice and leadership as for religious succour, even while the theologians try to break down the barriers between the two. One consequence has been to place the theme of citizenship – that is, of the human and civil rights of persons – at the forefront of popular movements, avoiding the assumption of earlier radicalisms that there could be no citizenship without a total transformation of society. The result may, finally, be effective pressure from below for that modernization of the state and of institutions of political representation which is so conspicuously lacking in the region. The irony is that an almost millenarian zeal fired with religious invocations was needed to 'get the people organized' in the manner of a modern *civitas*.

Four: Social Movements

Changing themes of social mobilization

The meaning of the term 'social movements' has changed in Latin American usage in the past twenty years. During the 1960s it was used to refer to large organizations calling upon a nationwide constituency and aiming to influence government policy or to engage in broad-based conflict drawn up along the lines of social class. They would include rural social movements (or peasant movements), urban trade unions, populist mobilizations such as those associated with Peronism, and alliances of grassroots movements formed under the guidance of particular political parties, such as the movements which developed in Chile during the Unidad Popular period. Local mobilizations tended to be linked to these broader agglomerations or to seek out a link with them. This was a style of politics suited to the 'ISI–populist–corporatist state' with its co-optative powers and a pattern of decision-making which, though superficially highly centralized, was in fact conducted by interlocking networks of competing centres of power within the bureaucracy and the political parties.

Authoritarianism undermined the basis for these movements. Leaders were imprisoned, exiled or killed. In Chile the repression was most thorough of all; a society in which organized class conflict had been a habit of life for decades in industry and for some ten years in agriculture, and in which political parties were the primary reference point for all political action, suddenly found itself without parties or unions. In Brazil the rural movements which had been particularly active in the north east in the years leading up to the 1964 coup were severely repressed, and although industrial trade unions were not banned, they were subjected to tight controls through the existing corporatist apparatus. The 1966 coup in Argentina did not repress very violently, and indeed its leaders tried to strike a deal with union chieftains; but after the 1976 coup a particularly severe repression was directed at shop-floor activists, against the revolutionary left and the left-wing intelligentsia which had mushroomed since 1969.

One might have thought that, in the face of this assault, political mobilization would simply disappear, but this did not always happen, and it did not take long, at least in Chile and Brazil, for new forms of popular organization, or forms which had existed in the shadow of the large-scale mobilizations, to emerge into greater visibility and strength. In addition, the vertical apparatus of unionism in Argentina survived, and in Brazil the manufacturing unions weathered a period of stringent corporatist control by the state to emerge with some independence at the end of the 1970s.

It is to the new forms of political mobilization which this chapter is devoted. These have arisen in part in response to repression but also as a response to changes in economic structure and in the role of the state in the economy. In Chile, the process of deindustrialization and the abandonment of a fifty-year commitment to a welfare state (however rickety) threw vast numbers of people into a state of indigence and *déclassement* which they never had imagined would befall them. Respectable middle-class persons, teachers, civil servants, found themselves out of work and forced to move away from their accustomed communities into working-class areas or 'worse'. Working-class households accustomed to fairly stable employment for their men were hit not only by cyclical unemployment, but by the physical disappearance of the factories and industries in which they had been employed. This collapse of a way of life produced at first efforts to organize charitable work, but later and increasingly, a myriad of self-help activities which by the late 1980s had become an established part of the country's urban landscape.

In Brazil the period of authoritarian rule brought structural changes in the economy, but of a very different kind: after an initial stabilization economic growth and industrialization advanced at breakneck speed, employment in industry and in cities generally expanded very rapidly, and the agrarian structure underwent an invasion of capitalist development which brought about social dislocation on a massive scale. The state apparatus also expanded, in contrast to that which occurred elsewhere, but, apart from the Transamazonian highway, social and physical infrastructure lagged far behind the need. Here too a ferment was set in train in the countryside and in the city: in the countryside localized conflicts over land and over massive infrastructural projects proliferated, while in the cities land invasions multiplied together with demands on the state apparatus that it make provision for basic social services. In Brazil, the corruption, delays, and political patronage which plague official provision have given rise to movements for self-management especially in community health, which have proved a crucible for the formation of local – and predominantly female – leadership.

The Catholic Church and its informal penumbra have played an important role in providing protection and even encouragement to these initiatives from below. But there are important differences between its interventions: in Chile the Church had thrust upon it the task of providing emergency relief to people who found themselves with no or hardly any income at all after the 1973 coup, which brought in its wake first mass sackings of politically suspect persons, and then an economic collapse. The Church also took up the cause of human rights and created a legal advisory service to help those whose rights were being violated and their families. As a result of these developments, the Church and especially the Archdiocese of Santiago, gradually became the *de facto* sponsors of a parallel welfare state apparatus financed by international charitable donations. Once the resources were available, the people at the grassroots – true to the densely organized networks built up over generations among the Chilean working class, at work and in the community – were quick to organize their own self-help organizations, as we shall see presently.

In Brazil the Church has been less involved with welfare activities and more, as we saw in the last chapter, with grassroots organization. Relief to the indigent during droughts, for example, has been recognized by the government as the responsibility of the state, however unsatisfactory the provision. The government provides school lunches, runs supplementary feeding programmes, provides old-age pensions to the rural population, even provides some medical care to the indigent; all these arrive with difficulty and usually appalling quality, but at least some responsibility is recognized.

Argentina is the great exception. The period from 1976 until the Falkinas War was marked by the almost immediate collapse of the Montoneros. The vast trade-union apparatus went into hibernation and scarcely uttered a squeak for six years. Mobilization in the cause of human rights was confined to the tiny but valiant group of Mothers in the Plaza de Mayo, though towards the end they gained a broad array of allies as the regime fell victim to its bickerings and its catastrophic military adventure. Although the economy underwent a recession and stagnation similar to the Chilean one, the response was utterly different. And the Church kept quiet.

The phrase 'new social movements' encompasses protest and conflict, lobbying and pressuring government agencies and politicians, as well as 'self-help' development projects, of which the most frequently cited are popular education, self-built housing, consumer or producer co-operatives, and community health care. Many of the processes it is intended to cover are themselves organized only on an ad hoc basis, such as the defence of rural land rights, and urban land invasions, while others which are created in response to a highly localized problem may survive and develop over long periods.

Ideologically, the newness of the *movimento popular* usually refers to an aggregate of dissent, dissent from official politics and dissent from the officially chosen path of development, usually decried as bringing little good to the poor. The usage reflects an ideological change in a community of radical intellectuals as much as a new social phenomenon. They are according 'newness' to processes which ten or twenty years ago they did not recognize as social movements at all; and this, in turn, may reflect their lowered expectations, their disillusion with the dreams of the past. In the past they thought that the piecemeal approach would not make a serious impression on poverty or social inequality. Now the co-operatives, self-help projects and so on which not so long ago were dismissed as mere cosmetics are taken seriously simply because more ambitious projects are too risky. Many may admire Nicaragua and support the Sandinistas for what they symbolize – as they supported Cuba in the past – but they are not willing to take the same risks and are increasingly willing to say so.

The novelty of these self-managed activities derives from the extent to which they are independent of the state apparatus: the days are past when reformist governments looked to create and finance such organizations in order to shore up their egalitarian or democratic credentials – for example with land reform co-operatives. Nowadays they may be viewed with sympathy only if they cost little and if they threaten no property-owning interests. Land reform, which inspired many government-sponsored self-management initiatives, has disappeared from the political agenda. So, self-management, no longer presenting itself as a cosmetic façade or as a disguised form of government manipulation, appears in a more favourable light, untainted by official patronage. This forms part of a broader canvas in which the idea of the rebirth of civil society takes a prominent place, and it is an idea which has undermined many long-standing assumptions of radical thought. As against the main currents of modern nationalism, this presupposes that the sources of solidarity lie neither in the state nor in a mythical pre-capitalist commune. It is a solidarity which takes seriously much of the modern liberal view of human and individual rights: it opposes corruption and favours transparency, it opposes arbitrariness and favours due process. But in addition it claims that rights are not enough, since their exercise, and the autonomy of individuals and groups which they presuppose, depend on power relationships rooted in the social structure. The concept of rights then acquires a dynamic dimension, as they are used to change those power relationships. The next step builds on the discourse of human rights and redefines them to include the right to housing, education, social welfare, urban services, land and so on: the right to be a competent citizen living a life in accordance with what contemporary cultures take to be civilized standards. It also reflects an underlying obstacle, namely the qualitative, managerial, inadequacy of the actually existing state apparatus, unable as it is to supply even the minimum requirements of competent citizenship, irrespective of quantitative or fiscal difficulties. The problem is that the means defeat the ends because the interests and power of those charged with translating policy and provision into physical actions take precedence.

In this perspective behind the claim that collective goods can be described as the object of rights is the different but implicit claim that they must at least be provided in a transparent manner consistent with proper procedure and without discrimination: bureaucratic fair play is, after all, merely a special case of due process. That may also be expensive – but it can hardly be unreasonable. The difficulty for the denizens of most Latin American political cultures – with the interesting exception of Chile and perhaps Costa Rica – is that, not having the experience of a state which plays even remotely fair, the alternative to reliance on the state is reliance on self or on the collective self of small-scale and primary loyalties. Yet the state constrains the capacities of these collectivities in innumerable ways, great and small – ranging from outright repression to petty regulation. Consequently, they are caught between two opposed and equally frustrating alternatives: rent-seeking in the hope of achieving something, however small and for however few people, or opting out entirely of political pressure politics – which amounts to leaving others to collect the rents.

From this several points follow. Firstly, that it is not at all inconsistent to be sensitive to a liberal concept of rights while following an illiberal policy of rent- seeking; secondly that the absence of due process and fair play – or rather the absence of the institutions which would impose them to a reasonable degree – should not be taken as evidence that a culture does not provide people with the basis on which to understand the concept of citizenship or of proper procedure. On the contrary, the violation of liberal prescriptions concerning bureaucratic behaviour – corruption in common parlance – should not lead us to ignore the rapidity with which non-Western cultures have assimilated the basic principles of bureaucracy so that opinion really is scandalized by corruption, even if the people find there is little in their individual or collective power that they can do to remedy it.

But thirdly and most importantly, it follows that if the state is an anti-liberal construction we do not have to be anti-liberals to pursue social change; indeed if the illiberalism of the state is experienced – leave aside 'demonstrated' – as an integral part of the injustices prevailing in civil society, then the movement from below can argue from liberal discourse in order to undermine power relations. The populist reformers and socialist revolutionaries of the 1960s and early 1970s adopted the language of liberal rights only occasionally and for tactical reasons; their successors – the post-marxists, social democrats, 'renovating' Peronists and the like – in the 1980s really do believe in those rights. Their changed position, though, has more radical implications than they care to draw, for reasons of political caution. If they have rejected the view that democracy failed and succumbed to military overthrow because it was a façade for bourgeois dictatorship torn away in a time of stress, they should also have asked whether it was democracy at all. In the case of a system which, as in Brazil, clearly rested – and rests – on the exclusion of vast numbers of people from the protection of rights the doubt may be evident enough. In Chile and Argentina the system failed the test of sustainability under stress. This is a crucial test, since what good is a system to the people if it cannot effectively protect the rights it purports to guarantee? The post-marxist generation have fallen into the trap of identifying institutional sustainability with political moderation. It is a theoretical trap because it is so manifest a sacrifice of principles; and it is a practical trap because the political moderation is not theirs to control or deliver – it depends, in the end, on the people's practical actions.

If that was all, it would hardly be very new. But there is more, in the collective but uninstitutionalized expressions and organizations which go under the broad heading of 'popular movement'. This phenomenon owes much to the ideological changes we have charted in Catholicism, evidently, and particularly to the idea that the struggle in itself is worthwhile, since to actually attain the final state is the millenarian abolition of the sensitive division between the sacred and the profane. It is not by accident that terms like *caminhada, exodo* and *luta*, which denote struggle and suffering – rather than *felicidade* or *Terra Prometida,*[1] which denote finality and utopia – are so prominent in the discourse of the informal Church. John Stuart Mill already wrote of the educative value of democratic practice; in the situations I have in mind the espousal of struggle for its own sake and for the 'stand' which it represents, reflects a largely unarticulated hope that in organizing themselves for even quite mundane purposes, or simply in coming together as in the CEBs, individuals are being citizens and are also exercising a right which they cannot take for granted, namely that of assembly. If they can give to their activities an instrumental purpose, so much the better, but those purposes

---

1 Meaning, successively, pilgrimage/struggle, Exodus (and thus journeying through the wilderness, as in *caminhada*), struggle, happiness, and Promised Land.

– as we shall see – are often so trivial that they hardly explain the time and energy expended on the organizations by participants. This collective activity is in itself a beginning of citizenship, especially in societies where so often the recognition of formal citizenship by the state carries with it a kind of conditionality.

The conditionality consists of a package of clientelistic involvements which popular culture regards as demeaning and illegitimate – albeit necessary in an adverse world.[2] The language of popular movements is drawn from the populist imaginary, and the units of organization are often based on primary groups rather than the secondary, professional and more anonymous groupings which embody a liberal image of active citizenship; but the symbolic and latent effects do not reinforce populism at all. On the contrary, they have the potential to create within civil society habits of transparency and due process which contradict those used by the state apparatus in its populist moments in its dealings with the poor in particular. It is quite misleading to suggest that popular movements are constructed on the basis of clientelism and personalistic ties simply because they grow up in small-scale communities or neighbourhoods. It is the official political apparatus which perpetuates clientelism in attempting to co-opt or suffocate initiatives from below.

The discourse of rights, then, having inverted the assumed relationship between political rights and social justice, now can open the way to a democratic space within civil society in which conflicting demands are discussed openly and not negotiated behind closed doors or on terms dictated by the state. The demand for collective self-management is in part simply a demand that public goods be managed by responsive and responsible bodies – a demand for fair dealing as much as for participation. As such it may not be a way of ensuring social justice in the crudely distributional sense – for in the final analysis the state does control the necessary resources. But if we take the view that the bad habits of politicians and bureaucrats constitute a significant factor in concentrating the distribution of resources, then by pressing for transparency popular movements may also achieve a little in the direction of equality. Above all, their supporters may attach more importance to fair dealing than they do to equitable distribution. They may seriously aspire to a world in which *política* is not a dirty word.

So much is hope, no doubt, and in the following sections I draw on

2 I refer here to the pejorative connotations of the word *política* in both Spanish and Portuguese. It is used to refer to pay-offs, kickbacks, dirty deals, explicit or implicit electoral corruption, all of which is taken to have a divisive effect on grassroots organizations. The word means the exact opposite of public, virtuous (in the Renaissance sense) involvement which it is taken traditionally to connote in the European tradition. On this see the perceptive remarks in Caldeira (1987).

forms of social mobilizations usually identified with 'new' social movements in order to judge whether such hope has any foundation, and also
as a prelude to the conclusions of the final chapter.

Changing themes of conflict in the countryside

In the 1960s the prevailing belief among the modernizing and developmentalist intelligentsia was that Latin American agriculture was stagnant,
traditionalist and decadent, and this was reflected in the calls for land
reform which reached their peak in the 1960s.[3] Subsequently research
showed that this view was not only simplistic but probably seriously
mistaken. Historians, economists and sociologists produced increasing
amounts of evidence that agrarian structures had been undergoing a
process of capitalist development for many decades – even centuries,
depending on the definition of capitalism – and that the vast estates which
resembled colonial inheritances were in fact creations of nineteenth-
century expansion, as were the purportedly antiquated labour relations
prevailing on them.[4] On the basis of this account one could construct a
typology in which there were three basic patterns of peasant movement,
depending on the agrarian structures in which they arose. Where they
were involved in forms of labour rent, working for landlords in return
principally for access to land with what might be termed a wage
'supplement' they tended to organize to fight first for the payment of a
proper wage and then, as the conflict escalated, for property in the land.[5]
Where they were involved in historic conflicts between great estates and
independent corporate peasant communities – as in the highlands of Peru
or in parts of Mexico before the revolution – the conflicts would be over
the ownership of land legally claimed. But once again, these conflicts
could escalate into movements for land reform, as in the historic case of
Zapata, the leader of Mexico's peasant heartland, Morelos, during the
revolution.[6] The third major type of conflict was more over wages and

3 This view is classically embodied in the reports of the Interamerican Committee for
Agricultural Development (CIDA) which were published under the auspices of the OAS
and various UN organizations in the wake of the Alliance for Progress.
4 The literature on this subject is now vast. For a summary see the forthcoming
contribution by Long and Roberts to the *Cambridge history of Latin America* vol. VI.
Among the most stimulating monographic contributions are: Mallon (1983); de Janvry
(1981).
5 A classic example is that of Bolivia; see Dandler (1975); also the Valley of La Convención
in Peru, see Fioravanti (1974); and the north east of Brazil, see Azevdo (1982).
6 The standard study is Womack (1968). This has recently been overtaken, though, by
Knight (1986, 2 vols). On land conflicts in the Peruvian highlands, see the relevant chapter in
Paige (1978).

working conditions than over land, and could be observed on plantations and large estates where labour was paid exclusively or predominantly in wages – as in the plantations of northern Peru or the great estates of central Chile (Quijano and Portocarrero, 1969; Lehmann, 1972, 1974).

Once the reality of capitalist development had been admitted, there developed a widely shared assumption that in the long run the third type of conflict would become dominant, resulting from an inevitable polarization of agrarian society into capitalist landowners and rural landless proletarians, squeezing out the middle peasantry. This view, derived from Lenin's account of Russian rural society in 1899,[7] was both ideologically congenial and convenient. Those who wished to ensure that agrarian reform did not merely perpetuate capitalism could point to it as grounds for the encouragement or even imposition of production co-operatives, for landless proletarians could be expected to prefer to become wage workers on collectives, whereas dependent tenants with access to land might be transformed into a 'cushion' of inevitably conservative small farmers by an individualist redistribution of land.

But the empirical research stimulated by land reform and peasant mobilization, revealed that the Lenin model was fundamentally flawed: a very rapid proliferation of small holding was taking place, even in Brazil where there had been no land reform; the great estates were not growing larger (though they were not shrinking much either); there were signs of a class of medium farmers coming to occupy even a dominant position in some places, such as Central Chile after land reform and southern Brazil; there were also signs of upward mobility from within the peasantry, though this was overshadowed by the mass of tiny smallholders.[8] Problems of poverty aside, this transformation of the agrarian structures has brought continued massive urban migration, and ever-increasing multi-employment (whereby an individual moves between different jobs, sectors and labour markets) – in short, a life of successive disruptions and

---

7 Lenin (1899). The book was retrieved as a fundamental reference point during agrarian debates of the 1960s and 1970s; it is Lenin's one major contribution to development economics, and consists not of an argument for collectivization, but of a sustained and documented attack on the naiveté of populists who thought that the hardships of capitalism could be avoided or circumvented by a return to peasant communes. Lenin's thesis was that there could be no revolution until capitalism had destroyed the peasant economy and created the proletariat, processes which were deeply interconnected. The arguments for collectivization came much later and in a different context, though Lenin's thesis was in the background (Lehmann, 1982).

8 These sentences are skirting rapidly round a vast amount of information and several theoretical minefields. For empirical studies of the emergence of a rich peasant or medium farmer elite see Long and Roberts (1984); on Chile see Lehmann and Castillo (1982). On Brazil see Lehmann (1982); also da Silva (1978) and (1981). See also Sorj and Wilkinson (1984). For a theoretical critique see Lehmann (1986b) and (1982).

unstable social bonds for millions of people. It has also brought about a change in the reality and the perception of rural social movements. In the 1960s there were discernible organizations which marshalled forces and even negotiated on behalf of large numbers of members, particularly in Chile and on the northern coastal plantations of Peru. But by the 1980s large-scale rural union organizations were no longer such significant actors in the process of collective bargaining or in the macro-context of debate about agrarian policy. In Chile, the military regime has brought about almost total repression of a rural union movement which at its peak claimed over 200,000 members. In Peru the land reform has transformed the sugar plantations into co-operatives. In Brazil the Confederation of Agricultural Workers (CONTAG) is, on paper, an enormous union with, in 1978, over 4.5 million members. But this quantitative strength is not reflected in either political power or negotiating strength. For most of its members the union is a service organization which looks after various social security claims and payments, and also provides legal advice in land tenure conflicts. It has been able to bargain effectively only in the sugar cane industry, where the annual harvest provides an excellent opportunity, and where a degree of uniformity in managerial and pricing arrangements makes the negotiation of collective agreements feasible.[9]

In the place of large formal organizations, we find a myriad of small-scale, dispersed movements engaged in an enormous variety of conflicts. The violence of rural conflict has increased enormously in Brazil on account of the pervasiveness of conflicts over rights to land and the readiness of landowners to resort to private bodyguards or worse (Martins, 1980, 1984); conflicts over rural land tenure in that country have become more serious and more numerous, not least since the departure of the military government.[10]

9 The two states where sugar accords have been the subject of hard negotiation are Pernambuco in the north east and São Paulo.
10 The evidence suggests that the overwhelming majority of killings are carried out by agents of landowners against squatters, rather than vice versa. A detailed study carried out by the Brazilian Association for Agrarian Reform (ABRA) produced the following data: in 1980 and 1981 197 persons died and 518 were injured in land conflicts; of those who died 150 were workers or squatters or Indians, in addition to 3 lawyers. The number of conflicts over land rose from 109 in 1971 to 8,966 in 1981. The share of the Amazonian region rose from a total of 30 conflicts in 1971 to 514 in 1981 (figures quoted in José de Souza Martins, 1984, pp. 90–91; and Reforma Agraria, (Bulletin of ABRA), 14,1, Jan.–Feb., 1984, p. 6). Since then violence seems to have increased: between 1980 and 1985 721 rural workers were killed, of whom 222 in 1985 alone, between January and May 1986 a further 80 died, including lawyers and pastoral agents. According to the Pastoral Land Commission, there were some 117 rural labour conflicts in 1984, involving more than 655,000 workers, and there were 483 land conflicts involving 332,000 peasants, including, it must be said, their families. (The Commission may be exaggerating: it probably counted an average of 8 or thereabouts per family): See Candido Gryzbowski: 'Lutando e construindo a democracia:

In Amazonia, small-scale organizations have grown up, often stimulated by a CEB or encouraged by advisers from CONTAG and the Comissão Pastoral da Terra. Only occasionally has a larger scale of action been organized, as in the north-western Brazilian state of Acre, where rubber tappers forced what they themselves called an *empate* (stalemate) by occupying rubber plantations and preventing them from being cleared for pasture land (Martins, 1984, p. 97). The subsequent murder of their leader, Chico Mendes, in 1989, has made Acre an international cause célèbre.

A second focus of agrarian conflict in recent years in Brazil has been the construction of vast hydro-electric dams which threaten to upset the ecology and flood the lands of thousands of farmers. In the organizations which have arisen to confront the authorities responsible the Church's Pastoral Land Commission has taken a very prominent part. These are new types of movement which do not operate directly on a class front – that is, they do not directly oppose workers to employers, tenants to landlords. But in confronting projects which embody the large-scale, capital-intensive character of Brazilian development, they question more directly the model of development which the state is pursuing. They also question the way in which the Brazilian state is accustomed to ride roughshod over the rights of the poor.

The movements against the dams represent quintessentially what a 'new' social movement should be: their social base is a heterogenous group – smallholders, sharecroppers, squatters, artisans, landless workers who find themselves under threat. They generate high-profile forms of solidarity in encampments and in protests, occasionally with a strong infusion of religious feeling. In the words of one sympathetic writer, they represent a 'redefinition of citizenship', a strengthening of community relations by a group which 'reappropriates their meaning'.[11] But as so often the appeal of *basismo* to the intellectuals is deflated in the mundane world of organization and negotiation at the base: for example, in one or two of these struggles the problem was solved and neutralized by the purchase for the claimants of a piece of land, by the government or by the Church.

This does not mean, though, that the intervention of pastoral and other external agents is without effects on popular organization and conscious-

---

os movimentos de trabalhadores rurais e camponeses no Brasil' ('Struggling and building democracy . . .') paper presented at the meeting of the Latin American Studies Association, Boston, October 1986.

11 Scherer-Warren, 1985. The idea that these movements contest not merely the dams themselves but an entire model of development is conveyed by the documents of the first National Meeting on Dams organized by the agricultural workers' union CONTAG in 1982.

ness. For example, the movement to resist the hydro-electric project of Itaparica on the São Francisco river in the north east of Brazil shows very well the crucial involvement of the Church since 1952, when the bishops and prelates of the vast São Francisco river basin published a document on the social problems of the region. In 1973 the Church's pastoral agents began to breathe new life into the agricultural union of smallholders and tenant farmers. In 1976 they alerted the population to the construction of the dam, while also raising the people's consciousness by calling on their religious sensibilities. Religious rituals – the recitation of the Lord's Prayer, the blessing by a priest – were incorporated into farmers' meetings, and a literature of solidarity found its way into the peasant movement.[12]

Out of the activities of the pastoral agents there emerged a Centre for the Defence of Human Rights, with its documentation centre, or 'Rural Workers' Centre' which became the spearhead of the struggle against the dam. It also acted as a channel for funds which could not properly be used by the Agricultural Workers' Union because of the restrictions on union finances. The centre was staffed by European professionals and funded by international NGOs including OXFAM. The role of the Church, formal and informal, enabled farmers to bypass or dynamize an immobile union leadership. The real, though limited, success of the campaign, which did force the electricity company to negotiate terms of compensation to some extent, created a prominent role for the advisers, so that by 1985, there was a gulf between them and the rank-and-file who still had no notion of how their demands would be met. Eventually, the World Bank, which was financing the scheme, was alerted through OXFAM pressure on its board of directors and more or less obliged the Brazilian government to borrow an additional sum for resettlement (see Chapter Five).

The themes of these conflicts are those of rights and equitable treatment rather than of class struggle. To be sure, they do constitute class

---

12 I believe that the world will be a better place
    When the suffering poor come to believe in the poor.

    When the poor come to create their common wellbeing
    Each feeling the other's needs as his own
    United in Jesus Christ
    Then we will all be as one.

    To believe only in the value of money is madness and vanity
    For Christ himself has said
    That the Way is the Truth.
    He who does not believe this
    Will never be free.

                    (My translation. The original is in rhyming verse: Pandolfi, 1986)

struggles in that they attempt to change power relations which in some sense do sustain the accumulation of capital by means of state power. But the struggles are often against state arbitrariness or over rival property claims and by no means always or even usually between employers and employees. The sugar workers of Pernambuco, or of the northern coast of Peru, the wage-earning proletarians of Chile's Central Valley, who were organized in trade unions, are probably exceptions. The more typical rural conflict over land rights takes multiple, decentralized and localized forms and rarely follows a hegemonic political organization. This is borne out by recent experience in Colombia where, as in Brazil, the most acute conflicts have been those over land in areas of frontier expansion where landlord capitalism has disrupted established peasant tenancies or indigenous peoples' institutional and tenurial integrity.[13]

Rural conflicts, then, often tend to turn on questions of citizenship, of fair dealing and of human rights. Indeed, even trade-union-style conflicts often turn on landowners' adherence to legal norms as much as on the level of wages. No wonder that the banner of land reform is once again being raised – despite all the practical difficulties it faces and its absence from the official political agenda – for its broad-based appeal is founded on an objection to violations of rights and personal autonomy in land tenure relations – in short, the landlordism which offends liberals and marxists alike.

For a period during the 1960s and early 1970s land reform was decried by the left because it neither undermined the capitalist mode of production – indeed it tends to strengthen it economically and politically – nor achieved much change in overall patterns of income and even land distribution; this was largely because it left the middle strata untouched and also because reforms rarely benefited the mass of independent smallholders among whom poverty was concentrated. But it is unlikely that those most directly involved – tenants, estate and plantation workers – have the same egalitarian or even anti-capitalist perspective. The discourse of rights, of fair dealing, carries more weight with them.[14]

---

13 Zamosc, 1986. It is interesting that Zamosc describes how a national organization born under the sponsorship of the state in the late 1960s (ANUC: the Association of Users of Government Services or *Asociación Nacional de Usuarios Campesinos*) should have disintegrated under the combined pressure of regional fragmentation and power struggles among a leadership detached from the dynamics of conflict at the grassroots.

14 For an account of the ways in which estate workers think about these issues, see Lehmann (1972). To be sure, the issues of equality and poverty remain, and the relevance of land reform in dealing with them remains in question, but that is a policy question (Lehmann, 1978a).

Alternatives to Land Reform

The days when the slogan of land reform could command broad support, from the centre right across to the extreme left are over. Peru and Chile have had their reforms: they more or less abolished great estates, but were disappointing because even after that the degree of landlessness and the inequality of landholding seemed to have changed little.[15] But in one sense the reforms did achieve their underlying aim, freeing the forces of production for a more dynamic capitalist development. Unfortunately, coming at a time of technological change, this reduced permanent employment and did not contribute much to improving the lot of the poorer independent smallholders who did not benefit directly from the redistribution of land.

An attempt to reproduce land redistribution in these two countries is politically out of the question. The social base of support has been removed with the radical shrinking of the rural proletariat permanently employed in the estates, and the social base of opposition has broadened to include the expanding numbers of medium-sized landowners who, even if a reform were to explicitly exclude them from expropriation,

15 In Chile there are effectively no estates left with more than 80 'standard' hectares – a standard hectare being a hectare of high-quality land, equivalent to more 'physical' hectares according to the quality. This is a substantial holding, but it was the 'floor' set by Frei's 1964 Agrarian Reform Law over which holdings could be expropriated on grounds of their size and irrespective of the efficiency of their land use.

According to Gomez and Echeñique (1988) neither the number of small holders owning less than 5 hectares nor their share of land changed much between 1965 and 1987, despite a land reform which expropriated 40 per cent of agricultural land between 1965 and 1973. The share of those owning 5–20 hectares, however, rose from 12.7 per cent to 31.0 per cent, while their number rose from 11.7 per cent of holdings to 21.0 per cent. During the same period there had been a remarkable intensification of land use in agriculture, and a substantial increase in (unpaid) family labour as well as in temporary labour, while permanent labour has declined, reflecting the increase in the middle strata. The daily wage paid in the early 1980s, when agricultural production was growing quite fast, was still at best under $5.00 and more usually $2.50 (Bengoa, 1983).

In Peru the evidence is more sketchy, but the pattern seems broadly similar, with persistent extreme poverty in the smallholding areas. In Peru there has not been a formal reversal of collective or co-operative holdings as in Chile; instead central control over the reform institutions more or less broke down after the expropriations were halted in 1975. Conflicts of varying intensity broke out between newly formed co-operatives and neighbouring peasant communities with conflicting claims to land, especially in the highlands; on the coast a remarkable degree of flexibility has allowed groups who initially had to form their co-operatives according to inflexible criteria to find a variety of solutions (Carter, 1984). The government which succeeded the military regime, headed by Belaúnde, explicitly turned its back on agrarian reform but did not directly undo what had been done – nor, for that matter, did it try to make the new structure work effectively.

would nevertheless feel threatened by the very idea of it, and would organize very aggressively to stop it. This is already happening in Brazil, where a comprehensive land reform has never been applied and probably never will be. In 1964 the new military regime, in deference to the climate of opinion represented by the Alliance for Progress, enacted a 'land statute' (*estatuto da terra*) which gave sweeping powers to the state to expropriate and redistribute land, to create co-operatives and so on, but these powers were never used except in very special circumstances. In 1985 the 'New Republic' replaced the military regime, and President Sarney committed himself to the cause of agrarian reform. However, when a new reform programme was proposed it caused a furore among landed interests and was gradually emasculated by the President's advisers; the final version which was sent to Congress was generally regarded as even more tepid than the military version of 1964. The reformists gradually resigned or were purged from the Ministry of Agriculture, and the measures of expropriation advanced at a snail's pace.

This represents a victory for a powerful lobby, ominously reinforced by a new organization called the União Democratica Ruralista (UDR: Ruralist Democratic Union) which during 1986 constituted itself not only as a pressure group lobbying against reform, but also, by all accounts, prepared itself and its members all over the country for armed confrontation with peasants. Although the most powerful landed interests are behind this organization, they are able to mobilize support on a wide social base: in the south of the country there has grown up in the past thirty years a broadly based class of capitalized family farmers who regard any sort of land reform as the first stage on the road to communism. Earlier events in Brazil (1964) and Chile (1973) show that this is a powerful and dangerous alliance. The times when the support or at least neutrality of a vast multi-class urban and rural coalition of workers, peasants, middle-class liberals and even business could be mobilized to facilitate land reform have passed. It is enough to ask what would happen if by the stroke of a pen, the President of Brazil really did expropriate all the farms which could be affected even under current moderate legislation. The answer is frightening to contemplate: the bureaucracy of INCRA (the Agrarian Reform and Colonization Institute) is a low-status employment in the federal government; its staff have no experience or training for a redistribution programme, let alone commitment to it, and it suffers from the same vices of time-serving and corruption which plague the bureaucracy generally. To expect them to manage the allocation of expropriated land, bringing it into production and financing that production, and to cope with the innumerable conflicts which would arise not only with landowners, but also among rival peasant claimants, is absurd.

But the underlying issue of citizenship remains, and it can be highlighted with reference to the system of land tenure. In Brazil, the legal position concerning land tenure has become so confused and the institutions charged with applying the law and protecting rights so ineffective, especially in Amazonia, that simply the proper application of the law of property – not of land reform – as it exists now would constitute a revolution. For the moment, the law of the jungle seems to prevail, in all senses of the expression.

In the place of land redistribution, numerous forms of rural co-operation are proposed, often as part of Integrated Rural Development Programmes – in the purchase of inputs and the marketing of outputs, in the provision of services. The literature on the subject oscillates between utopian hopes and crestfallen disappointments. Yet because of the flexibility of the concept – precisely because it is 'all things to all men' – it will continue to appear in proposals for an institutional framework for rural development. The obstacles to the proper functioning of co-operatives are not principally financial, nor do they reside in any innate resistance to co-operation, or innate suspiciousness, on the part of farmers. The principal obstacle is an absence of the rule of law, such that the poor lack the minimal requirements of citizenship, they lack the recourse against dishonesty and the means to enforce the elementary rules of commercial – and therefore co-operative – practice. Thereafter come other obstacles: lack of resources, lack of official support, inappropriate bureaucratic intervention and so on. Very often it has been the heavy-handed and clientelistic manner in which co-operatives have been established by the state which has contributed to these disappointments, rather than any inherent defects in the idea – and those very mechanisms are a symptom of the lack of citizenship against which the idea of land reform is, fundamentally, directed. Yet co-operatives, of all sorts, remain the most readily available mechanism for creating public goods among the poor and for getting state-financed resources other than land to the poor. Whether one views them as devices enabling individuals to achieve their own ends efficiently, or as institutions designed to reduce the social costs of individual actions (and raise their private costs), as providers of a certain category of public goods, or as the instruments for the redistribution of resources, co-operatives are a mechanism for collective self-management. They also bolster citizenship, in a variety of ways: they create rights and an awareness of rights among members; they create an incentive for collective decision-making which has an educative function. They also create a focus of conflict, and opportunities for unfair practice, but even that is an education in democracy. In short, insofar as they embody potentially a reversal of arbitrary forms of domination, co-operatives respond to the same needs as land reform, and they do so in a manner which is far less destabilizing politically.

But over and over again the same problems arise: being reliant for capital on government or other external agencies, co-operatives do not have the incentive to establish appropriate stimuli for their members and for employees; as a corollary, members only put up symbolic amounts from their own pockets, being poor and distrustful of the uses to which they will be put; decision making tends to end up in the hands of a dominant, self-perpetuating group of insiders.

Classic examples include the Chilean and Peruvian land reforms, which imposed to varying degrees a co-operative organization of production and of ownership on beneficiaries of the expropriation of great estates. These were heavily criticized by both right and left, for different reasons. In the event, in Peru more spontaneously than in Chile, cooperatives have given way to more individualist forms of production and tenure, and the allocation of land has evidently been subject to the combined effects of political power and market power. But in neither case has there been a restoration of the *ancien régime*. In retrospect, as originally envisaged by the reform legislation, co-operative forms have been transitional arrangements, and not entirely unsuccessful as such, even if the transition was neither as smooth nor as consensual as intended (Lehmann and Castillo, 1982; Gomez, 1983; Bengoa, 1983; Kay, 1982). It is difficult to see what other institutional form could have been adopted to secure the transfer of resources which occurred.

The Peruvian case, in which co-operatives were left to find their own way as the state gradually abandoned them to their own devices, produced a varied array of solutions in which joint management and ownership were applied to different factors of production depending on circumstances, preferences and so on (Carter, 1984). The crucial point is that co-operation, joint production, and joint ownership, have not disappeared: rather they have been adapted in accordance with local circumstances and interests.

Much more serious disorganization arose in attempts to institute worker-management in the industrial sector in both these countries (Espinoza and Zimbalist, 1978). In these cases, as in Yugoslavia, the claim that co-operatives in large-scale industry can in the long run combine economic efficiency with democratic self-management receives little support, while the solution of second-stage parcellization as observed in agriculture is not applicable. In small-scale production, on the other hand, co-operatives can be a sustainable alternative so long as they can count on reliable accounting and so long as external agents leave them alone. This is particularly relevant in the light of the vast number of small-scale, inefficient units of production found in the industrial informal sector, where transaction cost in the hiring of labour and account-keeping inhibit potential entrepreneurs from taking advantage of economies of scale. Examples include furniture making, automobile repairs and the manufacture of metallic goods such as filing cabinets, kitchen equipment, and so on.

There is still, then, a need for a realistic model of co-operatives, which narrows their scope and represents only a limited encroachment on members' autonomy. It draws on two distinctions: that which differentiates between production and services, and another which distinguishes between co-operatives as specific named organizations and co-operation as a widely diffused and extremely varied practice embedded in much economic life.

The experience of service co-operatives is far less disappointing than that of co-operatives based on joint ownership, joint decision-making, and joint production. Service co-operatives are in essence an application of economies of scale to the purchase of goods and the provision of services: members pay a small fee and have the right to buy from a co-operative, but they do not earn their living principally through the organization, so that the spheres of personal decision-making, co-operative management and work remain separate. This is how some of the very large organizations of European farmers, and indeed of the relatively prosperous farmers of southern Brazil, operate. Critics will say that they are almost indistinguishable from private concerns, which is true in some ways, except that they do not have shareholders and thus are not subject to the threat of takeover, or to the pressures of capital markets. All they must do is provide a service to their members as cheaply as possible over the long-run, so they must remain competitive or else lose their clientele and disappear.

This model need not be small-scale: it can equally be applied to the management of public goods, such as housing or medical care, irrigation, and even environmental management. The appropriate scale of any particular operation needs to be discovered and a mechanism needs to be developed which enables collective involvement by the membership to be compatible with a sustainable balance between their demands and the organization's capacity to deliver.

The other crucial distinction in this approach is that between co-operation as a practice in economic life, and co-operatives as formal organizations. It has been an understandable, though contradictory, feature of official co-operative ideologies in the developing world that they have evoked an arcadian image of co-operation in purportedly 'traditional' societies in order to justify officially sponsored co-operatives. Yet in practice official sponsorship of co-operatives has brought, or tried to bring, extremely 'untraditional' practices, such as bureaucracy and account keeping, disentangling primary relations from relations of production and exchange.

In the name of community and solidarity governments have instituted policies which, if they are to achieve their aims, require a differentiation of roles and a degree of impersonality as between people unaccustomed to deal with each other in that way. The managers are intended to be elected, or to be appointed by an elected board, not to be imposed by an elected *patrón*, and this can create role conflicts and ambiguities, when their obligations as members of a network of kin and friends conflict with those of, say, a manager or a foreman. These problems can be solved with suitable incentives and controls, but all too often the experience has been prematurely discredited and abandoned before the learning process has run its course, or before the state could take corrective measures. This is quite apart from political conflicts which have destabilized the experiments both on the ground and at the macro-level.

State-induced joint ownership and production co-operatives then, should be thought of as institutional forms peculiarly adapted to asset transfers lasting for a period during which the state encourages, protects and probably imposes them in order to ensure that the structural change is preserved, but after which they need to be left to adapt, to vary and no doubt, on occasion, to disintegrate. During this transition period the problem of profit distribution is usually purely theoretical, since if there are no profits they are reinvested. Unfortunately, subsidies tend to postpone the day of financial reckoning, and enable the problems of co-operation to be overlooked. The lack of incentives to co-operate is a consequence of government subsidy, and the reduction or withdrawal of that subsidy is necessary if people are to learn how to co-operate in a modern, impersonal context.[16]

Autonomous co-operation among small-scale urban operators and the marginalized poor, is extremely common and seems to face few obstacles so long as it does not involve too many people, and so long as it does not straddle too many spheres of their lives (Soto, 1986; Hardy, 1987). If too many spheres are brought under the scope of a single set of co-operative arrangements, then incompatibilities of interest between members begin to surface, especially when the officials or employees are also the only members. For example, an agricultural co-operative in which shares in profits are allocated per household and in which households finding themselves at varying stages of the development cycle cannot all provide the same amount of labour, will experience conflicts over comparability of effort contributed. In general, to ask members to pool *all* their productive assets (viz. land) and place it under a unified management is to offer too many hostages to fortune.

The way round this is to think of co-operation as a public good and of

16 On how learning is one of many ways in which Prisoner's dilemmas are overcome, see Wade, 1987.

co-operatives as providing a service – often consisting of the management of an asset or an activity, like land, or labour, or sewage, or water and so on. Thus the transport operators in Lima organize to do market research, to draw up rosters and timetables, rotas, and to arrange for servicing and repairs to stock; the women in Santiago's shanty-towns organize to do their shopping and child-minding; land invaders group together to hire an organizer; and, at the other extreme, thousands of southern Brazilian farmers join co-operatives to facilitate the purchase of inputs and the marketing of their product. In the small-scale examples we clearly have cases of co-operation from below in response to quite specific requirements of a tightly-knit group: in the large-scale ones we see the provision of a service at a low cost by an anonymous bureaucracy whose services are used because they are cheaper than the alternative. It can rely on a stable supply, or demand, from its membership and its officers are either not members, or else represent an insignificant proportion of the membership. In contrast to agricultural-production co-operatives, the freedom of the membership to go elsewhere for the service is a central feature, that is, there is little interlocking of market involvements, and, equally important, the management is impersonal and not reliant on the voluntary efforts of the membership. It is very different from a situation in which a person's dwelling, their land, and their labour are all lumped together in a pooled arrangement. As in Olson's reasoning, voluntary commitment of labour or money ceases to be reliable beyond a fairly small size because the return for the efforts of an individual are not easily discernible to him (Olson, 1965). But there is at least a range of appropriate sizes to particular purposes: we have learnt enough to know that agricultural production co-operatives should be small. We also know that co-operatives designed to take advantage of economies of scale for the purchase or sale of particular commodities need to be large, and that the voluntary and discrete character of their dealings with their members makes of the market the most effective sanction on a wayward management.

As a micro-economic device, co-operatives cannot be expected to counteract the dominant trends in income distribution which are dictated by international and nationwide patterns of growth and stagnation. But they remain obstinately on the agenda. As I have pointed out, they are an appropriate form for project-based redistributive programmes aiming to place assets within reach of the poor, even if they do not then last for ever. They are usually accompanied by a programme of education in politics, technology and many other areas, and they do multiply foci of political resistance to arbitrary bureaucratic power. But they are not a global solution and they may fall victim to the power of irresponsible petty oligarchies, aided by the apathy of beneficiaries. If they are agents of bureaucratization, this is not an unmixed curse, since that is one aspect of a necessary modernization process, and if it can be advanced 'from below', so much the better.

Urban social movements

Twenty years ago the terms used to describe the organized expression of urban popular forces were 'labour movement', (*movimiento obrero*: workers' movement) or 'union movement'. These referred to organized, institutionalized forces which had a place to go to present their demands, an identifiable rank-and-file whom they could mobilize in support of a negotiating process with identifiable interests and their representatives: the government and employers above all. Unions had to function within labour laws which imposed various limitations upon their freedom of action and tied them in varying degrees to government – more so in Brazil, less so in Chile, overwhelmingly so in Mexico, for example. But there were already numerous squatters' organizations, precursors of the 'new' social movements of today which did not fit into a ready-made legal framework: land invasions have a long and distinguished history in most of these countries' large cities, and over the years *de facto* procedures have evolved enabling people to establish themselves on land to which they had no legal title.[17] In Brazilian cities full legal title seems to be the exception rather than the rule, as much in cities as in the countryside, and not only in the working-class suburbs, with the consequent potential for conflict.

When social scientists and politicians speak of 'new' social movements they are referring to what they perceive as forms of mostly urban mobilization and conflict which do not fit into a ready-made institutional framework. In countries with a long history of corporatism they could have a far-reaching impact on political life if they become widespread and if they give rise to new institutional forms beyond the control of the state.

The theoretical argument in favour of these new forms has developed as social scientists have begun enquiring into the ways in which control and allocation of what economists would call public goods accentuates urban deprivation: provision of urban services, transport, infrastructure, health and education, available in principle to all urban dwellers, are denied to the poor because they cannot make their voice heard. These inequities do not arise merely because of market imperfections or bureaucratic errors.

17 Susan Eckstein gives an account of how illegal settlements gradually establish themselves; her study carried out in Mexico also shows the role of clientelistic politics in the process: see Eckstein (1977).

It has therefore been necessary to find a language and an analysis of inequity which fits into the dominant liberal democratic discourse, and that language is one of rights and citizenship.[18] The lack of citizenship of the poor in several major cities has been described as a 'social apartheid' for the geographical separation of income groups is such that they hardly come into contact with each other in the normal course of their lives, or even share the same services. The days when the *favelas* of Rio de Janeiro were visible from Copacabana beach have passed:[19] their inhabitants have been relocated forcibly to new projects situated far from their work places, in public housing projects which rapidly fall into decay because they are not the dwellers' own creation and no one feels responsible for them, and with inadequate facilities for economic life or even for leisure. Meanwhile, real estate in the fashionable south of Rio beyond Copacabana has prospered, as was the intention in eradicating the *favelas* (Portes, 1977; Perlman, 1976). In Santiago the eastern suburbs have become shop windows of conspicuous consumption, generously served by public transport and wide avenues: 30,000 low-income families (that is, about 150,000 people out of a population of some 4 million) have been shifted on government instructions from upper- to lower-income areas during Pinochet's municipal reforms (Espinoza et al., 1986). Brasilia, designed in the hope that members of different income strata would rub shoulders in a city aspiring to embody a more modern, but also more progressive Brazil, has become a middle-class enclave in which it is almost impossible to go about one's business without a private car,[20] while the lower-income groups have been exiled to satellite cities like Taguatinga thirty kilometres away. Pollution is becoming a case of international scandal in the industrial city of Cubatão, near the port of Santos in São Paulo, and known as 'the world's most polluted city' (Viola, 1987).

The diversity of urban grassroots initiatives in the concomitant struggles over what Castells would call 'urban meaning' can be illustrated by a comparison between the accounts we have of them in two radically different countries and contexts: those of Brazil and Chile. Apart from the well-known differences in the recent pattern of economic growth in the two countries, there are also noteworthy contrasts between the political cultures. In Chile ideological differences between parties are the

18 See, for example, the volume by various Brazilian social scientists: Covre, 1986. The book consists of series of reformulations of the problems of medical care, child care, education, housing, in terms of citizenship. Some will say that this is merely a recycling of corporate demands, but the formulation is nevertheless significant.

19 Copacabana beach itself is no longer as fashionable as it was either!

20 In fairness, it should be said that the dependence on the motor car was an original sin of the design of the city. Niemeyer's ideal of public housing fell victim to market forces not long after the 1964 coup – though even without the coup it was probably not sustainable.

dominant element defining their identity and matter as much after sixteen years of dictatorship as before. In Brazil, by contrast, politicians shift from one party to another with little hesitation, and if they can bring a following they are welcomed with open arms. Even during the military regime, the state apparatus was extensively used for the distribution of patronage; elections were gerrymandered in such a way that the opposition had no chance to win a majority in Congress – and Congress had little power in any case – but still these habits were not attenuated. In general, under civilian or military rule, Brazil is the much more corrupt and decentralized state. In neither country has authoritarianism brought about sea-changes in the pattern of party and ideological alignment, except insofar as the revolutionary left has been reduced to almost nothing.

Traditions of urban grassroots organization in Brazil and Chile

Today's urban social movements in Rio and São Paulo and Recife are the descendants of organizations which developed, in the heat of the political process in the 1950s or even earlier. In São Paulo, Neighbourhood Associations (Sociedades de Amigos do Bairro: literally 'Associations of Friends of the Neighbourhood') first appeared in middle-class neighbourhoods before the war, concerned to 'oversee' the city's already headlong growth. In the early 1950s they underwent a qualitative jump when Janio Quadros was elected successively Mayor of the city, Governor of the state and President of Brazil – a post from which he resigned after six months. Quadros's appeal was, crudely and broadly, to the masses, and after his election as Mayor in 1953 his electoral committees began to turn themselves into Neighbourhood Associations and then into an electoral machine (Singer and Brant, 1981, pp. 85–6). In Recife already in 1947 the Communist Party was helping to form similar organizations, apparently modelled on the São Paulo Neighbourhood Associations, and they provided a base for a left-wing coalition which won Mayoral elections in 1955 (Cézar, 1985). In Rio, the associations apparently originate with the efforts of Catholic Action (Bambirra, 1984), but their Federation of Neighbourhood Associations (FAMERJ), has been successfully co-opted by a variety of governments, under the military and afterwards during the Governorship of Leonel Brizola: in the latter years of the military regime the city's shanty-town (favela) movement was split into two – between the adherents of the Governor and the independents (Boschi, 1987). It was estimated in 1982 that there were 8,000 neighbourhood associations in Brazil as a whole, and that in Rio by about 1986 some 100,000 working- and middle-class people belonged to about 200 associations (Boschi, 1987). The consensus of accounts is that these associations were closely involved with political party activity and with the dispensation of patronage by state and local governments of all political persuasions. In Chile the analogous organizations were the Juntas de Vecinos (Neighbourhood Associations) but there is nothing in the literature to suggest that they fitted a system of political patronage Brazilian-style. Chilean politics under the electoral regime was not free of patronage, but local party structures were much stronger and less clientelistic and did not need to interfere in the Juntas de Vecinos in pursuit of votes. Only in the early 1970s, when class politics gave way to class war did the Juntas de Vecinos finally also become politicized along with everything else, from professional organizations to the local football team. In such a highly charged ideological atmosphere, though, it was hardly a clientelistic type of confrontation.

Just as there is a tendency to overestimate the 'newness' of social movements, so also there is a tendency to underestimate the economic potential and internal differentiation of working-class urban communities. Although social scientists have for years been trying to dispel the image of hopelessness so often associated with unplanned, uncontrolled, unofficial and above all unassisted housing – that is, shanty-towns – it still needs to be said that the areas where urban social movements arise encompass a vast range of standards and levels of fabric, services, income and investment. It is possible that in the volatile economic atmosphere of the 1980s the rate of improvement has slowed down, but there is no doubt that inhabitants of *favelas* or *poblaciones* are as concerned to improve both their dwellings and the services they depend upon as any other urban dweller, irrespective of their uncertain – or indeed non-existent – title to the land. The vast and intricate neighbourhood of Casa Amarela in Recife (population 185,000) (Castro, 1987, p. 12), built piecemeal on steep hillsides, with its narrow lanes and roads, its palm trees shading innumerable small self-built houses, most with a real if minimal defensible space, is built on land of disputed or uncertain ownership, but there is still constant activity in both private construction and also communal efforts to repair the infrastructure or petition the authorities to provide basic urban services.

Dynamism of this kind also brings differentiation; much of the housing is not occupied by its owners, but rented out; in Casa Amarela people even rent out a doorway if the occasion arises (much to the disgust of the local priest who preaches love and solidarity). The inequality among and within urban communities and settlements is likely to be substantial, yet it is rarely mentioned in studies of the popular movement – whereas it has become a central theme in peasant studies.

Inescapable political entanglements

The political dimension of urban popular organizations is deeply ambiguous. While it is essential if they are to make an impression on the authorities, it also provokes distrust among the grassroots who are constantly wary of political clientelism. The area of Casa Amarela, to which I have already referred, has an experience of popular organization from the times of the 'Recife Front' of 1947, and possesses a dense network of organizations – which themselves have since 1978 participated in a Federation of Associations of Casa Amarela.[21] The leaders of this federation are politically aware and well connected; they sense that their rank-and-file have a distaste for political involvement by the leaders of the popular movement, but they refuse to remain imprisoned in 'immediate' issues, wanting to advance in areas such as education and culture. If they do not take part in party politics, they say, then the movement will remain restricted in scope. The same can happen if they remain too close to the Church: the Church, they feel, wants the popular movement to go 'so far and no further'.

While these young and sophisticated leaders hope that the rank-and-file will not identify their style of politics with traditional clientelism, the suspicion is not so easily dispelled, especially in the light of the predominantly feminine character of popular movements in cities: accounts of women involved in new-style social movements (collective-consumption trade unionism) reveal a view of politics as a tainted business, and a concomitant reluctance to think of their own activities as 'political' at all. In contrast, women operating as political intermediaries on their own between politicians and their supporters, obtaining favours and mobilizing the vote at election time, held political activity in much higher esteem (Caldeira, 1987).

My observations in Recife in 1986 showed a high degree of expressed wariness among the rank-and-file towards political involvements, but the leadership of the *movimento popular* were irresistibly attracted to political involvement, however much care they took to keep the two roles separate. The rank-and-file suspect that they will inevitably gain nothing or even lose out by such involvements.[22] It is on account of such attitudes

21 The account which follows is drawn from observations made in Recife during July and August 1986.

22 In a telling quote, a São Paulo neighbourhood leader states quite clearly what she regards as 'real politics' and what she regards as 'politicking': 'We thought we might support one politician to strengthen our demands. But if he wants anything in return, then nothing doing. People don't want to offer anything in return; they just want what is good for the people. Of course, the Church is also political – but that is another type of politics, for it is seeking the best for the people' (Souto, 1983). However, another interview reported in the same article has a different view: 'I don't think the Church should be political; the next thing

that in Recife efforts to create a third-tier association grouping local organizations from the entire metropolitan area have failed;[23] rather than lay themselves open to manipulation or temptation, the various associations have preferred not to establish the organization on a formal basis. The fate of the FAMERJ federation of neighbourhood associations in Rio (mentioned above) lends credence to their apprehensions.

This distrust of politicians evidently opens up a space for priests and other Church-based personnel, for they have been able to play a dynamizing role without provoking fears of political manipulation. Indeed, some would say that the Church, formal and informal, in propagating reliance on popular autonomy, also limits the scope of democratization, by encouraging distrust of all large-scale organizations, of the state and of political parties. The Church has also played an educational role, as illustrated by the leaders of the popular movement in Casa Amarela, many of whom started their political life in the Youth Branch of Catholic Action. In Catholic youth organizations young people learn how to organize a meeting, how to speak in public and no doubt how to rig a meeting. Later in life, even when they go their separate ways, this early common experience provides a basis for joint actions and co-ordination among grassroots leaders.

Nevertheless an observer could be forgiven for asking whether their *caminhada* is not precisely that – a journey through the wilderness.[24] The problems of land tenure, of landslides – in Casa Amarela which, like so many semi-legal settlements in Brazilian cities, is built on the hills (*morros*)[25] overlooking the town – and of flooding go on and on. The vision of the people creating their own public goods – the self-management of their communities – may be appealing, but the state is the only institution capable of protecting them against landslides and flooding.

Despite so much hostility towards formal politics, closer inspection shows that the movements tend frequently to rely on the state or other

---

you know, the priest talks about those things and is put in jail ... the sermons are only about the cost of living ... and I find it disrespectful of the priest to smoke in Church [when meetings are held there]'.

23 Once representatives of a large number of organizations from all over a vast urban area gather together and have to elect officers, party politics will inevitably play a central role in putting together 'planks' and 'tickets'. How else, after all, could it be done?

24 Readers will recall that the word *caminhada* is drawn from Biblical sources and used by the informal Church to describe the wandering/via crucis/pilgrimage of the Brazilian *povo* (people).

25 The word *morro* has come by metonymy to refer to the working-class areas of a city. Thus in Rio at a *scola de samba*, one is told that the latest version of samba – *pagode* – came down from the *morro*. This may be a fiction, but it illustrates the usage and the idea that the poor live in the places most susceptible to landslides.

outside sources of material support, and that even the most apparently autonomist are up to their eyeballs in local pressure-group politics – confirming some of the suspicions voiced by Ruth Cardoso and discussed in chapter 2. A study carried out in Cidade Alemar on the southern periphery of São Paulo describes an initially successful neighbourhood association which achieved some success using the tried and tested patronage system, but falling into decay as it was taken over by politicians and eventually by a military policeman (presumably acting in his personal capacity). When CEBs were formed grassroots activity was revitalized (Souto, 1983), but the contrast between the 'old' and the 'new' style of local politics is less sharp than expected: the central activity remains the extraction of resources from the authorities, and in the place of political intermediaries the priest is usually involved: instead of merely sending in a petition or a small well-connected delegation, the CEBs go personally in groups and try to meet the Mayor or another official. It is not clear that the changed style of exercising pressure yields better results than the old style.

Another excellent, though unintended, example of these entanglements is given by an account of the Nurseries' Movement in São Paulo (Gohn, 1985). Based on Church-sponsored women's organizations (Clubes de Maes: literally 'Mothers' Clubs') in working-class neighbourhoods, in 1979 the movement extracted a commitment from the mayor to set up 830 nurseries – a figure later reduced to 300; of those 72 were built, and by 1981, just 32 were in operation. In the process, most of the movement's energies were consumed in endless disputes with the mayor, who wanted to use the nursery jobs as political patronage, while the movement's leaders took the view that the jobs should go to women who had played a part in the movement and who were drawn from the communities which would be using the nurseries. Ironically – in accordance with Ruth Cardoso's predictions – the movement had in its turn penetrated the state apparatus for it was helped by professionals on the municipal staff who opposed the mayor's party.

Not that all movements are sucked in to clientelistic politics. For example, during the 41-day São Paulo metalworkers' strike of 1980 (Vink, 1985), a network of local groups, especially CEBs, gathered funds for the strikers, and a bishop acted as treasurer of a technically illegal strike fund. The strike stimulated an expanding role for women, and growing solidarity and interaction among neighbours. From the network of support groups in the community small organizations grew up which eventually led to the formation of what could best be described as a 'shopping collective'.[26] In the process people's awareness of social issues

26 This sequence of events is drawn from a small study of a neighbourhood of some 6,000 persons (Reboredo, 1983). By 'shopping collective' I refer to a group of people pooling their

like labour laws and health care had increased; but the social movement, like the strike, lasted only for a limited time. The strike itself, however, had been lost.

Other movements were the Movement against the Cost of Living based mostly in São Paulo, and the 1983 nationwide campaign for direct elections to the Presidency ('Diretas ja!'). The former enjoyed the support both of the Archbishop and of various left-wing parties and was more a protest than a movement with concrete goals – remembered in *basista* circles for its expressive rather than instrumental qualities. The campaign for direct elections had one big and simple goal, namely the election of the first civilian President since 1964 by universal suffrage – rather than by the gerrymandered Electoral College.[27] It did not achieve its objective, but it certainly mobilized hundreds of thousands of people, especially in the cities, from the middle classes as much as from among the poor. Both these movements tried to achieve their goals without a party organization and their failure illustrates the difficulty of translating the dynamics of social movements – founded on personal involvement and social proximity – into such large-scale campaigns. According to Boschi (1987) although such political campaigns 'tended to demobilize the associations as vehicles for neighbourhood interests', the associations played an important role in stimulating political participation.

Just as the rural movements were founded on a common subjective awareness of truncated citizenship, so too we observe that the attempt to press the state to fulfil its basic legal and normative functions figures prominently in these urban movements. Side by side with efforts to extract resources the apparatus is pressed to guarantee personal security, to protect people from fraud, to enforce its own rules for public transport prices, or to protect property. To those who would say the state by its very nature only protects the property of the rich and powerful, the popular movements respond with constant pressure for it to protect their property rights too. For example, there are constant complaints against illegal or unofficial sales of invalid titles to people desperate for a plot to

---

money in order to purchase their necessities more cheaply than they would individually. Price differentials between supermarkets and corner shops in working-class areas make this perfectly feasible.

27 The Electoral College was designed by the military to be a docile body composed of notables with a strong rural bias. With the disintegration of the military regime, due to internal divisions, even a majority of the official party's Congressmen defected to an ever-more-dilute opposition during 1984 with a result which suited the political élite perfectly: the victory of an opposition candidate of impeccable conservative credentials, Tancredo Neves. In this way the transition received a degree of legitimacy without too much participation. There is little doubt that the military would not have tolerated direct elections, although an amendment to that effect did in the end almost pass Congress – with Tancredo's support (Skidmore, 1988).

build their house.[28] Some success has on occasion been achieved by academic lawyers, with Church support, who have forced speculators to regularize the titles.[29]

Another illustration of the potential efficacy of popular movements when focused on this type of superficially non-ideological issue is the Association of Public Transport Users in the industrial city of São André next to São Paulo. This association, consisting of representatives of 33 different organizations including CEBs and Neighbourhood Associations, monitored the fairness of pricing by conducting checks on the number of passengers per kilometre on which fares were based. Another account of a similar movement in the southern zone of São Paulo describes how in 1974 a movement initiated by a meeting of some 2,000 persons carried out detailed checks on the bus service to show that the operators were not fulfilling the requirements of their contracts with the Metropolitan Transport Commission. The movement lasted two years but had mixed results (Singer and Brant, 1981).

The drama of Brazil is her state apparatus. All efforts to bring to it the habits of a modern bureaucracy have so far failed miserably. The practices of patronage, nominal employment, bribery, and the traffic in influence are very deeply entrenched. While the big state enterprises may have developed a structure and culture appropriate to major international industrial and commercial corporations, the same modernization has not occurred in the core state apparatus. Popular movements – especially those seeking to extract resources, or to manage community life in the place of this ineffective state – are caught between their followers' needs – obviously a motive to join the game – and the distrust of 'politics' which is felt by those same followers.

In the next section we move to another country, where politics is more a matter of ideology, and where the habits of grassroots organization form part of the heritage of a relatively independent working class. Although the Chilean state has exercised a degree of control over the trade unions through the Labour Code ever since the 1920s, this control was never until 1973 anything like as close as that exercised in Brazil.

---

28 This practice is called *loteamentos clandestinos* – 'clandestine parcellizations'. In one case people bought land believing that they were receiving a title of ownership whereas all they got was a two-year lease. At the end of two years they might well have faced violent expulsion by the police had they not solved the problem. Singer and Brant (1981).

29 Singer and Brant (1981). The chapter goes on to describe another occasion when a similar protest was met by two Neighbourhood Association Presidents and a self-styled 'representative' of the State Governor who tried to persuade the people concerned to pay a certain sum to a lawyer who would then use his good offices with the state government; in addition it was insinuated that the lawyers brought by the Pastoral Commission to help them might in fact be agents of the speculators.

Chile is also a country which has a very recent memory of ill-fated but varied and generous experiments in communal, industrial and agricultural self-management.[30] We know little of how this experience has survived in the popular memory, but in all the ideological reappraisal there has been on the Chilean left, the idea of self-management has fared better than, say, those of proletarian dictatorship or people's power.

Communal self-management as a refuge against poverty and the suppression of citizenship

The Chilean military regime has in several crucial respects taken the opposed path to its Brazilian counterpart. Brazil under the military saw expanded expenditure, employment and coverage in education, social security and public health; the standard of provision may be appalling, but the country's tradition of corporatism, with a patrimonial state to match and all the opportunities for clientelism which went with it were preserved. Pinochet's government, in contrast, has dismantled the country's welfare state and left its functions to the private sector (Yotopoulos, 1989; Aedo-Richmond and Noguera, 1989; Scheetz, 1987). The poor have been left almost without any publicly funded health care; and the two recessions through which the country has passed since 1973, combined with the regressive trends in income distribution, have led to extremely high levels of unemployment and poverty. Although by the late 1980s the economy seemed set on a pattern of fairly stable growth, and although the indicators of living standards among the poor are not as bad as those for many other countries in the region, the deterioration has been uniquely sudden and has brought in its wake an extraordinary rearrangement of the social structure: a large amount of downward mobility as vast numbers of public-sector employees and professional people lost their jobs and their foothold in society. One consequence has been the growth of insecure self-employment for negligible profit. There has been an inversion of expectations such as has not (yet) occurred in Brazil, and this can be seen in another trend, namely the readiness of a

30 The Frei government had stimulated neighbourhood associations as well as Centros de Madres and similar apolitical activities, under the aegis of its urban promotional agency Promoción Popular. During the Unidad Popular period more combative and autonomous organizations developed, and were eventually repressed: *Juntas de Abastecimiento y Precios* (price and Supply Boards); *cordones industriales* or workers' councils in industrial areas, attempting to manage industrial production at the base in occupied factories; self-governing squatter settlements; and land seizures in town and country which were not new but did accelerate. These experiences were beset by all sorts of problems – commandism, vanguardism, even surrealism. For contrasting accounts and evaluations, see Espinosa and Zimbalist (1978) and Castells (1983). For an overview see Lehmann (1978b).

very large number of people to engage in what some call the 'popular' or 'solidary' economy' and others, less hopefully, might call 'the economy of institutionalized marginality', concentrated in the capital city.[31]

About one half of the population of Santiago have been classed as *pobladores*, that is people living in *poblaciones*, neighbourhoods dominated by the urban poor.[32] Despite this projection of a condition of poverty, the *poblaciones* are extremely heterogeneous; they are, after all, half the city's population and include public-housing apartment blocks, self-built dwellings of varying quality, and also respectable middle-class dwellings – many self-built and some, no doubt, more respectable in appearance than reality.

The rate of unemployment among the *pobladores* surveyed in 1985 was 26.1 per cent. In addition 12.1 per cent of those of working age were employed by the government's 'make-work' programmes which pay less than the minimum wage and are in effect a way of making people work humiliatingly for a minimal 'unemployment pay'. It is among this vast population that grassroots movements have proliferated in recent years.

The Chilean urban population has an intense recent history of organized grassroots action related to land tenure and housing, especially land invasions, and the organization of the communities living on invaded land. This history dates from before 1964, but during the government of Frei, invasions became a regular, almost institutionalized occurrence, to which the state had developed a patterned response. Occasionally this was repressive; but it also involved the provision of resources in a way which required the community to be organized. No doubt this was designed to produce a political payoff, but it did stimulate popular organization. The figure of some 20,000 community centres created in the country suggests more than mere paternalistic front organizations (Aylwin et al., 1986, p. 270). And the pursuit of autonomy by grassroots leaders sometimes went so far that communities behaved like independent republics – with very mixed results.[33]

31 The self-employed rose, roughly, from 18.8 per cent to 25.4 per cent between 1970 and 1980, an increase accounted for almost entirely by the urban sector (Martinez and Tironi, 1985). Open unemployment rose from 5.9 per cent in 1970 to 19.6 per cent in 1982, falling thereafter to 13.8 per cent in 1985. If workfare programmes, which pay less than the minimum wage, are included the 1982 figure would be 26.1 per cent and the 1985 figure 21.7 per cent. It should be added, however, that hidden unemployment declined as a share of total (i.e. open plus hidden) unemployment during the period (Jadresic, 1986).

32 The data to follow are from a sample survey of 920 households in 28 settlements carried out by the Sur Research Group in 1985 in Santiago (Tironi, 1987). Tironi writes of an estimate of 2.4 million; another source speaks of 'one third' of the Santiago population, or roughly 1.4 million, living in '*poblaciones*, shanty towns and precarious housing' (Valdés, 1986).

33 See the disillusioned account of the Campamento Nueva La Habana, notorious in Santiago during the Allende years as a standard-bearer of the revolutionary cause among the *pobladores*, in Castells (1983).

This tradition ensured that the Church found fertile ground when after 1973 it became involved first of all in the distribution of emergency help to people in desperate need, and later in the organization of a myriad of self-help organizations in the *poblaciones*. Compared with the Brazilian church certain differences stand out: firstly the Archbishop of Santiago and his appointees exercise closer control than in Brazil. Secondly, it does not seem to be accompanied by the same prophetic spirit as is the case in Brazil; there is not the invocation of the People of God as bearers of the Kingdom, or of the Bible as a source of moral tales. There is not such a pervasive informal Church: the pastoral agencies are under close episcopal supervision. And although the Archbishop of Santiago has created a very active unit for the defence of human rights, there is no counterpart to the more multi-active and decentralized Brazilian network of human rights centres.

In short, the central role played by the Church in the social organization of the *poblaciones* is probably more closely linked to its role as an institution above reproach – the only one in Chilean society – than to its prophetic role; more to its work in providing material relief of poverty than to its evangelical work announcing the place of the poor in the Kingdom of God.

A long-term study devoted specifically to *organizaciones de sobrevivencia* – literally 'survival organizations' – in Greater Santiago[34] found 1,383 organizations, with some 50,000 active members and some 200,000 beneficiaries – amounting to about 8 per cent of the total number of *pobladores*.[35] These are overwhelmingly self-management organizations; at most 175 out of the 1,383 organizations reported could be described as pressure groups let alone as representative bargaining agents. Since the rank-and-file are unemployed and since the state offers them nothing, there is little place for these activities.

Initially the Church's intervention in the *poblaciones* had what is called a markedly *asistencialista* character: that is to say, it was organized like a charity and not by the beneficiaries themselves. But gradually this

34 The study deserves special mention because it is the only one I have come across which both attempts to be complete and which also contains a systematic data analysis. I am extremely grateful to its author, Clarisa Hardy (1987 ms), for making it available in manuscript form.
35 The exact figures are: 1,383 organizations with 46,759 active members and 187,237 beneficiaries. The figure for beneficiaries is not a simple estimate based on the number of family members who may benefit from the membership of one person. In organizations devoted to production and sale of goods only those directly employed are counted; in organizations providing a service to their members – such as joint purchasing or other forms of co-operative consumption – the number of direct beneficiaries would be counted. So the estimate is a reasonable one. The only reason it might overstate the numbers is if many people are members of several organizations, in which case there would be double counting. The total number of *pobladores* – 2.4 million – is drawn from Tironi (1987).

changed and the Church began to encourage people to engage in more self-help activities, ranging from consumer co-operatives to workshops for making and selling embroidery, sewing and knitting, toy manufacture and so on. It will quickly be seen that these are activities likely to attract women: only 1 per cent of the people in these 'solidary workshops' are men. There were 364 of these workshops at the time of the survey (1986) and they had almost 6,500 members, that is about 18 for each workshop. Many more people (28,400, or 4,700 families) were involved in consumer co-operatives, which could be regarded as the simplest form of such organizations, purchasing on behalf of 20 families each on average. Another 4,000 families had organized common kitchens, though still, to preserve respectability, taking the prepared food home to eat. Another mechanism found to cope with the severe deprivation which has struck the *poblaciones* is growing one's own vegetables – and some 1,700 persons were working in small communal or family plots, of whom, again, over 1,000 were women.

The men, for their part, are in the majority only in a tiny number of the organizations involved in production; these tend to be very small businesses established for the unemployed with the sponsorship of their unions or former unions, earning a full-time wage and employing skilled labour. This type of organization is clearly not likely to prosper in times of hardship, and they are extremely few in number. Women, adding to their domestic burden – which men tend to resist, even when unemployed – prefer the part-time and flexible character of employment offered by most of the organizations; Hardy calculates that they earn more per hour than they would working for the government's workfare programmes.

The women are also establishing new models of organization. In place of the centralized, and restricted leadership characteristic of unions and pressure groups, they have to spread the leadership or managerial roles around more people, because of the multiplicity of tasks and also because of the other demands on their time. They meet very frequently[36] and in the process they learn to manage, to speak in public, in short to be grassroots leaders.

The story has charm, but the lessons from it are – as usual – not all that clear. The international NGO community subsidizes these activities very generously: Hardy states that some 90 per cent of the organizations she covered receive some sort of help from abroad: from OXFAM, Christian Aid, the Interamerican Foundation, various semi-statal European charities, from Caritas and so on. They fit the ideological and even the budgetary requirements of these agencies very well: they are cheap, they

---

36 Out of 1,279 organizations, 39.2 per cent held weekly, 12.9 per cent fortnightly and 23.8 per cent monthly meetings. Hardy op. cit. chapter 5.

are prepared to put up with short-term programmes requiring annual or biennial reapplications, and they embody the philosophy of an 'alternative' development. They do not use high technology, they seek out self-sufficiency, and their members are perceived as constituting the real *base*, the authentic poor, the salt of the earth. For the sociologist Manuel Barrera this is indeed institutionalized marginality, though he did not use that precise term: for him the mass of Chile's poor are not needed by international – or indeed domestic – capitalism, so they are given alms with which they can build up a shop-window of the ideological mirages which embody capitalism's guilt. And as for Pinochet, he does not complain at all: have not the international agencies taken over his responsibility for the poor, and relieved him of the political pressure to change his policies? It is a most bizarre convergence of interests.[37]

Although it seems to reach a large number of people, the 'solidary economy' as one, rather idealistic, author has called it (Razeto, 1985) probably contains a lot of ephemeral organizations, for in Hardy's study the vast majority were no more than two or three years old. Their numbers seem to have grown rapidly in response to the recession of 1984 which followed several months of street demonstrations during which hopes for the regime's collapse ran high; equivalent organizations might have existed before but disappeared during the brief boom of the early 1980s. The predominant role of women in it may, unfortunately, be an indication that it will continue to be marginal; if economic circumstances improve, the women and the men will certainly seek – and may find – more employment and income in conventional enterprises rather than attempt to expand their own co-operative organizations. At present, according to one study (Campero, 1987) men in the *poblaciones* prefer to eke out a living in even the most unprofitable self-employment. Recourse to the community kitchens, is regarded as particularly humiliating. In Campero's account, the 'solidary' economy is seen among the *pobladores* as the preserve of the Church, isolated from a broader world in which the desire, or dream, of social integration dominates – but perhaps his study spoke to the men while Hardy's spoke to the women, thus explaining divergent findings.

In addition to these sceptical conclusions, Campero is highly critical of the political parties, whose intervention he regards as insensitive and 'vanguardist': their local leaders (*dirigentes*) are parachuted in with ready-made programmes and do not take the time or trouble to build up a base from which a home-grown leadership can emerge. In times of generalized political activation – as in 1983 and 1984 – they can command a following, because the base needs co-ordination, or because there is a fleeting prospect of a change of regime, in which parties are likely to play

37 Conversation with Manuel Barrera, Easter 1987.

a role, but when the tide has turned they are left alone with only a small band of faithful. In the words of Teresa Valdés (1986), once the protests acquire a national, political profile, their leadership passes into the hands of the parties and 'the *pobladores* feel that they have nothing more to say'.

If political clientelism is the bane of popular movements in Brazil, then party divisions play the same role in Chile. They have no patronage to offer, being excluded from power, and yet they succeed in provoking divisions and even decay in grassroots movements. The sectarian element in Chilean political culture is something to which political scientists would do well to turn their minds. The same political science which makes a problem of Peronism's emotionalism has found Chilean politics superficially easy, because, as mentioned, every party and faction has an elaborate doctrine or line which seems perfectly coherent in European eyes. But Chile too presents problems: in particular, the extraordinary well-developed ideological sensitivity of political actors and organizations, which in the past made coalitions and alliances so unmanageable, and the high proportion of political activists or registered party members which created an appearance of political participation, but perhaps hid a gulf between the activists and their followers. It remains to be seen whether the very broad coalition of opposition parties formed to fight the 1990 elections holds together afterwards.

The parties of the left tried to ride on the back of the wave of protests in the period May 1983 to October 1984, and for a time it seemed that these largely unco-ordinated upsurges could lead to the overthrow of the government: in mid-1983, in one of the biggest such actions ever seen in Chile, 8,000 families seized land to build their houses on, and could not be dislodged. There were vast strikes involving small business and the middle classes. But in the end Pinochet's patience ran out and he sacked his conciliatory Minister of the Interior.[38] The legacy of the protests has been an atmosphere of profound disaffection among young people in the *poblaciones* – fertile ground for the planting of provocateurs, leading to periodic violence and fear among the population, either of communism or of further repression, or both. Leaders who emerge from grassroots organizations are tempted by the status and prestige of becoming a party leader. Indeed, there may well be a division between the more collective, more female and more shared leadership described by Clarisa Hardy in the organizations concerned with collective production and consumption, and the more 'verticalist', appointive, masculine leadership of the

[38] A state of siege was imposed in November 1985 and during the year from that date 34,220 people were arrested on political grounds; the working-class neighbourhoods were the object of 77 *operativos* – that is raids by the military or the police with house-to-house searches and arbitrary arrests. These operations are intended above all to frighten. Figures from the Chilean Human Rights Commission, quoted in Teresa Valdés (1986).

political parties now poised, in 1989–90, to take over the government.

Political parties are necessary, and the people desire change – but do they think that political parties can achieve change? When asked about their preferred government to replace the military, 20 per cent of a sample of *pobladores* refused to answer the question; only 5.9 per cent chose a left-wing coalition, and only a further 11 per cent chose any other sort of coalition. 53 per cent wanted a one-party government, and of those 38.7 per cent chose the Christian Democrats and 14.4 per cent the conservative right. 6.7 per cent chose another military government (Tironi, 1987). The rejection of the left was as much a rejection of ideological bickering and vanguardism as of left-wing ideas. (The Presidential period of Frei was remembered in positive terms – helped along by a question which, by mentioning his name, probably biased the answers.) Once again, the theoretical desire for change is in conflict with a practical distrust of divisive party politics; coalitions, in Chile, are associated with division, not unity, presumably because of the Unidad Popular experience.

The informal university[39]

It is not only in the shanty-towns that co-operation has been a mechanism of survival and of preserving self-respect. The social science establishment itself has shifted away from renowned but decaying universities to a congeries of small independent centres run on co-operative lines and financed by a combination of contract work and research grants – mostly from the Canada, the USA and Europe. What started as a 'coping' response to repression and expulsion from official universities, as well as to the budgetary famine affecting most of them, has now established itself, and will continue to exist and indeed flourish whatever the future political conditions.

These organizations constitute the intellectuals' version of autonomous self-management, and often work in collaboration with the social movements on the ground. The earliest initiatives date from Perón's Argentina in the 1950s, when independent social science was removed from the university. After Perón's overthrow in 1955 the sociologist Gino Germani returned to the university and formed an entire generation at the Institute of Sociology – until 1966, when the university was again purged by a military government. This generation then left the university and joined the earliest independent social science institutions in Latin America, of which the most prominent was the Centre for Social Research, also run by Germani, and founded in 1964 within the di Tella Institute. This was the most influential social science research centre in the region in the

39 The ideas in this section have been strongly influenced by Fernandes (1986).

mid-1960s, funded by the di Tella fortune and the Ford Foundation, among others.[40] Other early ventures were CEBRAP (Centro Brasileiro de Análise e Planejamento – Brazilian Centre for Analisis and Planning) in São Paulo, established with Ford Foundation help in the wake of large-scale dismissals from Brazilian universities after 1968; and the Instituto de Estudios Peruanos in Lima.

In the 1970s these centres proliferated. A guide published in Chile in 1986 lists 40 institutions, employing 543 professional research staff, of whom 73 have a Ph.D., 31 are Ph.D. candidates and 61 have a Masters, almost all from European and North American universities (Lladser, 1986). In Argentina there are fewer: 19, with over 200 members (Vacchieri and Gonzalez Bombal, 1986). I have found no equivalent guide in other countries, but in Peru there are several well-established centres apart from the IEP, especially DESCO which has a staff of over 100. In Chile and Peru they continue to be heavily dependent on external funding; in Brazil CEBRAP and later others began to receive funding and contracts from the government, even under the military governments which encouraged the development of domestic research capacity.[41] In Argentina several centres had close relations with the civilian government of Alfonsín.

For political and financial reasons the typical career pattern of the social scientist – moving between a secure base in academia and advisory roles in government – is no longer available. In its place there has arisen a network of independent and competing co-operatives – a destiny which would have been almost unimaginable twenty years ago. Almost without realizing it, they have built up an alternative – albeit one which is heavily dependent on the charity and to some extent the priorities of the international community who subsidize or contract their work. This success has occurred in unfavourable economic circumstances, but also in often very unfavourable political circumstances: bombs have been planted, threats have been made, people have been jailed, yet the show goes on.

The dependence on foreign financial support has meant that they are under pressure to do applied work, to do 'action-research', to plan, to evaluate the myriad self-help projects which their sponsors are also financing. In Santiago a group of agrarian researchers monitors development aid from international NGOs to Chilean farmers. In Brazil the idea of intellectuals and professionals placing their skills at the service of the

40 Vacchieri and Gonzalez Bombal, 1986. I am grateful to the authors for allowing me to see their unpublished work.
41 The decentralized character of the Brazilian state helped, for even while CEBRAP was being branded as 'communist' by some sections of the government, other branches were awarding them contracts.

movimento popular has now taken root: it 'benefits', for example, from the lack of jobs for qualified doctors in the country's cities. In Recife they manage health education programmes, including ante-natal classes and simple laboratory testing, as well as providing legal support, and taking educational video to the people. These activities have led one observer to coin the new term 'Grassroots Support Organizations' (GSOs) to describe their role.[42]

They are also beginning to establish a teaching role: in Santiago two institutes are running Masters programmes, and in Buenos Aires the government subsidizes apprentice researchers. In Recife the institutions of 'advice and support to the popular movement' give courses for professional people on subjects such as occupational health – and they are well attended by professionals and funded by government. This role may well develop in the future because the official universities are in a deplorable condition. In the Humanities and Social Science Faculties teaching staff receive a symbolic salary (only in Brazil do they earn enough to live on) and the material conditions for learning are terrible. Students with intellectual ambitions gravitate towards these institutes – where the pay is low by international standards but respectable by local ones.[43] It is ironic and instructive that the vitality of the region's social science community should have been maintained and reinforced by this new 'informal sector' of intellectual life. And, as we shall see in the final chapter, the GSOs also could play an important role as agents of both democratization and development in the future.

Conclusion: The emergence of *basismo*

Two somewhat contradictory attitudes have recurred in this account: the disenchantment with, or despair in, the capacity of the state to deliver real resources, even irrespective of financial constraints, and the demand for a bundle of rights encompassed by that relatively new term in Latin American political discourse – citizenship. Yet they need not be contradictory attitudes if thought of in the context of the theme of communal self-management. The previous generation of reformers and revolutionaries, few of whom held the Soviet model in unqualified admiration, had paid some attention to the idea of workers' management. Already then it was a point of contact between reformers and revolutionaries, but whereas for some it could not achieve its aims without a prior overthrow of capitalist power, for others it was a means of averting an apocalyptic confrontation. By the 1980s, under the influence of the informal Church,

---

42 Thomas Carroll (private communication).
43 It is also not very differentiated, ranging from $300 to $500 a month.

of post-marxism and of Liberation Theology, the idea of self-management has been applied with greater emphasis outside the factory gates in pursuit of a broader and more deeply rooted project of democratization of institutions and social relationships. Hence the re-placement of 'worker-management' by 'communal self-management'.

The movements will not fade away: they may become less prominent politically, but the practice of organizing and pressuring will be com-municated to other people and other issues. They cannot be easily repressed because they have no central 'brain'. Gradually they will become more sophisticated, more complex and better informed; they already have their documentation centres and their expert advisers in the informal university.

It is to this myriad of organized activities, to the *comunidades de base*, and to the ideological biases which accompany them, that I refer when I speak of *basismo*. The term is often used pejoratively; indeed it came to prominence by analogy with *obrerismo*, or 'workerism', the error conde-mned by official marxism as unthinking obeisance to the workers themselves, as opposed to the 'objective interests' of the working class.

Rather than an unquestioning obeisance to the grassroots, to the poor and all their works, I prefer to think of *basismo* as a bias, a tendency, not a complete – or even completable – system in itself. As a bias it is surely a necessary corrective to the versions of radical ideology associated with *dependencia*, or with what one Brazilian wag labelled *machismo–leninismo*. It is an attempt to refashion socialist thinking by 'listening to the poor' just as Liberation Theology would refashion theology by reading the scriptures with the poor. This is not obeisance, nor is it anti-intellectualism: rather it is a call to rethink the role of the intellectual. As praxis, just as in theory, it is a call to openness, refusing the closedness of both large-scale centralized political organization and large-scale systems of teleological thinking.

The accusation of irrational obeisance nevertheless is valuable as a warning to the consumer, to keep an eye open for hints of bad faith. For since the voice of the poor is the 'voice of the voiceless' many are those who will proclaim that they have privileged access to that voice, that they have grasped the truth by means of an intuition which is simply not available to others: in short might this not be a road to another form of privileged wisdom, of intellectual arrogance? To solve this dilemma we must cease to reify 'the poor' and instead think analytically and in a more universalistic fashion of the processes of acquisition of voice, so that the interpretation of the voice of the voiceless is open to rational debate, to 'truth criteria'. We must then ask ourselves how that process leads to a questioning of what we take for granted in our daily social and political life. Voicelessness represents a dimension of social experience which has failed to penetrate the erudite imagination, yet which is essential to the development of that imagination. In short, the application of erudition to an interpretation of the voiceless as they begin to speak is not a question of pity or emotion, but of self-criticism.

In this respect I would like to conclude by returning to two issues which transcend the parochial world of slums and peasant communities, to strike close to the daily life of the erudite imagination anywhere in the world. The first is that of gender, the second that of international charity.

One of the most constant themes emerging in *basista* literature, both ethnographic and hortatory, is the indissolubility of the women's movement and the popular movement. The failure of the women's movement 'as such' (that is, the exclusive and named cause of women's liberation) to penetrate among the poor is now amply documented;[44] so also is the preponderance of female participation in popular organizations, as we have seen in Santiago, and as is described for Lima as well (Tovar, 1986). In Rio de Janeiro too, among predominantly middle-class associations, women headed almost one-quarter in 1981 (Boschi, 1987). This pattern is important because it is allied to a pattern of resistance to clientelism, and also to the adoption of organizational models in which the responsibilities of leadership tend to be managerial rather than symbolic–representational, and shared rather than concentrated. The available accounts sometimes make this out to be an essentially male–female opposition, but the issue is not so simple: there are also plenty of examples of clientelistic politics mediated by women intermediaries (Caldeira, op. cit., 1987). It may well be the product of the particular forms of kinship present especially among the urban poor of Latin America: the enormous weight of female-headed single-parent families, often living together under one precarious roof must by now be having a political effect, but we lack studies of the relationship between such structural phenomena and the popular movement. Indeed, a recent author has added to the familiar 'double burden' of women a third dimension, namely precisely that of community management in which women in general in the Third World are claimed to play a preponderant role (Moser, 1989).

To these practical observations must be added an ideological effect: the boundaries between the personal and the political, between the private and the public, are being broken down, together with the erosion of the male roles guarding and defining those boundaries. It is not so long since the predominance of reproductive and personal issues in the women's movement was being decried as a symptom of its incapacity to penetrate

---

44 Maruja Barrig (1986) describes the various attempts to set up women's sections in official organizations of the Peruvian left and how they came to grief. See also Sarah Radcliffe, 1988.

the sphere of politics, but what we are now seeing, perhaps, is a simultaneous redefinition of the boundaries between the political and the personal or reproductive sphere and also of the boundaries which excluded women from politics.

These changes – which I describe with all the warnings appropriate to a tentative and speculative exercise – also crop up in the world of 'popular' or simply 'adult' education. The accounts reported in this chapter suffer from the absence of this theme, largely because the available sociological studies tend to concentrate on pressure-group politics, protest movements and communal self-management. But, from the time when Paulo Freire set the world's imagination alight, popular education opened up a legitimate space in a wide variety of contexts. Activities ranging from the formation of co-operatives, to credit schemes, to nutrition and health programmes, sponsored by governments or by both official and non-governmental international development organizations, have invariably comprised an educational/consciousness-raising component – as for example in the case of the World Bank's PAPP programme (Programa de Ajuda ao Pequeno Productor: Programme of Support for Small-scale Producers) in north-east Brazil. According to a review of the experience of popular education in Chile, such activities open up a space in which individuals can become persons, in which a 'climate of affect and respect reigns', in which participants acquire a vocabulary of competent and skilled social interaction enabling them to regard themselves and each other as citizens, as equals, rather than, by implication, as dependent and interstitial operators.

This may sound excessively idealistic, but these activities must by now be having a cumulative effect. They are too widespread, too broadly tolerated and too legitimate, and this is so because, as explained in an earlier chapter, Freire's project took the form of cellular and incremental, rather than bombastic, subversion. Some may have been suspicious of the modernizing character of Freire's project, but if it is a modernization from below, their suspicions were ill-founded.[45] To quote a Chilean report: 'This process is experienced by participants as a "salvation", marking a boundary between a "before" and an "after" the educational experience: "before I was a nobody . . . now I am a person"; "before I just made noises . . . but no longer"; "before I could not speak. . ."'[46]

---

45 See Vanilda Paiva's account (1980). It will be recalled that according to Paiva, Freire was inspired by 'developmental nationalism', but Freire, via the perceived need for a critical consciousness within society, can be thought of as having contributed to that slogan the complementary – but also contradictory – idea of modernization from below. Those who were embarrassed by Paiva's analysis did not comprehend the difference between modernization from above and from below.

Such changes seem to present another face of the processes whereby women are undermining and transforming the barriers between the personal and the political – for if in the process they are undermining traditional ties of clientelism that means the boundaries are not precisely being removed but are being redefined in a manner more consistent with a modern ideal of citizenship. Indeed, one of the most significant new boundaries to emerge is that which divides the daily routine – so physically and psychologically oppressive – from the privileged space opened up for communicative competence by popular education.

As noted, *basismo* is heavily dependent on the charity of the international community, and this dependence has attracted much criticism.[47] Paradoxically, international NGOs have more freedom to impose their models than their official – and far wealthier – counterparts: they are subject to little control by the state apparatus, and they can seek out a clientele which will accept their own conception of the right way to development. Having done that, they can then engender a relationship of dependence by making local institutions and groups dependent on short-run grants for their survival – for these organizations rarely provide funding beyond a year or two. The funding is usually in the form of grants, or of loans on terms so 'soft' that they are, in effect, grants, but though this sounds generous it hampers the development of autonomous sustainability. In the long run this is no solution; indeed it is the Achilles heel of much *basista* activity. In the next, and final, chapter, I develop some ideas of how *basismo* could emerge into a new, mature, stage by linking into a modernized state apparatus – for maturity and sustainability must now be the names of the game.

---

46 'en la historia personal de cada uno de ellos se marca un "antes" y un "después" de la experiencia educativa: "yo antes no era nadie . . .ahora soy"; "yo antes era puro gritos . . . ahora no"; "yo antes no hablaba"' (Martinic, 1986). This article summarizes findings in Gajardo, 1982, and García Huidobro and Martinic, 1985.

47 A famous early polemic came from Peru (Rodriguez et al. 1973). This polemic was directed more at the invasion of the territory of the poor by various 'popular' programmes sponsored by international, and especially North American, official aid agencies, with the aim of co-opting the poor and neutralizing their political potential.

Five: *Basismo* as if Reality Really Mattered *or* Modernization from Below

It will be evident to the reader of previous chapters that the ideology of *basismo* suffers from a lack of both elaboration and realism. As it stands, it is a style of political action, a disposition towards the world, easily dismissed as lacking in a serious political project and unable to accumulate forces so as to make an impact beyond the micro level. Unelaborated, it may suffer the same fate as dependency which, for all its brilliant insights, was never developed theoretically.

Basismo does not deserve such a fate, especially in the light of the deficiencies of the currently available alternatives, namely neo-conservative or libertarian political economy and post-marxist caution. I shall proceed by first extracting those basic elements which form the core of the practice and discourse of *basismo* as described in chapters Three and Four. I shall call these *basismo* as invocation, because they have not been developed as a theory and also because they form more a set of dispositions implicit in the activities of a wide variety of organizations and individuals than explicit formulations of a political philosophy.

Basismo as an invocation

'*Another development*'

The notion of 'another' or an 'alternative' development has found an audience in recent years as a reaction to the perception that the economic growth under capitalism undoubtedly experienced in poor countries until the early 1980s had disappointingly little effect on the standards of living of the poor, especially as measured by basic quality of life indicators such as health, nutrition and so on. 'Another' development gives priority to the satisfaction of basic human needs, and contains more than a hint that capitalist development is not, in practice, consistent with this aim. 'Another' development believes that the technologies transferred from industrial economies are often not appropriate to poor countries – they put people out of work, they entrench the power of professional elites who monopolize knowledge, they encourage and then perpetuate aspirations to unrealistic styles of life the achievement of which by the few is at the cost of negligible improvements or even deterioration for the many. 'Another' development also places a lot of faith in the capacity of NGOs, both international and domestic, to correct these trends.

In the words of one of its most prominent European advocates, Marc Nerfin, 'Another development' is:

> (i) 'need-oriented' (but by no means limited to basic needs); (ii) self-reliant; (iii) in harmony with nature and ecologically sustainable; and (iv) going hand in hand with people empowered to make structural transformations. (Nerfin, 1987)

It is a populist message in which the role of the people is foremost: the state and large bureaucracies in general serve only to alienate or subordinate them, and are dismissed with little discussion as corrupt institutions controlled by the wealthy, and biased towards 'rich country' solutions. The people are assumed to be the poor, though culturally and ethnically heterogeneous. And the poor know best: their understanding of their environment makes them less disposed to violate it; their understanding of their own labour makes them the respositories of the most relevant technological knowhow. (Richards, 1985) They are oppressed not only – and not even principally – by international capitalism, but rather by technocracies which monopolize legitimate expertise, and the power to apply that expertise. It is a critique of attitudes as much as structures, and the tone is hortatory, appealing to experts, planners, gurus and political decision-makers, to undergo a change of attitude rather than to participate – as in the tradition of the Latin American left – in large-scale political organizations looking to seize or win state power.

Some versions, especially those figuring in the publications of international organizations, such as the ILO, do place more responsibility on – and thus implicitly more trust in – the apparatus of the state, calling for a redirection of and increase in public expenditure to enable basic needs to be met. In this case the ideology of another development appears more like traditional reformism dressed up in a new vocabulary.

Developmental populism is not a discourse of power, but addresses itself to its audience as if they were all potential converts to the cause (Chambers, 1983). This is one of its affinities with the Theology of Liberation, which is the only systematic written exposition of a *basista*

philosophy in Latin American thought. Latin American secular intellectuals, even those engaged in *basista* projects and other activities, are
reluctant to write a *basista* philosophy, preferring to express their
thoughts in relation to marxism and liberalism and the arguments
between them. The *basista* approach is best thought of as a contribution
to bodies of thought which possess a possible coherence of their own,
rather than a coherent system in itself, but that still requires a transcendence both of the endless confrontation of the two traditions mentioned
and also of efforts to conciliate or synthesize them in some way.

Democracy and participation

Basismo proclaims its democratic identity, but it distrusts the formal
apparatus of liberal democracy, just as it distrusts the formal apparatus of
the modern state. It is more Rousseauiste than modern liberal democracy,
emphasizing democracy as an educative and solidarity-building activity
of face-to-face groups. It is also anti-marxist insofar as it does not accept
the idea that the democratic character of a regime has to be judged by its
approximation to the objective interests of the proletariat. *Basismo* does
not accord to any authority a monopoly of knowledge concerning the
interests of the proletariat – or of anyone else. It rejects the model of state
socialism prevalent in Eastern Europe as a practical proposition, but
hesitates to associate itself with attacks on socialism emanating from
western capitalist countries: *basistas* seem to take the view that what
happens in Eastern Europe even under *perestroika* is little concern of
theirs.

Democracy, for a *basista*, is a matter of overcoming, and undermining
unwarranted forms of domination. Domination derived from economic
power is illegitimate; domination by political power, whatever its origins,
is presumed to be self-interested, moved by shadowy levers and motiva-
tions. Hence the preference for political activity involving the physical
presence of the grassroots, protesting, petitioning and getting in the way
of the smooth running of a machine. 'O povo desarruma todo' – 'the
people turn everything upside down'.[1]

In the light of these ideological resistances to involvement in formal
politics, it is not surprising that communal self-management and 'collective-consumption trade unionism' have become the main practical vehicles of secular *basismo*. Communal self-management is not the same as
'local government' and does not aim to replace local government because
it does not have any pretensions to become an organ of the state; it can
rather be described as a proposal for the management of public goods by

---

1 The phrase belongs to the theologian and Biblical scholar Carlos Mesters (interview, São
Paulo, 1986).

their beneficiaries. It is a recipe for the proliferation of organizations rather than the accumulation of power: one each in each area for sewage, housing, lighting, education and so on. Proposals for uniting or federating such organizations run up against the distrust of size, and an aversion to political bargaining.

'Collective-consumption trade unionism' is not, as its critics sometimes claim, merely another set of pressures placed on the hapless representatives of the state to provide anything from schools to transport to urban services and nursery schools. It is also a more sustainable form of unionism because it is built on a tacit assumption of fiscal bankruptcy: in these circumstances to press for and obtain collective goods may improve the quality of life as much as or more than conventional trade-unionist attempts to raise wages – especially in times of inflation. A sewage system is less likely to be eroded by inflation, for example, than a percentage wage increase, though it can hardly be regarded as a substitute for it. Even without inflation, the difficulties of translating private purchasing power into, for example, a sewage system, are substantial: innumerable people with the same purchasing power are also trying to get their hands on the state's depleted budget. In some ways, the difficulties involved in making public goods available on a small scale are the same as those involved in obtaining an anti-inflationary consensus among trade unionists: in both cases a lack of trust (the 'prisoners' dilemma') leads people to prefer a second-best but identifiable personal or single-group goal over a preferable, but less certain, collective goal which risks being undermined by a failure of continued co-operative arrangements. But the pessimistic assumptions of the dilemma do not necessarily hold in a small-scale context where people know each other, and where they have opportunities to learn, and thus to modify their own and each others' behaviour, over a period of time (Wade, 1987).

In some circumstances and for certain purposes such activity may be more worthwhile than participation in formal party politics. Apart from the constraints of extremely volatile economics and poverty-striken state apparatuses, there may also have been a learning process. The instrumentalization of party apparatuses and political office – and the articulation between the two – has in the end not rewarded political supporters very well: the time and energy spent by voters in pressing their case for projects and the like must have become less and less worthwhile. A shift towards collective-consumption trade unionism might attenuate the colonization of the state by parties or clienteles or sections of civil society. It is not a global solution, though, because it leaves the elite groups whose demands are less noisy but so much more effective and so much more costly to society, with an even freer hand. So it is not a substitute for formal political activity.

'Collective-consumption trade unionism' is more diversified, less cumulative, more pinpointed and unites fewer people in any one cause than the mass pressure of populist or socialist reformism. But it needs to operate in such a way as to avoid the operative inadequacies of the state machine which divert disproportionate amounts of allocated funds to wages. Collective self-management of projects should alleviate those problems, as often occurs in agriculture with irrigation, regulation of fallow and other public goods.

Basismo speaks also of democracy at the macro level, placing much emphasis on rights. Until the recent past, the production and distribution of wealth was the overwhelming intellectual and ideological priority among Latin American writers, not because they disparaged them, but rather because their protection at least under a democratic regime was taken for granted, and non-democratic regimes were regarded primarily as regimes of class oppression whose abuse of human and political rights could therefore hardly be otherwise. In this way the question of authoritarianism and human rights violations was assimilated to that of class power. The discourse of individual rights was monopolized by the liberal–individualist elite, who applied it to the defence of market freedoms and thus, in the eyes of their opponents, to the defence of their own interests. In this respect the ideological atmosphere has changed decisively: individual rights are now taken very seriously by those who espouse the cause of social transformation, in whose eyes they need to be upheld for their own sake. It is no longer assumed that the correct balance of class power will in and of itself guarantee the protection of rights. It has been the *basistas* who have tried to place human rights in particular at the centre of political discourse, with the essential support of the Catholic Church.

This language of rights, though, has become somewhat indiscriminate: the definition of human rights themselves has been expanded to cover the right not only to life and due process of law and basic freedoms, but also the right to land, to a roof over one's head and to education and health – in other words it risks becoming a vast umbrella-concept justifying unlimited pressures on hard-pressed governmental budgets, and also it risks repeating the schematic versions of Liberation Theology in which the poor are the exclusive inheritors of the Kingdom of God and the rich can no more enter heaven than they can pass through the 'eye of a needle'. The question of whether rights can be absolute where the state is near-bankrupt – or indeed under any economy where scarcity exists (which means all existing economies) remains unresolved. For they do not come cheap.

Bureaucracy

Basismo is often dismissed as a type of anarchism. This reflects its advocates' distrust of large-scale formal bureaucracies as well as the irritation of their opponents. The distrust has two contradictory roots: it is a distrust of scale for its own sake, of the arrogance of power, of the classic habits of bureaucracy, its formalism, its reduction of persons to one-dimensional members of abstract categories, in short its alienating character. It is also the distrust of bureaucracy 'Latin-style': of clientelism, jobbery, and feather-bedding, all features which constitute efforts to suppress the alienating character of formal bureaucratic organizations.

Yet at the same time *basismo* means organization, and organization means creating bureaucracy. *Basista* commitment to proper procedure and to the equal status of all members encourages the proliferation of formal organization, yet distrust of size ensures that each organization remains small. It proceeds as if small was beautiful and efficient *and* democratic. Like traditional Latin American populism *basismo* must translate the solidarity expressed in a process of political mobilization into a coherent and feasible political programme. The failure of traditional populism to create sustainable channels of political pressure or sustainable bureaucratic apparatuses, relying instead on co-optation and corporatist control diminished its many achievements in the collective memory.

Neo-populist *basismo* calls upon the solidarity of community construed in an excessively concrete, physical sense. The result is certainly a process of institution-building at the grassroots, but also a proliferation of pressure groups which may individually have comparatively short lives, and thus a failure to accumulate forces, to translate the grassroots mobilization into sustained mobilization at the level of formal politics: hence the failure, for example, of the 'cost of living' movement in São Paulo. (The strikes of 1979, on the other hand, also in São Paulo, laid the basis for the rise of the Workers' Party (PT).) The transcendence of this frustrating pattern, like many *basista* objectives, requires action by the state as much as by the grassroots. The state needs to develop mechanisms of response to the grassroots which are non-clientelistic and transparent: the officials at the 'cutting edge' should be trained and qualified, and those roles should not be reserved for the low paid and low status.

This requires a radical revision by the state apparatus of how it relates and responds to pressure, overcoming responses which depend on the political or clientelistic affiliations of a populace treated as supplicants or petitioners. The neo-conservative argument, of course, is that any governmental allocation of resources is corrupt, and invites rent-seeking behaviour. This is to overlook the difference between transparency and opacity, between impartiality and clientelism; in short, between desirable and pathological bureaucracy, which makes a practical difference to citizenship.

The implication of these remarks is to reaffirm an abiding but necessary conflict between community and bureaucracy. It is astonishing that even experts in public administration or in planning, when they enthuse about participation, forget that more participation is likely to require more – and better – bureaucracy: more information to be processed, both for the benefit of grassroots decision-makers and for information about their decisions, and more and more deliberative and decision-making bodies which need to be serviced. To some extent volunteers provide this support, but if participation is to be democratized convincingly, then that solution is inadequate.[2] Naive *basismo* is mistaken in dismissing bureaucracy: the impersonality and transparency which that term embodies should not be confused with its pejorative connotations. Bureaucracy in the abstract sense is essential not only for efficiency but also for democracy, and its malfunctioning is a reason for improving it, not for its abolition.

The spirit of community, which is at odds with impersonality and formal rules, will not go away, but *basismo* has construed community in a way which excludes the multiplicity of ties of solidarity in modern societies. In a somewhat anachronistic fashion it aspires to the recreation of primary communities which purportedly existed in the past and were destroyed by the invasion of the market and the capitalist mode of production. This is a pipe-dream. The affirmation of the multiplicity of ties implies that an individual has concerns and interests which link him not only to the neighbourhood, but also to his or her communities of origin – in the case of migrants; to professional groups; to fellow-believers; to fellow members of an ethnic group; and so on. Unless this is taken into account, the grassroots movement will not be able to sustain its initiatives, or to create frameworks for the mobilization of these multiple-potential organized forces. This involves complexity, of the kind which mobilization focused exclusively on the *base* tends to reject or evade; it involves efforts to create larger-scale organizations with supporting apparatuses to gather information, present a case, and garner popular support. There are examples of this type of organization: FASE,[3] an

2 For example, John Friedmann, a distinguished regional planner, argues for a 'radical devolution of powers', and explains how where 'lower-order life spaces are concerned' ... 'central planners operate with models that are too highly aggregated', in systems where 'feedback loops are excessively long' and with information which 'contains unknown biases and errors'. Maybe, but he does not mention the sophisticated systems and networks required to make the local system work (Friedmann, 1985).

3 Federaçao de Orgaos para Assistencia Social e Educacional, founded in 1961. In Mexico there is a 'Coordinadora Municipal'.

institution which has offices in 13 Brazilian cities and provides support to popular movements and trade unions. Such accumulation and co-ordination involves bureaucracy, with all its attendant free riding, negotiation, power-seeking and rent-seeking, but with the advantages of greater sustainability and improved probabilities of achieving stated goals.

Bureaucratic change, then, stands in a relationship of both com-plementarity and tension to popular mobilization – creative tension if we are lucky. It involves the professionalization of grassroots movements and their leadership, as well as changing the habits of the state bureaucra-cy itself, to render it responsive to the resulting pressures while avoiding the colonization of that apparatus in the time-honoured style of *latino* politics. The latter part of this chapter will return to these themes in more detail.

Markets

Basismo faces the same dilemmas as its populist and marxist precursors when it comes to markets, since it distrusts individualism as much as it distrusts the arbitrariness of state bureaucracies. For a *basista*, both markets and the state tend to preserve and probably accentuate inequality and marginality, yet the distrust of and disillusion with *dirigisme* may in the present climate – and also under current real political constraints – outweigh the distrust of markets. Whereas neo-conservative practice has emphasized the imperfections of factor and product markets, as opposed to capital markets, structuralists may emphasize that high monetarism and free-marketeering has done nothing to reduce the monopolistic character of capital markets, while the deregulation of labour and financial markets has had a dramatically deleterious effect on the lives of the poor and even the middle classes.

Unfortunately, the reduction of the monopolistic character of capital markets itself requires refined forms of state intervention, and the question of how this can be achieved without giving rise to new forms of rent-seeking remains unresolved, as the Chilean crash of 1982 illustrated. Hernando de Soto argues unconvincingly that deregulation on its own would open up access to capital. The structuralists have insisted more on the need to open up access to capital for small business and the 'informal sector' through the bureaucratic channels which control credit and especially subsidized credit. This is not easy: credit in the informal sector is extremely expensive and often operates so as to protect petty local monopolies through some sort of criminal network. It is difficult to imagine Development Banks competing in that arena.

Despite the evident biases of neo-conservative economics, a *basista* response to Soto, and to his enthusiasm for the neo-conservative/ libertarian/minimalist state should not ignore the innovativeness of his insights into the dynamics of both individualism and co-operation in the small-scale, or informal sector. In so doing it would be as well to emphasize the creation of enabling mechanisms in a market framework: technical assistance, skill creation, the provision of access to market and technical information. Soto's obsession with a reduction of the powers and size of the state have distracted him from the essential role of a modernized state in supporting his informal entrepreneurs, and also from the possibility of harnessing institutional networks such as popular education to these ends. He seems to believe, for example, that the only source of market imperfections is in state intervention, which is manifestly absurd: the criminal networks in control of the drug traffic or of informal credit, the shortage of technical and managerial skills and information, the ignorance of how to keep accounts – these and many other factors play a role in making access extremely difficult.

Basismo as if reality really mattered

Bureaucratic modernization and the role of grassroots support organizations (GSOs)

If there are aims and ideals proper to popular organizations, a programme embodying them should begin by admitting that they are inherently unsuited to be the aims and ideals of government policy and, conversely, that aims and ideals proper to government are not suited to popular organizations. The state should make a space available for empowerment, it should not seek to sponsor or regiment the corresponding organizing effort: that action falls to the popular organizations themselves. To say the state should 'empower them' – to use the word as a transitive verb – is a contradiction in terms. The political history of modern Latin America is littered with examples of co-optation disguised as varieties of popular participation, alias empowerment.

To advocate 'another' development, then, is to engage in sustained, organized advocacy on a range of issues; it is not to issue an all-encompassing and inevitably risky blueprint. Radical political activity is not the striving for a rupture but rather a multi-layered, well-informed, range of scaled political interventions. These can never reach a high degree of mutual coherence or consistency for they are themselves incoherent both in the policy-formulating process and in the implementation. To be sure, governments must feel constrained to reduce inconsistency, but a *basista* is by definition not in government; he, or she, is, rather, a person who intervenes politically in favour of empowerment, and his or her task must therefore be to introduce a bias into policy and its implementation, not to seek control of policy as a whole. Popular participation is an integrative process, but not in an organicist or corporatist sense of the word. It integrates by multiplying foci of conflict as well as by multiplying mechanisms for the channelling and conceivably the resolution of conflict, but not by imagining and thus in the end imposing a system of coherence.

The realistic *basista* approach would take into account two assumptions: macro-style structural reform is risky, and the state is indigent and not always very efficient. It would then proceed to devise methods whereby the scarce resources available can be used to best effect, with some – though not necessarily maximum – popular participation.[4]

But there are pitfalls. The participatory element in officially sponsored projects is on occasion merely a camouflage for using the unpaid labour of the beneficiaries themselves, called on to provide their labour free of charge in building, say, a school or health centre or maintaining the necessary facilities. If that is all it consists of, then participation is a façade.

The incorporation of non-governmental organizations should not be used to evade changes in bureaucratic style. Indeed, such change may be more effective if popular organizations are mobilized to pressure for improvements in official provision than if they themselves are entrusted with tasks to which they are not necessarily suited. A good example of NGOs taking on tasks which would be better performed by the state is that of credit. There are numerous examples of international NGOs financing rural development programmes in which 'one-off' capital investments such as irrigation work well enough, while complementary short-term producer credit fails to be repaid. One reason is quite simply that since the financing body does not have a permanent presence in the area debtors have little incentive to repay: the sanction of refusing future credit is only available to established banks and resident money-lenders, and the NGOs should try to channel their credit operations through banks in the same way as official aid agencies do.

The options, as so often, are not reducible to an either/or choice, but should be considered in the light of the ways in which official and unofficial provision can be flexibly combined so as to exploit the virtues and circumvent the vices of the various organizational forms available. This means looking to the state for scale and co-ordination, and to the grassroots for 'attunedness'. The same eclecticism can be applied to technology. If we take the provision of primary health care, for example,

4 Readers will recall Patrick Moynihan's polemic on the Great Society programme and its motto 'maximum feasible participation'. Patrick Moynihan: *Maximum feasible misunderstanding*, 1970.

we can see that it need not be entirely 'low-tech': cheap desk-top computers can be installed by community organizations and operated by high-school graduates to keep records – an example of high tech favouring participation.

This brings us to the grassroots support organizations (GSOs), (Carroll, 1987), staffed by professionals but not subject to the rigid rules of tenure and pay which apply in government service, nor to a rigid bureaucratic culture. These organizations have proliferated in recent years as intermediaries between international NGOs and grassroots organizations, managing funds and projects, conducting training programmes, evaluations and so on. They can perform similar functions for the state, on an expandable scale, for many of them have proved their competence. They play an important role as pioneers of methods and ideas, but they too can become less marginal, more central, contributing to the professionalization of NGO activity. Likewise, a working relation needs to be built up between NGOs and the state. This relationship is inevitably tense, because of ideological differences and differences in style, but it is nonetheless necessary. It is also tense because, if government officials have more power and job security, nowadays the staffs of GSOs may be more highly qualified and enjoy higher social status and more international professional connections than their official counterparts. They tend to have studied in Europe or the USA, and travel abroad in connection with their relations to the international NGO network. They are not always worse off materially: pay levels in public service, even for doctors, have now fallen to such abysmal levels that NGOs often pay higher salaries. Above all, they exhibit a more intense, often obsessive, commitment to their work.

Some people would go further, and say that the GSOs should be contracted not by the state but by popular organizations themselves, though this would still have to be funded by the state. But experience does not show that such an approach would live up to expectations. While popular organization is omnipresent and growing all the time in the numbers of its adherents and activities, popular organizations themselves tend to be small and financially dependent, and to have difficulty in sustaining a long life span, being plagued by fluctuating membership and unstable leadership – or by self-perpetuating leaders who grow detached from the rank and file as they grow closer to funding bodies and GSOs. Excessive faith in the managerial potential of grassroots organizations may breed disillusion both among intended beneficiaries of their activities and also among those who pay the bills. Unless, of course, the latter use these activities as a tool of political clientelism – thus defeating the object of the exercise. The strengthening of GSOs may be labelled elitist by some, but it is probably the most effective way of improving management and achieving greater stability.

My argument here has concerned not the content of the basic-needs policy but the modes of organization which would be needed to make it sustainable. This means improving the performance of the state bureaucracy through pressure from below but also taking measures to prevent that pressure from merely adding to existing clientelism, whether it be personalistic (as in Brazil) or mediated by ideological party loyalties (as in Chile). Whatever the appeal of grassroots organizations, it must be recognized that experience does not give good grounds for entrusting them on their own with large-scale resources or very ambitious tasks. GSOs could in the future fill this void and come to play a major role in the relationship between grassroots organizations and the state.

Dangers facing the international NGO community

The actual and desirable role of international NGOs is a vast and sensitive subject, from which dispassionate analysis and evaluation have been crowded out by guilt, hyper-sensitivity and lobbying. For example, it is not clear what would constitute a proper method of evaluating the expenditure of charitable donations. Since they are 'free' should their use be evaluated according to the same criteria as loans? Or should the criteria be even stricter? Should they be seen as an expressive rather than an instrumental outlay, in which the solidarity expressed takes precedence over the use to which resources are put? Should they be seen as sponsoring experiments or models, which if successful could then be adopted by official domestic and international agencies? When I began to inquire into these issues I quickly concluded that to answer such questions properly would require a book all to itself, but, since grassroots development in Latin America and elsewhere – especially in Africa – has become so heavily dependent on non-governmental aid, a few central points must at least be raised, and these are those of accountability, dependence and professionalism.

The lack of accountability of international NGOs is extraordinary. They need to prepare audited accounts, but economic evaluation of the effectiveness of their projects is rare compared to the evaluations which are standard procedure in official aid agencies. Stories of misallocation of resources, or worse, are filtering through from the ground, and although they remain unverified there is a serious danger that a few big scandals will lead to public disaffection with non-governmental aid just as occurred with official aid twenty years ago. For the moment, the NGOs enjoy great popular esteem: in the USA Congressmen perceive them to be far more popular than official aid agencies, and are receptive to the pressures of their lobbyists. This favourable treatment is bolstered by the prevailing ideological bias against the public sector in most Western countries. This bias has led governments to channel substantial amounts of their aid budgets through the NGOs: some US-based NGOs also receive up to 60 per cent (the legal limit) of their funds from the government, either as sub-contractors or for projects put forward by their own organizations. Paradoxically, the one official US agency charged with channelling funds through non-governmental channels – the Inter-American Foundation (IAF) – has been under severe political pressure because its *basista* commitment and human rights concerns have drawn accusations of left-wing bias from conservative lobbyists (notably the Heritage Foundation).

The non-governmental aid business, then, has already become politically controversial, and will in the future become more so, as politicians and the public realize that the resources they use are not free: they are the result of the sacrifice of private individuals and receive government subsidy through tax rebates from donations as well as directly. They also have a cost which is less readily observable, to the governments of developing countries: they take up a large amount of officials' time; their power to allocate or withhold resources is a potential bargaining counter if they wish to influence government policies; they can intervene directly at the grassroots with models and incentives which may run counter to official policy – or indeed to those of other NGOs! This is not to make any judgement – positive or negative – of government policy, but merely to point out that there is a cost, that it is borne by people and governments in rich and poor countries, and that it remains an unknown quantity.

The argument that these costs are difficult or impossible to quantify, especially with available methods of cost–benefit analysis, is a serious one. But to sustain it the NGO community would have to modify their claim that they are now involved in long-term development aid rather than relief work. Instead, they would have to say that their policy is one of creating and experimenting with alternative models of organization to those adopted by the official aid system. And if that is the policy, then the NGOs would have to abandon their occasionally jealous guarding of pet projects, following the principle that their models should be developed, refined, and tried out with a view to eventual adoption on a much larger scale by the official system. This in turn would also require them to change fundamentally their distrustful, even hostile, attitude to the state – the state in general, not only those all-too-numerous states which merit such an attitude. Even where states are repressive or parasitic, NGOs should, on this view, be trying to contribute both to making them less repressive, and also to their modernization – a task which *basismo* too often regards as heretical. A similar disposition towards multilateral agencies would not be necessarily inconsistent. The World Bank has, in fact, created a small unit to liaise with the NGO community – though it is not as yet evident that this is more than a cosmetic response to domestic political pressure in the US.

The NGO community's hostility to the state is complementary to the image of the 'pet project': NGO personnel become emotionally involved with the grassroots organizations and GSOs they sponsor, strike up a close personal relationship with their leaders, and thus run the risk of identifying themselves with a particular leadership. At the same time, the financial anxieties of their own organizations, and perhaps their own anxieties when faced with the prospect that an organization may acquire increasing autonomy, lead them to favour short-term, project-based funding, subjecting their clients to a constant round of fund-raising. This undermines the function of institution-building on which the aid community so often insists. Open-ended no-strings commitment is not possible either, but this is a good example where local GSOs have a role to play as intermediaries and advisers; yet there are signs that some international NGOs would prefer to avoid local GSOs by putting their own expatriate managers on the spot to ensure ideological conformity, especially in Africa.

This issue is particularly sensitive because intellectuals from the GSOs in Latin America are beginning to voice their doubts about the legitimacy of certain facets of the non-governmental aid business. They are becoming aware that in many ways it is easier for the NGOs than for their official counterparts to impose models of organization and ideology on their clients, because they can create a very direct relationship of dependence with vulnerable groups. Multilateral and bilateral agencies, in contrast, have to deal with governmental apparatuses which, however impoverished and whatever their state of disrepair, still have much more bargaining power than the urban and rural poor.

In addition, because of the very numbers of international NGOs active on the ground, and because of the variety of their ideological and practical involvements, there is the danger of fomenting conflict among groups of beneficiaries in villages and urban communities. Furthermore, they may create confusion by uselessly multiplying technical resources or organizational models in neighbouring localities.

Finally, there is the question of professionalism. Certain kinds of NGO take the view that hierarchy is undesirable, and that close personal familiarity with the 'people' is more valuable than professional managerial skills. This disposition fits well the publicity boasting that 'only 2 pence in every pound is spent on administration', but it neglects to ask whether if 5 pence were spent the remaining 95 pence might not be even more productive. Personnel are on the whole badly paid, and few resources are set aside for their training: the view is that they are in the organization for idealism rather than ambition, and that they do not have families or careers. While it would be absurd to ask NGOs to pay World Bank salaries, or to deny the unique contribution of their ideological commitment, present arrangements risk defeating the aims of the organizations.

These remarks, based on conversations with colleagues in the USA, the UK, Brazil, Chile and Ecuador, and on the experience of people who have worked with NGOs in Bangladesh, are intended to raise questions rather than to answer them, and should be construed as an appeal to the international NGO community to open themselves up to themselves as well as to the outside world before rumours become scandals, before investigative journalists subject them to aggressive intrusion, and before public disenchantment at home dries up the flow of funds. Like the *basistas* of the Third World, they need to modernize.[5]

Conclusion

Governments in Latin America, also in Africa, have been able because of the particular configuration – or lack of configuration – of the state, to make radical departures in economic policy which are unthinkable in either capitalist or socialist advanced industrial societies, where established habits and interests are more deeply entrenched. But their faith in the instruments of macro-economic policy has been accompanied by a disdain for institutions. Hitherto *basismo* has, to some extent, shared in that disdain, for its faith in grassroots organization has not been accompanied by a concern to build sustainable institutions on other than a very small scale: yet it seems to me that a *basista* approach is essential for that purpose and that the achievement of that aim is both desirable in itself and a condition for success in an economic-development strategy.

Institutional basismo

We have noted in chapter Two the defensive and in some ways evasive character of post-marxist adherence to liberal democracy. Can *basismo* do better? Some might say that, to do better, *basismo* must improve the distribution of income, and render the political system more authentically representative. I do not think it can be expected to do either, since social

5   A recent report by Judith Tendler for the Ford Foundation is a unique and exemplary case in which sympathy for the objectives of *basista* projects (or livelihood, employment and income-generating programmes) is combined with a dispassionate search for the real reasons for survival and success in achieving their objectives. She concludes, significantly, by recommending that the Foundation pay more attention to its links with the public sector in order to achieve replicability and to do what Sheldon Annis would call 'scaling up' (Tendler, 1987).

movements are not institutions, nor political parties, but they may have the effect of rendering liberal democratic institutions more sustainable by creating new channels for pressure groups and by-passing the parties and professional politicians, and by creating a firmer foundation for human and political rights in civil society.

This may sound contradictory, since it might be claimed that by-passing politicians and parties weakens democracy. But in these countries all too many elected politicians consolidate their positions by acting as intermediaries between constitutents and the state apparatus, while parties, once they have a foothold on government – insofar as they are centralized organizations – act as employment agencies for their followers.

If social movements constitute themselves as successful pressure groups maybe formal politics will become less clientelistic, less personalistic, and more universalistic. Latin American politicians seem to believe that they become more democratic by going to the people, and eliciting quite specific demands for state expenditure on items of local concern: the more they listen and deliver, they seem to believe, the more democratic the institutions. This is founded on a misapprehension, since it omits to consider how priorities can be established, how the pressures of those 'with voice' can be weighed against the needs of those without, how exiguous budgets can be best spent. The bureaucracy needs to converge with pressure from below by accepting the existence of that pressure and developing methods of dealing with it on the basis of clear and transparent, technical, 'bureaucratic' procedures. In short, what is required is a declientelization which deprives political representatives of the control over access to the resources of the state but still accepts the principle that bureaucracy is open to pressure.

The difficulties are enormous. Bureaucracies, as they presently exist, are adapted to fending off demands, rather than to soliciting, welcoming or evaluating them, and this further encourages political clientelism: politicians find that the only way of meeting demands from their constituents is to bypass or subvert formal procedures, by operating through their contacts or clients within the bureaucracies or, if they are at the head of executive organizations, by appointing *asesores*, or advisers, who operate in parallel to the bureaucracy and try to override or undercut it. A tiny over-worked activist staff coexists with, and struggles against an underpaid, under-motivated and underutilized mass of office-holders.[6] A substantial qualitative improvement and not infrequently a painful reduction in numbers is needed to make the apparatus more responsive.

6 These statements are based on observations and interviews, in Recife, 1986. An article in *Veja* (17 September 1986) reports that some 10,000 civil servants in Brasilia account for three jobs each, on average, as discovered by the Secretariat for Public Administration.

More democracy means not ever more elections or elected bodies, but more open and more transparent avenues for channelling pressure from civil society. Some might object that this merely compounds the traditional instability of faction-ridden regimes which are claimed to have succumbed to the weight of excessive demands from all quarters. But that is a mistaken interpretation, for if these demands had truly been so strong the evidently profound exclusionary features of Latin American societies and the political marginalization they embody would not remain. The problem resides not in the quantity of demands but in their content and in the manner of governmental response to them. They tend to be demands for employment or wage increases, and thus place continuing and cumulative burdens on budgets, and they tend to be channelled through the apparatus and factions which try to colonize the state. That is, the demands are channelled through the discretionary processes which are part and parcel of the ISI system, and which encourages petitioners to mount high-profile campaigns, in the absence of clear and enforceable criteria for resource allocation and wages policies, and in conjunction with short-circuits through party and trade-union connections. Demands from popular movements are different: they tend not to be for wages but for projects and capital investment, and although these also carry with them some recurrent maintenance and management costs, they do not have the snowballing effects of wage demands. But government must still find ways of dealing with these demands in a routinized way, in order to avoid mini-confrontationism: street demonstrations, sit-ins, and the like, creating an atmosphere of crisis over the installation of a crèche in a shanty town.

To be sure, *basismo* will strengthen and broaden political awareness, but if the pattern of intermittency and ephemerality, of inadequate institutionalization of both the grassroots organizations themselves and the mechanisms of access, is not transcended, then the institutional basis of democracy will be weakened not strengthened, and clientelism will proliferate even further.

This chapter opened by asking whether *basismo* can do 'better'. That is to say, can it contribute to the sustainability of electoral civilian regimes? Can it contribute to making the state less oppressive? Can it contribute to the reduction of social injustice? Moreover, can it do these things better than the post-marxist version of liberal democracy, which in its present form offers little but a plea for peaceful political competition plus, in the case of some authors, a paeon to popular organization outside the formal political system?

These are, to some extent, discrete aspirations. There is no certainty that the preservation of electoral systems with secure guarantees for individual rights depends on greater equality in the distribution of income. Indeed, that is very much in doubt for we have learnt that, at least in the short run, a redistribution of income (real or attempted) may be more unsettling than stabilizing.

Given the uncertainty of these relations, the question is what can popular movements achieve in three dimensions, of which one is pragmatic and the other two – rights and equity – embody what we broadly think of as democratic values.

The pragmatic aim of sustaining electoral and minimally humane regimes may be furthered by the strengthening of popular movements, but it will probably be unaffected either way by their proliferation – and proliferation is the problem, as we have seen. By the strengthening of these movements I mean that they will become fewer in number but with much larger social bases, and will acquire a degree of bureaucratic support: 'scaling up' (Annis, 1987). In the process they would lose some of the spontaneity and populist freshness which Liberation Theologians, say, find attractive, but they might gain in effectiveness.

The theory is that such organizations, so long as they maintain links with their bases, provide the intermediate links and the mechanisms of interest aggregation whose strength is a condition of democratic existence and stability. But for this to happen, the state must loosen the reins of its charter system, (Stepan, 1978, pp. 38ff) otherwise the organizations' growth will be severely constrained. The contribution to sustainability lies, in the long run, in the mutual recognition, and to some extent mutual dependence, of two sets of bargaining agents: the agencies of the state and the mass organizations. Once they recognize each other as distinct, outside organizations should have no interest in colonizing branches of the state apparatus. If the charter system is loosened, then the way will be open for competing organizations which might undermine political clientelism. And so, again, we return to the same theme – that the arguments for *basismo*'s contribution to institutional or economic development, are most convincing when social mobilization is combined with reforms in the state apparatus. The claim that it can achieve development or democracy, or that it can meet basic needs, without requiring the co-operation of the state is as unsustainable as the claim that the state, in these societies, can make progress in those aims without parallel deepening and strengthening of popular organizations.

Scaling up does not only mean growing in size or creating umbrella organizations. It also means developing GSOs which can act as advisers in preparing projects, providing technical assistance in engineering, project appraisal or legal matters, assist in negotiating with the state apparatus, and also mobilizing resources through international non-governmental, governmental and multilateral organizations. Scaling up is one of the most striking ways in which the modernization process is transmitted from below, and it can contribute to the insulation of the political and social spheres.

I have said that the stronger and deeper the popular organizations, the more they should undermine political clientelism. The reason for this is that they should attract their supporters by offering a more transparent, less conditional relationship. Voters or followers complain bitterly of the conditionality of politicians' favours even while continuing to seek, enjoy and repay them, and members of popular organizations are sensitive to the boundaries between the proper spheres of politics and of popular organizations. This awareness gives us reason to believe that the rank-and-file would prefer to channel their petitioning activity through their own organizations, while supporting politicians and their parties for more strictly ideological reasons. The outcome may not be less pressure on the state, but it may enable the state to rationalize the ways in which it deals with pressure.

Thus, superimposition of political and bureaucratic office holding and the representation of interests – a pattern which, in the Argentine case, Guillermo O'Donnell described as 'corporative anarchy' – might be reduced and so elective regimes rendered more sustainable and more capable, even with their limited resources, of responding to pressure from below. To be sure the macro-economic issues of inflation and debt, and the corresponding conflicts over wage policy would not then disappear. It would indeed be comforting to believe that the strengthening of grass-roots movements and their superstructures would reduce the pressure for wages, on the grounds that those movements might obtain more durable benefits than ephemeral monetary gains. Unfortunately, given the inevitable selectivity of capital projects, and the 'catching-up' reflexes of wage bargaining, that belief is unlikely to be supported by experience. On the other hand, when the crunch comes and government is forced to reduce wages on pain of becoming an international financial pariah, the availability of a channel to get projects off the ground may at least ease politicians' consciences. And project-based expenditure on public works, education and primary health care, has the virtue of using little, if any, foreign exchange, at least in the larger countries. (In smaller and poorer countries even simple articles like syringes, schoolbooks and writing materials need to be imported.)

Basismo as a struggle against oppression

We come now to the struggle for rights and the gains they may bring for equity. The insertion of social movements in wider networks of information, dissemination and expertise is as applicable to their struggles against oppression as it is to their struggles for the satisfaction of basic needs.

Some of *basismo*'s most notable successes have been due to their links with national and international audiences, as in the case of the dam at Itaparica in the north east of Brazil, where the World Bank was galvanized into a unique – and uniquely costly – resettlement project by international pressure groups taking up the cause of the small land holders whose property was about to be flooded.[7]

It is in these struggles against arbitrary power and unpunished oppression by private or unauthorized individuals that the expressive bonds which social movements can create and reinforce, and which are valued not only by their Christian supporters and propagators, come into their own. In this context symbolism and witness can bear fruit, as in the story of the Mothers of the Plaza de Mayo, or in the irridentist encampments of displaced smallholding farmers in Brazil (Martins, 1984), and more generally, in the Base Christian Communities. Faced with an overwhelmingly powerful apparatus and in the absence of any openness on the part of the offending authorities, there is little alternative to making a hue and cry.

The vast majority of the humanitarian, co-operative and other grassroots organizations to which we refer have no proper legal existence at all. This may seem a detail but it is certainly an obstacle to their undertaking any role which involves handling substantial sums of money, or signing agreements with governmental organizations, employing more than a small number of people, or paying their employees more than token wages. The reason for this is not just that they are poor: it is also that the charter system does not make it easy to obtain what is known as 'legal personality', that is, the legal recognition by the state which enables organizations to act as corporate bodies. To change these circumstances would require legal reforms whose implications would send the legal establishment into paroxysms, for the recognition of a right to establish organizations without prior permission would constitute a fundamental change in the Latin concept of the state. Yet the rise of both neo-liberal and post-marxist ideology gives some reason to believe that a climate for a shift away from corporatism is developing.

Rights imply conflict, and not only at the macro-level: property rights and indeed the right to life are inextricably bound up with conflict over land, for example, especially in Brazil. Rights may also imply expense, as in the case of the enforcement of equal rights legislation by judicial

---

7 The dam was financed under a World Bank loan in 1985, due to be completed in 1988. In the intervening period protests from the farmers whose land was to be flooded and from international humanitarian organizations working with them, reached the bank through its executive directors and a $300m resettlement scheme was approved, to be financed in part by a $132m bank loan. The 'free-standing' character of this scheme was unique in World Bank practice, and was due to be completed in 1993.

decisions in the USA and the UK, or the reform (i.e. the purging and renovation) of the apparatus defending human and civil rights in Latin America. This involves sensitive areas which none of the nascent electoral and civilian political regimes have confronted: police violence and corruption, the invasiveness of security organization in general, the impunity of private repression in the Brazilian hinterland and so on. The enormity and sensitivity of this task cannot be underestimated but sooner or later it will have to be confronted. The difficulties faced by President Alfonsín in resisting the pressure for a *de facto* amnesty from the Argentine officer corps, which he ultimately allowed, and the success with which the Brazilian military have retained complete control over all security matters, internal and external, even in the decisions of the Constituent Assembly, testify to the weakness of civil society at the macro-level (Stepan, 1988). At the micro-level, old habits, encrusted in the networks of patrimonial domination and ideologically indifferent party sodalities, which, contrary to expectations, modernization has not undermined, will die even harder.

These are some of the most distressing issues we have to consider, for whereas one might expect that an armed institution which reacts violently when under threat, may revert to more peaceful methods when the threat is removed, we find that in their dealings with the mass of the people, the organs of security routinely use violence, especially in Brazil, whatever the regime, and so far it has been difficult to see how this can be changed. It is one thing to stop the torture of high-profile political activists, but another to stop the routine torture of blacks, indians and beggars.

If abuses cannot be ended from within the state, then at least civil society could produce an attempt to reduce them. Thus far we have seen international campaigns concerning high-profile human rights violations, but fewer activities, related to the more mundane, but deeply rooted, habits I have mentioned (Amnesty International, 1988).

The scale of the problem, especially in Brazil – where more or less the entire prison population seems to be black – defies small-scale initiatives.[8] Grassroots support organizations, many of whose staff are trained lawyers, can play a role in challenging abuses, or in supporting the challenges of popular organizations. But beyond such pin-pricking, this is a matter for political reform which politicians dare not touch.

It must be added that mobilization against the arbitrary use of power is not only mobilization against the pathological elements in the security apparatus. No one who does any field work can fail to be impressed by

---

8 One example is the Centro Luis Freire in Recife which runs a legal advisory service and intervenes, for example, in cases where young children are being kept in prison simply because the police do not know who their parents are.

the innumerable forms of petty oppression of the poor when they come face-to-face with other large-scale organizations: to see a doctor they must arrive with sick children at dawn and take their places in interminable queues; to obtain a credit for a season's planting they face far greatei obstacles than do persons with means; the free schooling to which they are usually entitled is generally of poor quality, imparted by extremely low-paid teachers; in rural areas in Brazil teachers are often unqualified, scarcely paid, and absent. Other more notorious examples include the razing of illegal urban settlements, and police indifference to or collusion with violence in rural land disputes. Those who suffer by such routine oppression would probably place greater value on reducing these immediately experienced forms of oppression than they would on macro measures to change global indices of inequality. Certainly, the cellular, small-scale forms characteristic of popular organizations, are most appropriate to struggles and protests against oppression of this kind, even if they cannot conduct class struggle in the traditional sense of a struggle between workers and capitalists or peasants and landlords. For it is in this routine oppression that we find mechanisms and relationships which make inequality so easy to increase and so difficult to reduce. By changing the experience of inequality, social movements could eventually change the institutions which perpetuate and accentuate it. Persistent, localized, co-ordinated pressure placed on institutions such as health services and education, might achieve more in changing oppressive social and political relationships, and even in improving life chances, than attempted high-level macro-economic transformations.

There are, then, two arguments in favour of the more expressive, symbolic, and confrontational dimension of grassroots mobilization as conceived by *basismo*. The first is that it can, gradually, bring about a reduction in institutional arbitrariness and oppression. These habits reflect cultural traits which cannot be changed by institutional manipulation or political or administrative reforms, unless challenged in the field of social relations where they take place, just as discrimination in the treatment of ethnic minorities and women resists legal and administrative correctives so long as cultural practices remain unchanged.[9]

The involvement of activist Christian priests, religious and lay persons realizes its potential more fully, probably, in this sphere than in the spheres of political pressure or communal self-management. Their role,

9 The forms of oppression under consideration here are less easy to encapsulate and challenge within a liberal context than the discrimination mentioned, and which have, of course, been the *causes célèbres* of arguments about rights in richer countries. The reason is that the notion of class, denoting a form of inequality which is not ascriptive but built into the structures of society does not fit into the official liberal legal discourse. For arguments along these lines see Unger (1983).

after all, is to 'stand up and be counted', and their participation in mobilizations for rights and against oppressive behaviour does produce some discomfiture to the institutions responsible.

Grassroots mobilizations can therefore bring about changes in a more sustainable and lasting manner than can the macro-interventions advocated by the official left and by structuralist economists. The struggle against everyday oppression has a role to play even in the reform of public administration. For bureaucracy is a structural element in the exclusionary role played by institutions which regulate markets or control access to them: it is invisible to the outside, but it is deeply felt by the individuals who, on account of their lack of money or status, find themselves reduced to the condition of supplicants and, as often as not, turned away. Sustained resistance to everyday oppression can bring about cultural and institutional changes such that the old ways of exercising power simply cease to be feasible.

We thus return, after admitting that many of the aspirations of its ideologues are hopelessly unrealistic, to a strong defence of grassroots activism, be it of secular or religious inspiration. Indeed, the argument is strengthened by the narrowing of its scope and the definition of spheres in which it can be effective. These can be classified in two broad categories: one, that of everyday resistance to oppression in which size and duration are not of the essence, and the other, more instrumental, more complex, including both communal self-management and collective-consumption trade unionism, requiring larger-scale organization, more professionalism and more linkage with grassroots support organizations and with the state itself, so as to fulfil the requirements of institutional competence and sustainability which are essential to a 'basic needs' approach to development.

'Empowerment', a term which so temptingly encompasses all the processes which I have been discussing, turns out, unsurprisingly, to be a complex, multi-dimensional concept, and above all a process, as the word's construction itself implies. It is not a process organized from the helm of government, but it does require a strong state, that is, a state in which executive power is centralized, and departments are not colonized, and also one in which security agencies are not a law unto themselves. If the bureaucratic authoritarian regimes were, and remain, more than usually offensive to basic moral principles, and if the redistributive programmes which they stopped or pre-empted were more than usually offensive to basic rules of prudence in economic policy, then maybe it is worth asking whether, prior to allocating or redistributing resources to the poor, states should not, as a matter of *social* policy, give priority to protecting the poor from the unwanted attentions of the agents of the security apparatus or of the drugs mafia, from corrupt officialdom or landlord violence. At least this might enable people to take greater advantage of the opportunities available to them in the existing market structures, and would in any case be a necessary condition for changes in those structures to achieve their stated aims of income or asset redistribution. It is by no means risk-free, nor is it cost-free in financial terms. It is a (subversive) extension of the arguments of capitalist modernizers such as Soto, taking them beyond the constricting realm of market freedoms and contract law, to the broader one of human, civil and political rights.

We thus conclude by attempting to transcend the blind spots which advocates of many points of view have suffered because they are fatally attracted to an intuitive, often tribal, ideological coherence. Soto mistakenly interprets his insights into the life of the informal sector as proof of the viability of a pure market approach to every aspect of economic policy; *dependentistas* saw no solution to any social problem unless the world economy was restructured. But Soto for his part does not see that if he is to defend property rights he must equally defend human, civil and political rights, because he has reduced the concept of freedom to a concept of property, and he carelessly – or maybe carefully – elides the problem of inefficiency and ineffectiveness in the state with the problem of state intervention in principle. The *dependentistas* took the view that markets were unworthy of any consideration, and assumed that suppression of social inequality would of itself ensure the security of democratic institutions. Where ultra-monetarists reduce all problems to the failure of markets, *dependentistas* reduced them to capitalist exploitation. The Theology of Liberation, if thought of as a naively optimistic call upon human beings to follow the true message of Christ and build the Kingdom of Heaven, is also reductionist. And its opposition to much modern theology in questioning the divide between religious and secular life, might also be judged reductionist. Yet this reading is wrong: rather it conceives of the construction of the Kingdom of Heaven not as even the remotest conceivable practical possibility, but rather as a tension, a tendency, a constant invitation to transcendence of the here and now. Some see it as the embodiment of the revolution, but even they see no merit in revolution as a pre-defined and once-for-all stasis. The approach taken by the Theology of Liberation to the interpretation and construction of spiritual truth is anti-modernist in the sense that it doubts that its ideals can be pursued or specified by the discussions of professional theologians, and post-modern in its conception of that search for truth as a matter of progressive approximation and in the emphasis it places on the method of undertaking that endless project. It also departs from modernism when it goes to the people and looks to their culture, their religious practice and their participation, in the interpretation of the Bible and in the discussion of spiritual truth. In the last analysis, though, there is an irony, for in the very process of a liberation which claims to be spiritually inspired, in all the multiplicity of agitations and involvements of priests, religious and not least of nuns, the institutions and practices of modernity are reaching the people. And the experience, one hopes, is radically different from the ravages of 'modernization from above'. Indeed, it could be argued that the informal Church, at least, has an idea of how to break the reductionism that from above combines modernization with poverty, and from below divorces modernization from social justice. Modernization from below is not just a 'half-way' model: it really expresses a desire to break out of established modes of thought.

Bibliography

Abbott, Walter M. (ed.) 1966: *The Documents of Vatican II*, London, Geoffrey Chapman.

Aedo-Richmond, Ruth, and Noguera, Inés 1989: 'Recession and educational policy in Chile', *IDS Bulletin* (Institute of Development Studies, University of Sussex), 20,1, January.

Abós, Alvaro, 1983: *La columna vertebral*, Buenos Aires, Legasa.

Abranches, Sergio 1978: 'The divided leviathan: state and economic policy in authoritarian Brazil', Ph.D. thesis, Cornell University.

Ahumada, Jorge 1958: *En vez de la miseria*, Santiago, Editorial Universitaria.

Almeida, Maria Herminia Tavares de 1984: 'O sindicalismo brasileiro entre a conservação e a mudança'. In B. Sorj and M. de Almeida (eds), *Sociedade e política no Brasil pós-64*, Rio, Brasiliense.

Althusser, Louis 1966: *Pour Marx*, Paris, Maspéro.

Alvarez, Carlos Chacho 1986: 'El Peronismo: la modernidad y la crisis de la política', *Unidos*, 4,10, June.

Alves, Ruben 1980: 'Towards a theology of liberation', Ph.D. thesis, Princeton.

Amin, Samir 1976: *L'impérialisme et le développement inegal*, Paris, Editions de Minuit. (English trans.: *Imperialism and unequal development*, Hassocks, UK, Harvester, 1977.)

Amnesty International 1988: *Brazil: authorized violence in rural areas*, London.

Anderson, Perry 1976–7: 'The antinomies of Antonio Gramsci', *New Left Review*, 100.

Angell, Allan 1972: *Politics and the labour movement in Chile*, London, Oxford University Press.

Annis, Sheldon 1987: 'Can small-scale development be large-scale policy? the case of Latin America', *World Development*, 15, supplement.

Ansaldi, Waldo (ed.) 1986: *La ética de la democracia*, Buenos Aires, CLASCO.

Aron, Raymond 1965: *Main currents in sociological thought*, London, Penguin.

Aylwin, Mariana et al. 1986: *Chile en el Siglo XX*, Santiago, Emisión.

Azevêdo, Fernando 1982: *As ligas camponesas*, Rio de Janeiro, paz e Terra.

Bacha, Edmar 1975: 'Hierarquía e remuneração gerencial'. In R. Tolipan and A. C. Tinelli, *A controversia sobre distribução de renda e desenvolvimento*, Rio, Zahar.

Bacha, Edmar and Taylor, Lance 1978: 'Brazilian income distribution in the 1960s: "facts", models and the controversy', *Journal of Development Studies*, 14,3.

Ballón, Eduardo (ed.) 1986: *Movimientos sociales y democracia: la fundación de un nuevo orden*, Lima, Desco.

Bambirra, Vania 1984: 'Favelas e movimentos de favelados no Rio de Janeiro', *Politica e Administração*, 1–2, July–Sept.

Banck, Geert and Doimo, Ana Maria 1987: 'Between utopia and strategy: a case study of a Brazilian urban social movement', unpublished ms, Centre for Latin American Research and Documentation (CEDLA), Amsterdam.

Barraclough, Solon and Fernandez, José Antonio 1974: *Diagnóstico de la reforma agraria chilena*, Mexico, Siglo XXI.

Barrig, Maruja 1986: 'Democracia emergente y movimiento de mujeres', in Eduardo Ballón (ed.), op. cit.

Barry, Norman P. 1988: *The new right*, London, Croom Helm.

Bates, Robert 1981: *Markets and states in tropical Africa: the political basis of agricultural policies*, Berkeley/London, University of California Press.

Bengoa, José 1983: *El campesinado después de la reforma agraria*, Santiago, Sur.

Bernanos, Georges 1974: *Journal d'un curé de campagne*, Paris, Plon, (first published 1936).

Bianchi, Andres (ed.) 1969: *América Latina: ensayos de interpretación económica*, Santiago, Editorial Universitaria.

Boff, Leonardo 1977: *Ecclesiogênese*, Petropolis, Vozes.

—— 1985: *Church, charism and power*, London, SCM Press.

—— 1986: *E a Igreja se fez povo. Ecclesiogenese: a Igreja que nasce da fe do povo*, Petropolis, Vozes.

Bonino, José Miguez 1977: *La fé en busca de eficacia*, Salamanca, Sígueme.

Boschi, Renato 1987: 'Social movements and the new political order in Brazil'. In J. Wirth et al. (eds), *State and society in Brazil*, Boulder, Westview Press.

Bourricaud, François 1967: *Pouvoir et société dans le Pérou contemporain*, Cahiers de la Fondation Nationale des Sciences Politiques, no. 149, Paris, Armand Colin.

Brading, David 1984: *Prophecy and myth in Mexican history*, Cambridge, Centre for Latin American Studies.

—— 1986: *Origins of Mexican nationalism*, Cambridge, Centre for Latin American Studies.

Brandão, Carlos Rodriguez 1980: *Os Deuses do Povo*, São Paulo, Brasiliense.

Bruneau, Thomas C. 1974: *The political transformation of the Brazilian Catholic Church*, Cambridge, Cambridge University Press.

Buchanan, James M. 1975: *The limits of liberty: between anarchy and leviathan*, Chicago/London, University of Chicago Press.

Buchanan, James M., Tullock, Gordon and Tellison, Robert D. (eds) 1980: *Towards a theory of the rent-seeking society*, Texas A&M University Economic Series no. 4, College Station: Texas A&M University.

Caldeira, Teresa 1987: 'Mujeres, cuotidianeidad y política'. In E. Jelín (ed.) *Ciudadanía e identidad: las mujeres en los movimientos sociales latinoamericanos*, Geneva, United Nations Research Institute for Social Development.

Camargo, Candido Procopio Ferreira de 1971: *Igreja e desenvolvimento*, São Paulo, CEBRAP.

Cammack, Paul, 1985: Introduction. In P. Cammack and P. O'Brien (eds), *Generals in retreat: the crisis of military rule in Latin America*, Manchester, Manchester University Press.

Cammack, Paul and O'Brien, Philip (eds) 1985: *Generals in retreat: the crisis of military rule in Latin America*, Manchester, Manchester University Press.

Camp, R. L., 1969: *The papal ideology of social reform: a study in historical development 1878–1967*, Leiden, E. J. Brill.

Campero, Guillermo 1987: 'Las organizacions poblacionales', paper presented to the CLACSO/SUR/CADIS seminar on urban social movements and democratization processes, Santiago, March.

Canitrot, Adolfo, 1978: 'La viabilidad económica de la democracia: un análisis de la experiencia peronista 1973–1976' *Estudios Sociales*, (Buenos Aires), May.

Cardenal, Ernesto 1974: *En Cuba*, Buenos Aires, Carlos Lohlé.

—— 1973: *Salmos*, Buenos Aires, (English translation, *Psalms*, London, Sheed Ward, 1981).

Cardoso, Fernando Henrique, 1973: 'Associated-dependent development: theoretical and practical implications'. In Stepan (ed.) *Authoritarian Brazil*, New Haven and London, Yale University Press.

—— 1977: 'The originality of the copy: CEPAL and the idea of development', *CEPAL Review*, 4.

—— 1985: 'O desafio da participação', speech delivered 1984, reprinted in Cardoso: *A democracia necesaria*, Campinas, Papirus.

Cardoso, Fernando Henrique and Faletto, Enzo 1970: *Dependencia e desenvolvimento na America Latina*, Rio de Janeiro, Zahar, (English translation: *Dependency and development in Latin America*, University of California Press, 1979).

Cardoso, Ruth 1983: 'Movimentos sociais urbanos: balanço crítico'. In Sorj et al. (eds) *Sociedade e politica no Brasil pós-64*, São Paulo, Brasiliense.

Carneiro, Dionisio Dias 1987: 'Brazil'. In Taylor and Helleiner (eds) *Stabilization and adjustment programmes*, Helsinki, World Institute for Development Economics Research.

Carr, E. H. 1953: *The Bolshevik revolution, 1917–1923*, 3 vols, London, Penguin.

Carroll, T. F. 1987: 'Some research propositions and interpretations of grassroots support organizations', ms.

Carter, Michael 1984: 'Parcelization and reform sector productivity: theoretical questions and an efficient mixed institutional alternative', ms, University of Wisconsin, Department of Agricultural Economics, August.

Castells, Manuel 1983: *The city and the grassroots: a cross-cultural theory of urban social movements*, London, Edward Arnold.

Castro, Antonio Barros de 1985: *A economia brasileira em marcha forçada*, Rio, Paz e Terra.

Castro, Gustavo do Passo 1987: *As comunidades do Dom*, Recife, Fundação Joaquim Nabuco.

CELAM (Conferencia Episcopal Latinoamericana: Latin American Bishops' Conference) 1985: *A Igreja na atual transformação en América Latina a luz do Concilio*, Conclusões de Medellin, 8th edn, Petropolis, Vozes, (originally published 1968).

—— 1986: *Evangelização no presente e no futuro da America Latina* (Conclusões da Conferencia de Puebla).

CEPAL (United Nations Economic Commission for Latin America: ECLA) 1949: El desarrollo de la América Latina y algunos de sus principales problemas', (Introduction to *Estudio económico de América Latina*, reprinted in Gurrieri (ed.), I, *La obra de Prebisch en la CEPAL*, 2 vols, Mexico, 1982, Fondo de Cultura Económica.)

Cezar, Maria do Ceu 1985: *Movimentos sociais alem da dicotomia rural-urbano*, Centro Josué de Castro, Recife.

Chambers, Robert 1983: *Rural development: putting the last first*, Harlow, England, Longman.

Chauí, Marilena 1986: 'PT "leve e suave"'. In Sader (ed.), *E agora PT?*, São Paulo, Brasiliense.

Ciria, Alberto 1983: *Política y cultura popular: la Argentina peronista, 1946–1955*, Buenos Aires, Ediciones de la Flor.

Clark, Martin 1977: *Antonio Gramsci and the revolution that failed*, New Haven/London, Yale University Press.

Claudín, Fernando 1975: *The Communist movement*, London, Penguin.

Collier, David (ed.) 1979: *The new authoritarianism in Latin America*, Princeton University Press.

CNBB (Conferencia Nacional dos Bispos Brasileiros) 1981: *Comunidades: igreja na base*, São Paulo, Edições Paulinas.

Comissão Pastoral da Terra 1981: *A luta pela terra na Biblia*, third edn. Goiania.

Congar, Yves 1968: *Christians active in the world*, New York, Herder and Herder.

—— 1985: *Lay people in the Church*, London, Geoffrey Chapman, and Westminster, Maryland, Christian Classics, (revised edn), (original: *Jalons pour une théologie du laicat*, Paris, Editions du Cerf, 1964.)

Corbo, Vittorio 1985: 'Reforms and macro-economic adjustments in Chile during 1974–1984', *World Development*, 13,8, August.

Costa, João Cruz 1956: *Contribuição a historia das ideias no Brasil*, Rio de Janeiro, Livraria José Olympio.

Covre, Maria de Lourdes Manzini 1986: *A cidadania que não temos*, São Paulo, Brasiliense.

Cox, Harvey 1966: *The secular city: secularization and urbanization in theological perspective*, London, SCM Cheap edition.

—— 1984: *Religion in the secular city: towards a post-modern theology*, New York, Simon and Schuster.

Cruise O'Brien, Donal 1972: 'Modernization, order and the erosion of a democratic ideal: American political science in the sixties', *Journal of Development Studies*, 8,4.

Cunha, Euclides da 1944: *Revolt in the backlands*, Chicago University Press, (original: *Os Sertões*, 1902).

Dandler, Jorge, 1975: 'Campesinado y reforma agraria en Cochabamba, 1952–53: dinámica del movimiento campesino en Bolivia', La Paz, Centro de Investigación y Promoción del Campesinado, *Cuadernos de Investigacion*, no. 9.

Davis, Nathaniel 1985: *The last two years of Salvador Allende*, London, I. B. Tauris.

Debray, Régis, 1967: *Révolution dans la révolution*, Paris, Maspéro.

de Janvry, Alain 1981: *The agrarian question and reformism in Latin America*, Baltimore/London, Johns Hopkins University Press.

de Kadt, Emanuel 1970: *Catholic Radicals in Brazil*, London, Oxford University Press.

della Cava, Ralph 1968: 'Brazilian messianism and national institutions: a reappraisal of Canudos and Juazeiro', *Hispanic American Historical Review*, 48.

—— 1970: *Miracle at Juazeiro*, New York, Columbia University Press.

—— 1987: 'La Iglesia brasileña y la apertura', *Sociedad y Religión*, 4, July, Buenos Aires.

Díaz Alejandro, Carlos 1965: *Exchange rate devaluation in a semi-industrialized country: the experience of Argentina, 1955–1961*, Cambridge, Mass./London, MIT Press.

—— 1970: *Essays on the economic history of the Argentine Republic*, New York/London, Yale University Press.

Di Marco, L. E. (ed.) 1972: *International economics and development: essays in honour of Raúl Prebisch*, New York, Academic Press.

di Tella, Guido, 1983: *Argentina under Perón, 1973–1976*, London, Macmillan.

dos Santos, Teotonio 1969: *Socialismo o fascismo: dilema latinoamericano*, Santiago, Prensa Latinoamericana.

Dunn, John, 1972: *Modern revolutions*, Cambridge, Cambridge University Press.

Eckstein, Susan 1977: *The poverty of revolution, the state and the urban poor in Mexico*, Princeton, NJ, Princeton University Press.

Edwards, Alberto 1984: *La fronda aristocrática en Chile*, Santiago, Editorial Universitaria, (first edn 1928).

Erickson, K. O. 1977: *The Brazilian corporate state and working-class politics*, University of California Press.

Espinosa, Juan G. and Zimbalis, Andrew S. 1978: *Economic democracy: workers' participation in Chilean Industry, 1970–1973*, New York, Academic Press Inc.

Espinoza, Vicente, Rodriguez, Alfredo and Rosenfeld, Alex 1986: 'Poder local, pobladores y democracia', *Proposiciones* (Santiago), 12, Oct.–Dec.

Evans, Peter 1979: *Dependent development: the alliance of multinational, state and local capital in Brazil*, Princeton/Guildford, Princeton University Press.

Eyzaguirre, Jaime 1973: *Fisionomía histórica de Chile*, Santiago, Editorial Universitaria, (original: 1957).

Faria, Vilmar 1984: 'Desenvolvimento, urbanização e mudanças na estrutura de emprego', in Sorj and Tavares de Almeida (eds).

Fausto, Boris (ed.) 1975: *História geral da civilização Brasileira*, São Paulo, Difel.

Fernandes, Rubem Cesar 1986: 'Sems fins lucrativos', *Comunicações do ISER*, Rio, Istituto Superior da Religião.

Fernandes, Dom Luis 1985: *Como se faz uma comunidade eclesial de base*, Petropolis, Vozes.

Fioravanti, Eduardo 1974: *Latifundio y sindicalismo agrario en el Peru*, Lima, Instituto de Estudios Peruanos.

Fogarty, Michael 1957: *Christian democracy in western Europe*, London, Routledge & Kegan Paul.

Forni, Floreal 1987: 'Catolicismo y peronismo', *Unidos*, 4,14, April.

Foxley, Alejandro 1985: *Para una democracia estable*, Santiago, CIEPLAN.

Foxley, Alejandro, et al. (eds) 1986: *Development, democracy and the art of trespassing*, Notre Dame, University of Notre Dame Press.

Frank, André Gunder 1969: *Capitalism and underdevelopment in Latin America*, New York, Monthly Review Press.

—— 1970: 'Sociology of development or underdevelopment of sociology?', in Frank: *Latin America: underdevelopment or revolution?*, New York, Monthly Review Press, (originally published in *Catalyst*, (Buffalo), 1967.

Frei, Eduardo 1937: *Chile desconocido*, Santiago, Ediciones Ercilla.

Freire, Paulo 1972: *Pedagogy of the oppressed*, London, Sheed and Ward.

—— 1974: *Educação como prática da liberdade*, Rio de Janeiro, Paz e Terra, (original: 1967), (English translation: *Education: the practice of liberty*, London, Writers and Readers).

Friedmann, John 1985: 'Political and technical moments in development: agropolitan development revisted', *Society and Space*, 3, 156–67.

Furtado, Celso 1959: *Formação economica do Brasil*, Rio, (English translation *Economic growth of Brazil*, University of California Press, 1963.)

—— 1973: *A hegemonía dos Estados Unidos e o subdesenvolvimento da América Latina*, Rio, Civilização Brasileira.

—— 1985: *A fantasia organizada*, Rio de Janeiro, Paz e Terra.

Gajardo, Marcela 1982: *La educación popular en Chile: un esfuerzo de sistematizaión*, Santiago, PIIE.

Galjart, Benno 1964: 'Class and "following" in rural Brazil', *América Latina*, 7, 3.

Galasso, Norberto 1983: *La izquierda nacional y el FIP*, Buenos Aires, Centro Editor de América Latina.

García, Norberto and Tokman, Victor 1985: 'Acumulación, empleo y crisis', PREALC: *Investigaciones sobre empleo*, 25.

García Huidobro, J. E. and Martinic, Sergio 1985: *Las instituciones privadas y la educación popular: el caso chileno*, Santiago, CIDE, working paper no. 5.

Garretón, Manuel Antonio and Martínez, Javier 1986: *La reforma en la Universidad Católica*, Santiago, Ediciones Sur.

Gazmuri, Cristián 1984: 'La historia de Chile Republicano: una decadencia?', *Alternativas*, Santiago, June.

Gera, Luci 1986: 'Religion y cultura', *Nexo*, September.

Gera, Lucio and Melgarejo, G. Rodriguez 1970: 'Apuntes para una interpretación de la Iglesia Argentina', Montevideo, Ediciones del Centro de Documentación, MIEC/JECI.

Gillespie, Richard, 1982: *Soldiers of Perón: Argentina's Montoneros*, Oxford, Clarendon Press.

Gohn, Maria da Gloria Marcondes 1985: *A forca da periferia: a luta das mulheres por creches em São Paulo*, Petropolis, Vozes.

Gomez, Sergio 1970: *Los empresarios agrícolas y la reforma agraria*, Santiago, ICIRA.

—— 1983: *Instituciones y procesos agrarios en Chile*, Santiago, FLASCO.

Gomez, Sergio and Echeñique, 1988: *La agricultura chilena: las dos caras de la modernización*, Santiago, FLACSO/AGRARIA.

Gramsci, Antonio 1975: *Prison notebooks*, (Italian edn: *Quaderni del carcere*, 4 vols, Einaudi).

Grayson, George 1968: *El Partido Demócrata Cristiano Chileno*, Santiago, Editorial Francisco de Aguirre.

Grupo de Investigaciones Agrarias (GIA) 1987: *El Hambre en Chile, un estudio de la seguridad alimentaria*, ms, Santiago.

Grzybowski, Candido 1986: 'Lutando e construindo a democracia: os movimentos de trabalhadores rurais e camponeses no Brasil' ('Struggling and building democracy ...') paper presented at the meeting of the Latin American Studies Association, Boston, October.

Gurrieri, Adolfo (ed.) 1982: *La obra de Prebisch en la CEPAL*, 2 vols, Mexico, Fondo de Cultura Económica.

Gutierrez, Gustavo 1973: *Teología de la liberación*, Salamanca, Ediciones Sígueme, (12th edn 1985), (English translation *A theology of liberation: perspectives*, Maryknoll NY, Orbis Books).

—— 1983: *The power of the poor in history*, Maryknoll, NY, Orbis Books.

—— 1984: *We drink from our own wells: the spiritual journey of a people*, (English translation, Maryknoll NY, Orbis Books).

—— 1985: *Church, charisma and power*, London, SCM Press.

Haberler, Gottfried 1959: *International trade and economic development*, National Bank of Egypt.

Halperín Donghi, Tulio 1984: 'El revisionismo histórico como visión decadentista de la historia nacional', *Alternativas* Santiago, July.

Clarisa Hardy 1987: 'Organizarse para vivir: pobreza urbana y organización popular, ms, Santiago, Programa de Economia del Trabajo.

Harnecker, Marta, 1971: *El capital: conceptos fundamentales*, Santiago, Editorial Universitaria.

Hebblethwaite, Peter 1975: *The runaway church*, London, Collins.

—— 1984: *John XXIII: Pope of the Council*, London, Chapman.

Hewitt, W. E. 1987: 'The influence of social class on activity preferences of CEBs in the Archdiocese of São Paulo', *Journal of Latin American Studies*, 19, 1, May.

Hewitt de Alcántara, Cynthia 1969: 'Brazil: the peasant movement of Pernambuco, 1961–1964'. In Landsberger (ed.), *Latin American peasant movements*, Ithaca, Cornell University Press.

Hirschman, Albert, 1979: 'The turn to authoritarianism in Latin America and the search for its economic determinants'. In David Collier (ed.), *The new authoritarianism in Latin America*, Princeton, Princeton University Press.

Hirschman, Albert (ed.) 1961: *Latin American issues: essays and comments*, New York, Twentieth Century Fund.

Huizer, Gerrit 1965: 'Some notes on community development and social research', *América Latina*, 8, 3.

Humphrey, John 1982: *Capitalist control and workers' struggles in the Brazilian auto industry*, Princeton, Princeton University Press.

Huntington, Samuel 1957: *The soldier and the state*, Cambridge Mass., Harvard University Press.

—— 1968: *Political order in changing societies*, New Haven/London, Yale University Press.

International Labour Office 1970: *Towards full employment: a report on Colombia*, Geneva.

—— 1972: *Employment, incomes and equality: a strategy for increasing productive employment in Kenya*, Geneva.

—— 1977: *Employment growth and basic needs: a one world problem. The international 'basic needs strategy' against chronic poverty*, New York, Praeger.

Jadresic, Esteban 1986: 'Evolución del empleo y desempleo en Chile, 1970–85', *Estudios CIEPLAN*, 20.

James, Daniel 1978: 'Power and politics in Peronist trade unions', *Journal of Interamerican Studies and World Affairs*, 20, 1, February.

Jauretche, Arturo 1974: *FORJA y la década infame*, Buenos Aires, A. Peña Lillo.

Jelín, Elisabeth (ed.) 1987: *Ciudadanía e identidad: las mujeres en los movimientos sociales latinoamericanos*, Geneva, United Nations Research Institute for Social Development.

Jones, Steve, et al. (eds) 1982: *Rural poverty and agrarian reform*, New Delhi, Allied Publishers.

Kaldor, Nicholas 1959: 'Problemas económicos de Chile, *Panorama Económico*, (Santiago), 102, April–June, (reprinted as 'Economic problems of Chile', in, *Essays on economic policy*, London, Duckworth, 1980.

Karol, Karl 1972: *Guerrillas in Power*, New York, Hill and Wang.

Kay, Cristóbal 1982: 'Achievements and contradictions of the Peruvian Agrarian Reform', *Journal of Development Studies*, 18, 2, Jan.

Keck, Margaret 1986–7: 'Democratization and dissension: the formation of the Workers' Party', *Politics and Society*, 15, 1.

Kennedy John J. 1958: *Catholicism, nationalism and democracy in Argentina*, Notre Dame, Notre Dame University Press.

Kinzo, Maria d'Alva Gil 1985: 'An opposition party in an authoritarian régime: the case of the MDB in Brazil', D.Phil. thesis, Oxford University.

Knight, Alan, 1986: *The Mexican Revolution*, 2 vols, Cambridge, Cambridge University Press.

Krueger, Anne O. 1974: 'The political economy of the rent-seeking society', *American Economic Review*, 14,3, June.

Laclau, Ernesto 1977: *Politics and ideology in marxist theory*, London, New Left Books. See especially 'Towards a theory of populism', ibid.

—— 1985: 'Social movements and a recasting of the political'. In Slater (ed.) 1985, *New social movements and the State in Latin America*, Amsterdam, CEDLA.

Laclau, Ernesto and Mouffe, Chantal 1985: *Hegemony and socialist strategy: towards a radical democratic politics*, London, New left Books.

—— 1987: 'Post-marxism without apologies', *New Left Review*, 166, Nov.–Dec.

Landsberger, Henry (ed.) 1969: *Latin American peasant movements*, Ithaca,

Cornell University Press.

Leeds, Anthony 1964: 'Brazilian careers and social structures', *American Anthropologist*, 46, Dec.

Lehmann, David 1971: 'Political incorporation versus political stability: the case of the Chilean Agrarian Reform, 1965–1970', *Journal of Development Studies*, 7, 365–95.

—— 1972: 'Peasant consciousness and agrarian reform in Chile', *Archives Européennes de Sociologie*, 7,4, July.

—— 1978a: 'The death of land reform', *World Development*, 6,3.

—— 1978b: 'The political economy of Armageddon', *Journal of Development Economics*, 5.

—— 1982: 'After Lenin and Chayanov: new paths of agrarian capitalism', *Journal of Development Economics*, 11.

—— 1986a: 'Dependencia: an ideological history', working paper DP219, Institute of Development Studies, University of Sussex.

—— 1986b: 'Two paths of agrarian capitalism: a critique of Chayanovian marxism', *Comparative Studies in Society and History*, October.

—— 1989: 'A Latin American political scientist: Guillermo O'Donnell', *Latin American Research Review*, 24,2, pp. 187–200.

Lehmann, David (ed.) 1974: *Agrarian reform and agrarian reformism*, London, Faber, (US edn: *Peasants, landlords and governments*, New York, Holmes and Meier).

Lehmann, David and Castillo, Leonardo 1982: 'Chile's three land reforms: the inheritors', *Bulletin of Latin American Research*, 1,2, May.

Lenin, V. I. 1899: *The development of capitalism in Russia*.

Levine, Daniel H. 1985: 'Continuities in Colombia', *Journal of Latin American Studies*, 17.

Levinson, Jerome and Onis, Juan de 1970: *The Alliance that lost its way*, Chicago, Quadrangle Books.

Lima, Haroldo and Arantes, Aldo 1984: *História da Ação Popular*, São Paulo, Alfa-Omega.

Lladser, Maria Teresa 1986: *Centros privados de investigacion en ciencias sociales en Chile*, Santiago, Academia de Humanismo Cristiano and *FLACSO*.

Long, Norman and Roberts, Bryan 1984: *Miners, peasants and entrepreneurs: regional development in the central highlands of Peru*, Cambridge, Cambridge University Press.

Long, Norman and Roberts, Bryan (eds) 1978: *Peasant cooperation and capitalist expansion in Central Peru*, Austin, Texas University Press.

Love, Joseph 1980: 'Raúl Prebisch and the origins of the doctrine of unequal exchange', *Latin American Research Review*, 15, 3.

Lovisolo, Hugo 1986: 'A serviço de nós mesmos', *Religião e Sociedade* (Rio), 13,3, November.

McGrath, Alister 1986: *The making of modern German Christology*, Oxford, Blackwell.

McSweeney, Bill 1980: *Roman Catholicism: the search for relevance*, Oxford, Basil Blackwell.

Mainwaring, Scott 1986: *The Catholic Church and politics in Brazil, 1916–1985*, Stanford, Stanford University Press.

Mallon, Florenica 1983: *The defense of community in Peru's Central Highlands: peasant struggle and capitalist transition*, Princeton, Princeton University Press.

Malloy, James (ed.) 1977: *Authoritarianism and corporatism in Latin America*, Pittsburgh University Press.

Mariátegui, J. C. 1928: *Siete ensayos de interpretación de la realidad Peruana*, Lima, (10th edn Lima, Amauta, 1965), (English translation: *Seven interpretative essays on Peruvian reality*, Austin, University of Texas Press, 1971).

Mariátegui, J. C. 1965: *El alma matinal*. In *Obras completas de J. C. Mariátegui*, Lima, Amauta, 3.

Maritain, Jacques 1984: *Humanisme intégral: problèmes temporels et spirituels d'une nouvelle chrétienté*, (original: 1936). In Jacques et Raïssa Maritain: *Oeuvres complètes*, Paris, Editions Saint-Paul, 6.

Martínez, Tomás Eloy 1986: *La novela de Perón*, Buenos Aires, Legasa.

Martínez, Javier and Tironi, Eugenio 1985: *Las clases sociales en Chile: cambio y estratificación, 1970–1980*, Santiago, Sur.

Martinic, Sergio 1986: 'Educación popular vista por sus participantes', *Mensaje*, (Santiago), 367, March–April.

Martins, José de Souza 1980: *Expropriação e violencia: a questão politica no campo*, São Paulo, HUCITEC.

—— 1984: *A militarização da questão agraria no Brasil*, Petropolis, Vozes.

Marx, Karl 1976: *Capital*, I (original: 1867), London, Penguin Books.

Mayol, Alejandro, Habegger, Norberto and Armado, Arturo 1970: *Los Católicos postconciliares en la Argentina*, Buenos Aires, Galerna.

Mesa-Lago, Carmelo 1978: *Social security in Latin America: pressure groups, stratification and inequality*, Pittsburgh, University of Pittsburgh Press.

Mesters, Carlos 1984: *Flor sem defesa: uma explicação da Biblia a partir do povo*, Petropolis, Vozes.

Meyer, Jean 1974: *La Cristiada*, 3 vols Mexico City, Siglo XXI. (English translation, abridged: *The Cristero revolt*, Cambridge University Press, 1976).

Mignone, Emilio 1986: *Iglesia y dictadura: el papel de la iglesia a la luz de sus relaciones con el régimen militar*, Buenos Aires, Ediciones del Pensamiento Nacional.

Moises, José Alvaro et al. 1982: *Alternativas populares da democracia*, Petrópolis, Vozes.

Morandé, Pedro 1984: *Cultura y modernización en America Latina*, Instituto de Sociología, Catholic University, Santiago.

Morris, James O. 1966: *Élites, intellectuals and consensus; a study of the social question and the industrial relation system in Chile*, New York School of Industrial Relations, Ithaca, New York.

Moser, Caroline, 1989: 'Gender planning in the Third World: meeting practical and strategic gender needs', *World Development*, 17, November.

Moynihan, Patrick 1970: *Maximum feasible misunderstanding; community action in the war on poverty*, New York, Free Press.

Muraro, Valmir Francisco 1985: *Juventude Católica operária*, Rio, Brasiliense.

Navarro Gerassi, Marysa 1965: 'Argentine nationalism of the right', *Studies in Comparative International Development*, 1,12.

—— 1968: *Los nacionalistas*, Buenos Aires, Jorge Alvarez.

Nerfin, Marc 1987: 'Neither prince nor merchant: citizen – an introduction to the Third System', *Development Dialogue*, 1.

Noel, Gerard 1980: *Tha anatomy of the Catholic Church: Roman Catholicism in an age of revolution*, Garden City, Doubleday.

Nun, José 1969: 'Superpoblación relativa, ejército industrial de reserva, y masa marginal', *Revista Latinoamericana de Sociología*, 5,2.

Nunberg, Barbara 1986: 'Structural change and state policy: the politics of sugar in Brazil since 1964', *Latin American Research Review*, 21,2.

Nurkse, Ragnar 1953: *Problems of capital formation in underdeveloped countries*, Oxford, Clarendon press.

O'Donnell, Guillermo 1971: *Modernization and bureaucratic authoritarianism*, Berkeley, University of California, Politics of Modernization Series.

—— 1977: 'Corporatism and the question of the state', first presented at a meeting in February, 1974 and later published in James Malloy, op. cit.

—— 1978: 'Apuntes para una teoría del estado', *Revista Mexicana de Sociología*, 4.

—— 1978a: 'Reflections on the patterns of change in the bureaucratic–authoritarian state', first presented in Spanish in May 1975 and later revised and published in English in the *Latin American Research Review*, 13,1.

—— 1978b: 'State and alliances in Argentina', presented at a meeting in December 1976 and published, in English, in the *Journal of Development Studies*, 15,1, October.

—— 1979: 'Tensions in the bureaucratic authoritarian state and the question of democracy', in Collier, op. cit.

—— 1982: *1966–1973: el Estado burocrático autoritario: Triunfos, derrotas y crisis*, Buenos Aires, Editorial Belgrano, (English translation: *Bureaucratic Authoritarianism: Argentina, 1966–1973 in comparative perspective*, University of California Press, 1988).

—— 1984a: *Y a mí que me importa? Notas sobre sociabilidad y política en Argentina y Brasil*, Buenos Aires, CEDES.

—— 1984b: 'Democracia en la Argentina *micro y macro*'. In Oszlak (ed.) *Proceso, crisis y transición democrática*, 1, Buenos Aires, Centro Editor de América Latina.

—— 1986: 'On the fruitful convergences of Hirschman's *Exit, voice and loyalty* and *Shifting involvements*: reflections from recent Argentine experience'. In Foxley, et al., op. cit.

—— 1988: *Bureaucratic authoritarianism: Argentina, 1966–1973 in comparative perspective*, Berkeley, University of California Press.

O'Donnell, Guillermo and Linck, Delfina 1973: *Dependencia y Autonomía*, Buenos Aires, Amorrortu.

Oliveira, Francisco de 1986: 'Qual e a do PT?'. In Sadar (ed.), *E agora PT?*, São Paulo, Brasiliense.

Oliveira, Pedro A. Ribeiro de 1986: 'Comunidade, igreja e poder – em busca de um conceito sociologico de "igreja"', *Religião e Sociedade*, 13,3, November.

Olson, Mancur 1965: *The logic of collective action*, Cambridge, Mass., Harvard University Press.

—— 1982: *Rise and decline of nations*, Ithaca/London, Yale University Press.

Ortega y Gasset, José 1929: *La rebelión de las masas*, Madrid, Revista de Occidente.

Oszlak, Oscar (ed.) 1984: *Proceso, crisis y transición democrática*, 1, Buenos Aires, Centro Editor de América Latina.

Paige, Jeffrey 1978: *Agrarian revolution*, Glencoe, Ill., The Free Press.

Paiva, Vanilda 1980: *Paulo Freire e o nacionalismo desenvolvimentista*, Rio de Janeiro, Civilização Brasileira.

—— 1985 (ed.): *Igreja e questão agraria*, São Paulo, Edições Loyola.

Pandolfi, Maria Lia 1986: 'Na margem do Lago (um estudo sobre o sindicalismo rural), Masters Thesis, Federal University of Pernambuco, Recife.

Panitch, Leo 1980: 'Recent theorizations of corporatism: reflections on a growth industry', *British Journal of Sociology*, 31,2, June.

Perlman, Janice 1976: *The myth of marginality*, Berkeley, University of California Press.

Petrini, João Carlos 1984: *CEBs: um novo sujeito popular*, Rio de Janeiro, Paz e Terra.

Pierucci, Antonio Flavio de Oliveria 1984: 'Democracia, igreja e voto', University of São Paulo, Doctoral Dissertation.

Pinto, Anibal 1970: 'Naturaleza e implicaciones de la "heterogeneidad estructural" de la América Latina', *El Trimestre Económico*, 145, Jan.–March.

Poggi, Gianfranco 1967: *Catholic Action in Italy: sociology of a sponsored organization*, Stanford, Stanford University Press.

Poletto, Ivo 1985: 'As contradições sociais e a pastoral da Terra'. In Vanilda Paiva (ed.), 1985, op. cit.

Pollock, David 1979: 'The United States and ECLA' *CEPAL Review*, 7, April.

Portantiero, Juan Carlos 1984: 'Socialismo y democracia. Una relacion difícil', *Punto de Vista*, 20.

—— 1987: 'La concertación que no fué: de la Ley Mucci al Plan Austral'. In José Nun and Juan Carlos Portantiero (eds) *Ensayos sobre la transición democrática en la Argentina*, Buenos Aires, Punto Sur.

Portes, Alejandro 1977: 'Politica habitacional, pobreza urbana e o estado: as favelas do Rio de Janeiro, 1972–76', *Estudos CEBRAP*, 22.

Poulantzas, Nicos 1970: *Pouvoir politique et classes sociales*, Paris, Maspéro, (English translation, London, New Left Books, 1973).

Prebisch, Raúl 1947: *Introducción a Keynes*, Mexico, Fondo de Cultura Económica.

—— 1955: 'Sound money or uncontrolled inflation?', *Review of the River Plate*, 11 November.

—— 1956: 'Final report and economic recovery programme', *Review of the River Plate*, 20 January.

—— 1971: 'El falso dilema entre desarrollo económico y estabilidad monetaria', (reprinted in Gurrieri op. cit.).

Purcell, Susan Kaufman 1977: 'Mexican business and public policy'. In Malloy, 1977.

Quijano, Aníbal, and Portocarrero, Felipe 1969: 'Peru: peasant organizations. In H. A. Landsberger (ed.), *Latin American peasant movements*, Ithaca and London, Cornell University Press.

Radcliffe, Sarah 1988: '"Así es una mujer del pueblo": low-income women's organizations under APRA, 1985–1987', University of Cambridge, Centre of Latin American Studies, working paper no. 43.

Razeto, Luis 1985: *Economía de la solidaridad y mercado democrático*, Santiago, Programa de Economia del Trabajo, Academia de Humanismo Cristiano.

Reboredo, Lucilla Augusta 1983: 'A transformacão de um bairro operario numa comunidade: um estudo da psicologia social do quotidiano', Masters Thesis, Catholic University, São Paulo.

Redclift, Michael 1986: 'Sustainability and the market: survival strategies on the Bolivian frontier', *Journal of Development Studies*, 23,1, October.

Remmer, Karen and Merkx, Gilbert 1982: 'Bureaucratic authoritarianism revisited', *Latin American Research Review*, 17,2, 3–40.

Reverte, Javier Martinez (ed.) 1983: *Violeta Parra: Violeta del Pueblo*, Madrid, Visor.

Richards, Paul 1985: *Indigenous agricultural revolutions*, London, Hutchinson.

Rock, David 1986: *Argentina: from Spanish colonization to the Falklands War*, London, I. B. Tauris.

—— 1987: 'Intellectual precursors of conservative nationalism in Argentina, 1900–1927', *Hispanic American Historical Review*, 68,2.

Rodo, Jose Enrique 1967: *Ariel*, Buenos Aires, Ediciones Depalma.

Rodriguez, Alfredo, Ríofrío, Gustavo and Walsh, Eileen 1973: *De invasores a invadidos*, Lima, DESCO.

Rodriguez, Octavio 1986: *La teoria del subdesarrollo de la CEPAL*, Mexico, Siglo XXI, (first edn 1980).

Roett, Riordan 1972: *The politics of foreign aid in the Brazilian northeast*, Nashville, Vanderbilt University Press.

Rolim, Francisco Cartazo 1980: *Religião e clases populares*, Petropolis, Vozes.

Sader, Emir (ed.) 1986: *E agora PT?*, São Paulo, Brasiliense.

Salazar, Gabriel 1986: 'De la generación chilena del '68: omnipotencia, anomía, movimiento social?' *Proposiciones*, (Santiago), 12, October–December.

Sarlo, Béatriz 1983: 'La perseverancia de un debate', *Punto de Vista*, 18, August.

—— 1984a: La izquierda ante la cultura: del dogmatismo al populismo', *Punto de Vista*, 20, May.

—— 1984b: 'Una alucinación dispersa en agonía', *Punto de Vista*, 21, August.

Sarmiento, Domingo Fausto 1868: *Facundo*, (original: 1848), (English translation: *Life in the Argentine Republic in the days of the tyrants*, New York, Hafner, 1868).

Scalabrini Ortiz, Raúl 1940: *Historia de los ferrocarriles argentinos*, Buenos Aires, Reconquista.

Schaffer, Bernard 1973: *The administrative factor: papers in organization, politics and development*, London, Frank Cass.

Scheetz, T. 1987: 'Public sector expenditures and financial crisis in Chile', *World Development*, 15,8, August.

Scherer-Warren, Ilse 1985: 'O movimento dos trabalhadores rurais no sul do Brasil: seu papel na democratização da sociedade', ms, Department of Social

Sciences, University of Santa Catarina.

Schmitter, Philippe 1974: 'Still the century of corporatism?', *Review of Politics*, 36,1, January.

Schwarz, Roberto 1973: 'As ideias fora do lugar', *Estudos CEBRAP*, 3, 149–61, January.

Seers, Dudley 1962: 'A theory of inflation in underdeveloped countries based on the experience of Latin America', *Oxford Economic Papers*, 14,2, June, (Spanish version: *El Trimestre Económico*, July–September, 1963).

—— 1963: 'The limitations of the special case', *Oxford Bulletin of Economics and Statistics*, 25,2, May.

Serra, José 1979: 'Three mistaken theses regarding the connection between industrialization and authoritarian regimes'. In David Collier (ed.), *The new authoritarianism in Latin America*, Princeton, Princeton University Press.

Sigal, Silvia and Verón, Eliseo 1986: *Perón o muerte: los fundamentos discursivos del fenómeno peronista*, Buenos Aires, Legasa.

Sigaud, Lygia 1979: *Os clandestinos e os direitos: estudo sobre trabalhadores de cana de açucar de Pernambuco*, São Paulo, Duas Cidades.

Silva, Jose Graziano da (ed.) 1978: *Estrutura agraria e produção de subsistencia na agricultura Brasileira*, São Paulo, HUCITEC.

—— 1981: *Progresso tecnico e relações de trabalho na agricultura*, São Paulo, HUCITEC.

—— 1985: 'Reforma agraria', in *Lua Nova*, 1,4, March.

Singer, Paul and Brant, Vinicius Caldeira (eds) 1981: *São Paulo: o povo em movimento*, Petropolis, Vozes.

Skidmore, Thomas 1967: *Politics in Brazil, 1930–1964: an experiment in democracy*, New York, Oxford University Press.

—— 1988: *The politics of military rule in Brazil, 1964–1985*, New York, Oxford University Press.

Slater, David (ed.) 1985: *New social movements and the state in Latin America*, Amsterdam, CEDLA.

Smith, Brian H. 1982: *The Church and politics in Chile: challenges to modern Catholicism*, Princeton University Press.

Sodré, Nelson Werneck 1968: *Historia militar do Brasil*, Rio, Civilização Brasileira.

Sorj, Bernardo and de Almeida, Maria Herminia Tavares (eds) 1984: *Sociedade e política no Brasil pós-64*, Rio, Brasiliense.

Sorj, Bernardo and Wilkinson, John 1984: 'Processos sociais e formas de produção na agricultura brasileira'. In B. Sorj, and M. de Almeida (eds), *Sociedade e politica no Brasil pós-64*, Rio, Brasiliense.

Soto, Hernando de 1986: *El otro sendero*, Lima, Instituto Libertad y Democracia, (English translation: *The other path*, London, I. B. Tauris, 1989).

Souto, Anna Luiza Salles 1983: 'Movimentos populares urbanos e suas formas de organização ligadas a Igreja'. In ANPOCS (Associação Nacional de Pos-Graduação em Ciencias Sociais), 'Movimentos sociais urbanos, minorias etnicas e outros estudos', *Ciencias Sociais Hoje*, 2, Brasilia.

Stallings, Barbara 1978: *Class conflict and economic development in Chile*,

Stanford, Stanford University Press.

Stepan, Alfred 1978: *The state and society: Peru in comparative perspective*, Princeton University Press.

—— 1988: *Rethinking military politics*, Princeton University Press.

Sunkel, Osvaldo 1958: 'La inflación chilena: un enfoque heterodoxo', *El Trimestre Económico*, (Mexico), 100, Oct.–Dec.

—— 1971: 'Integración transnacional y desintegración nacional en América Latina', *El Trimestre Económico*, 150, Jan.–June. (Also trans. Rosemary Thorpe and Victor Urquidi (eds): *Latin America in the international economy; proceedings of a conference held by Int. Economic Assoc., Mexico City, Mexico*, London, International Economic Association, 1973.)

Tavares, Maria da Conceição 1964: 'El proceso de sustitución de importaciones como modelo de desarrollo reciente en America Latina'. In CEPAL: *Economic Bulletin for Latin América*, 9,1, (reprinted in Andres Bianchi (ed.), *América Latina: ensayos de interpretación económica*, Santiago, Editorial Universitaria, 1969).

Taylor, Lance and Helleiner, G. K. (eds) 1987: *Stabilization and adjustment programmes*, Helsinki, World Institute for Development Economics Research.

Teixeira, Douglas 1974: *Os errantes do novo secolo*, São Paulo, Duas Cidades.

Tendler, Judith 1987: *What ever happened to poverty alleviation?*, Report to the Ford Foundation, New York.

Terán, Oscar 1986: *En busca de la ideología argentina*, Buenos Aires, Catalogos.

Tironi, Eugenio 1984: *La torre de babel: ensayos de crítica y renovación política*, Santiago, Ediciones Sur.

—— 1986: *El liberalismo real*, Santiago, Sur, 1986.

—— 1987: 'Pobladores: la demanda por participación', *Mensaje*, 360, July.

Tovar, Teresa 1986: 'Barrios, ciudad, democracia y política', in Ballón op. cit.

Tolipan, Ricardo and Tinelli, Arthur Carlos 1975: *A controversia sobre distribuçao de rendu e desenvolvimento*, Rio, Zahar.

Unger, Roberto Mangabeira 1983: *The critical legal studies movement*, Cambridge, Mass., Harvard University Press.

—— 1987: *Social theory: its situation and its task: a critical introduction to 'Politics: a work in constructive social theory'*, Cambridge, Cambridge University Press.

United Nations Economic Commission for Latin America 1949: *The economic development of Latin America and some of its principal problems*.

Vacchieri, Ariana and Gonzalez Bombal, María Inés 1986: 'Los centros academicos privados: las ciencias sociales en la Argentina', ms.

Valdés, Teresa 1986: 'El movimiento poblacional: la recomposición de las solidaridades sociales', FLASCO (Latin American Faculty of Social Sciences), working paper 283, Jan.

Valenzuela, Arturo 1978: *The breakdown of democratic regimes: Chile*, Baltimore/London, Johns Hopkins University Press.

Vergara, Pilar 1985: *Auge y caída del neoliberalismo en Chile*, Santiago, FLASCO.

Viner, Jacob 1952: *International trade and economic development*, Glencoe, The Free Press.

Vinhas de Queiroz, Mauricio 1977: *Messianismo e Conflito Social*, São Paulo, Atica.

Vink, Nico 1985: 'Base communities and urban social movements: a case study of the metalworkers; strike, 1980, São Bernardo, Brazil'. In Slater op. cit.

Viola, Eduardo 1987: 'O movimento ecológico no Brasil', *Revista Brasileira de Ciencias Soiciais*, 3,1, Feb.

Wade, Robert 1987: 'The management of common property resources: collective action as an alternative to privatization or state regulation', *Cambridge Journal of Economics*, 11.

Waisman, Carlos 1987: *Reversal of development in Argentina: postwar counterrevolutionary policies and their consequences*, University of California Press.

Wallerstein, Immanuel 1974: *The modern world system*, New York, Academic Press.

—— 1979: *The capitalist world economy*, Cambridge, Cambridge University Press.

—— 1984: *The politics of the world economy*, Cambridge, Cambridge University Press.

Warman, Arturo 1976: . . . Y venimos a contradecir, Mexico, Ediciones de la Casa Chata, (English translation, *We come to Object*, John Hopkins Press 1980).

Wells, John, 1977: 'The diffusion of consumer durables in Brazil and its implications for recent controversies conerning Brazilian development', *Cambridge Journal of Economics*, 1,3, pp.259–79.

Wiarda, Howard 1981: *Corporatism and national development in Latin America*, Colorado, West View Press.

Williams, Gwyn 1975: *Proletarian order: Antonio Gramsci, factory councils and the origins of Communism in Italy, 1911–1921*, London, Pluto Press.

Winckler, J. 1976: 'Corporatism', *Archives Européennes de Sociologie*, 17,1.

Womack, John, 1968: *Zapata and the Mexican Revolution*, New York, Vintage Books.

World Bank: 1981: *Accelerated development in sub-Saharan Africa*.

—— 1985: *Development report*.

—— 1987: *World development report*.

Yotopoulos, P. A. 1989: 'The (rip) tide of privatization: lessons from Chile', *World development*, 17,5, May.

Zamosc, Leo, 1986: *The agrarian question and the peasant movement in Colombia: struggles of the National Peasant Association, 1967–1981*, Cambridge, Cambridge University Press.

Papal Encyclicals and other documents

John XXIII 1961: *Mater et magistra*.
——— 1963: *Pacem in terris*.
Leo XIII 1891: *Rerum novarum*.
Paul VI 1967: *Populorum progressio*.
——— 1968: *Humanae vitae*.
——— 1975: *Evangelio nuntiandi*.

'Instructions' of the Congregation for the Doctrine of the Faith

1984: *Instruction on certain aspects of the 'Theology of Liberation'*.
1986: *Instruction on Christian freedom and liberation*.

Statements of Bishops

1973: *Ouví os clamores do meu povo*, statement by the bishops and religious superiors of the north-east of Brazil, 6 May.

INDEX

135–7; in Liberation Theology, 128–
35; at Puebla, 130; compared with
Catholic Action, 130–1; studies of,
135–8; and politics, 137; and São
Paulo strikes, 174
CELAM (Latin American Episcopal
Conference), politics of, 109–10; *see
also* Medellín
Chile, 44–6; post-marxism in, 65–8;
Christian Democracy in, 105–8;
nationalist ideology in, 106; Catholic
student movement in, 107–8; Pope's
visit to, 145; Church and social
movements under military rule, 150;
land reform in, 161n.; co-operatives
in agriculture, 164; political opinions
of *pobladores*, 183; *see also* military
government, rural social movements,
urban social movements
Christian Democracy, 104–8; in Chile,
67–8
Church: and dictatorships, 111; in
Chile and Brazil, 111–12; and human
rights, 112; question of the laity,
130–2; internal problems after
Vatican II, 144–5; Chile and Brazil
compared, 179; *see also* rural social
movements
citizenship, 151–5; and popular
culture, 154–5; and rural social
movements, 159–60; and co-
operatives, 163; and land tenure,
163; and urban deprivation, 168–9;
and urban social movements, 175
clientelism: attitudes to among the
people, 154; Chile and Brazil
compared, 169–70; in Chile, 171;
and urban social movements in
Brazil, 172–4; declientelization, 205
CNBB (Brazilian National Episcopal
Conference), 139, 140
Colombia, 160
collective consumption trade
unionism, 63–4, 192–4
concientizaçao (consciousness-raising),
98, 100
Congar, Yves, 122, 131

co-operatives: and citizenship, 163;
conditions for success, 163–8; in
Chile and Peru, 164; in industry,
164; official sponsorship of, 165; and
the informal university, 184
corporatism: and labour, 34–6; and
business, 36, 55; and the Church,
90–1
corruption, and popular culture, 152

dependency theory, 8, 26–32, 213
distinction of planes model: in
Maritain, 104; in Liberation
Theology, 122
dos Santos, Teotonio, 30

education, adult, 188
Estado Novo, 34–5, 40

Foxley, Alejandro, 65, 67
Frank, André Gunder, 26–8
Frei, Eduardo, 44
Freire, Paulo, 96–101
Furtado, Celso, 6–7, 8, 9, 13, 38

Geisel, Ernesto, 41–2
Gera, Lucio, 114–16, 146
Germani, Gino, 183
Goulart, 'Jango', 40, 44
Grassroots Support Organizations
(GSOs), 185, 198–201
Gutierrez, Gustavo, 117, 120, 121–8

Haya de la Torre, Victor Raúl, 15–16
human rights, expanded definition,
151–2; *see also* Argentina, Brazil,
Church
Huntington, Samuel, 24–5

import-substitution industrialization,
7, 9, 11; and pact of domination,
33–4; and economic volatility, 37–9;
under the Brazilian military, 42–4;
and class alliances in Argentina, 46–
8; and social movements, 148

Pius XII, Pope, 91
political repression, in Brazil, 42
popular culture and religion, 138–9,
    143–4, 146–7; 'official version', 147
Portantiero, Juan Carlos, 69–70
positivism, 1–2
post-marxism, 59–64; in Chile, 65–8;
    in Brazil, 71–6; and democracy, 153
Prebisch, Raúl, 3–9, 10–11
priests: recruitment of in Brazil, 94;
    political opinions of, 138
Puebla, Conference of CELAM at,
    146; see also CEBs

Quadros, Janio, 40

Recife, popular movements in, 172–3
reformism: in Brazil, 39–41; in Chile,
    44–6
rent-seeking, 86
Rosas, Argentine caudillo, 106
rural social movements, 155–60;
    typology of, 155–6; effects of
    capitalist expansion in, 156–77; and
    citizenship, 160

Sarlo, Beatriz, 70
self-management, 151
Silva Henriquez, Cardinal Archbishop
    of Santiago, 108, 112
social doctrine of the Church, 88–91;
    effects of in different countries, 103
social movements: in Castells, 62–4;
    and post-marxism, 62; meaning of
    term, 148; under military rule, 148–
    50; 'new' forms of, 150–2; and
    bureaucracy, 207; 'scaling up', 207;
    expressive and symbolic dimensions,
    209; see also CEBs, rural social
    movements, urban social movements

solidarity, in support of nationalism or
    citizenship, 151–2
Soto, Hernando de, 80–5, 197–8, 213
state, theory of, 51–9
Stepan, Alfred, 34
structural heterogeneity, 12

Tavares, M. C., 11
terms of trade and developing
    countries, 5–6
Theology of Liberation, see Liberation
    Theology
Tironi, Eugenio, 65–7

Unidad Popular, 45–6
urban deprivation, 169
urban social movements, 168; and land
    tenure, 168; in Brazil, 169, 170–6;
    attitudes to formal politics, 172–3;
    limitations, 173–4; in Chile, 178–83;
    and Church in Chile, 179–81; role of
    women in, 180–1, 182;
    institutionalized marginality, 181;
    relations to parties in Chile, 181–3;
    see also clientelism
urban townships (favelas, poblaciones);
    resettlement of, Chile and Brazil,
    169; variety of and differentiation in,
    171

Vargas, Getulio, 40; and Church, 94–5
Vatical Councils: Vatican I, 88; Vatican
    II, 108; on laity, 132
Vuskovic, Pedro, 38

women: and urban social movement in
    Chile, 180, 182; and popular
    movements in general, 187
World Bank, 159, 188